Effective Talent Management

Effective talent management is about aligning the business's approach to talent with the strategic aims and purpose of the organisation. The core rationale of any talent strategy should be to have a direct positive impact on the organisation's goals but in many cases this is not so. The ideas, principles and approaches outlined here will enable the reader to understand the strategic nature of talent and design a response that meets the needs of their own organisation. Case studies are used to illustrate the concepts and proven methodologies guide the day-to-day practice of the reader. The content will link the strategic intent of HR with the practical actions it takes to make a positive impact on the business's results. The author begins by examining the disconnected nature of talent management in many organisations; how at times it has been a response to trends and seen by many as a bolt on to HR and he proposes a different model, one that links clearly the development of a talent strategy with the achievement of a business strategy. Mark Wilcox summarises succinctly the case for a more strategic approach to talent management, one directly linked to business performance. He concludes that the time is now right for talent management, and therefore many HR managers, to move from a functional support role to one with a direct strategic impact on the business.

Mark Wilcox, MBA, MSc, BSc, FCIPD, MBPs, is the driving force behind Change Capability Consulting Ltd. He works with leading organisations on developing a clear line of sight between the strategic goals of the business and the people activities the organisation pursues. Aligning talent and business strategy to successfully transform the organisation's results is the prime focus for his consulting work. Mark is a truly internationally experienced professional and has worked for some of the world's best and biggest companies. He was until late 2005 the Director of People & Organisational Development at Sony Europe based in the Headquarters in Berlin. There he was responsible for the European Talent Management Strategy and in supporting European wide organisational change. Previously he enjoyed 20 years' experience with Nestlé.

Effective Talent Management

Aligning strategy, people and performance

Mark Wilcox

Routledge
Taylor & Francis Group

LONDON AND NEW YORK

First published 2016 by Routledge

2 Park Square, Milton Park, Abingdon, Oxon, OX14 4RN
605 Third Avenue, New York, NY 10017

Routledge is an imprint of the Taylor & Francis Group, an informa business

First issued in paperback 2020

British Library Cataloguing in Publication Data
A catalogue record for this book is available from the British Library

Library of Congress Cataloging in Publication Data
Names: Wilcox, Mark, 1961- author.
Title: Effective talent management : aligning strategy, people and performance / by Mark Wilcox.
Description: Farnham, Surrey, UK ; Burlington, VT : Gower, [2016] | Includes bibliographical references and index. | Description based on print version record and CIP data provided by publisher; resource not viewed.
Identifiers: LCCN 2015044909 (print) | LCCN 2015041112 (ebook) | ISBN 9781472464323 (ebook) | ISBN 9781472464330 (epub) | ISBN 9781472464316 (hardback : alk. paper)
Subjects: LCSH: Manpower planning. | Personnel management.
Classification: LCC HF5549.5.M3 (print) | LCC HF5549.5.M3 W55 2016 (ebook) | DDC 658.3/01—dc23
LC record available at http://lccn.loc.gov/2015044909

ISBN: 978-1-4724-6431-6 (hbk)
ISBN: 978-0-367-73702-3 (pbk)

Typeset in Sabon
by Swales & Willis Ltd, Exeter, Devon, UK

Contents

Figures

Tables

Chapter 1

Why is talent management so important for business?

Introduction – effective talent management

Any organisation can buy more computing power, copy a competitor's business model, move to digital channels for business or relocate to the latest fast-growing market. However, none of these strategic actions will make an organisation successful if it isn't employing and retaining the right type of people. Having the right talent to support the organisation's strategic goals is about the only sustainable competitive advantage a company can create and maintain. Talent makes or breaks businesses yet its value as a critical business asset is rarely measured and, even more rarely, fully understood. This book is an attempt to change that, even if just a little.

Talent management carried out effectively can impact dramatically on the success of any organisation, the key word in that last sentence being 'effectively'. It's not about being efficient, it's about positive impact on the end goals of the organisation. This book explores how you build an Effective Talent Management (ETM) strategy and then how to execute it.

What's in a name?

The emergence of Talent Management as a discipline in the wider field of Human Resources (HR) Management was in no small way linked to the publication of McKinsey's 'War for Talent' study in 1997 and the subsequent best-selling book in 2001.[1] It seems this 'call for arms' for HR created a whole new cadre of budding talent professionals. Many roles, in organisations large and small, embraced this new challenge and promptly renamed their incumbents 'Talent Managers'. However, nothing much changed in the way organisations managed their talent. Many of the responsibilities remained exactly the same as those previously undertaken by the recently rebranded Development or Recruitment Managers. What was missing then, and the situation is not much better now, was the understanding that talent management was not a transactional or support role but was the key to unleashing the strategic impact of HR.

Hindsight makes us tough critics and now, having spent the last 15 years delivering talent management approaches that work, it is hard to believe how much was missed. Even with a strong academic background in HR, Organisational Psychology and Business Administration and many years of experience in practical HR, I still needed to have my own epiphany.

In early 2001, whilst working for Sony, the global electronics and entertainment company, I was part of a team of HR managers tasked with contributing to the Europe-wide, business transformation effort. We all worked in the headquarters in Berlin and were responsible for the HR support for the whole of the European business.

Sony was for many years a victim of its own success. For over 40 years it had dominated the consumer electronics market in Europe and made healthy profits. However, it had over time become too complex in its regional structure, too reliant on saviour products coming out of the technology pipeline, overly dependent on a few 'cash cow' products and generally inefficient in comparison to its new aggressive competitors. As the market for consumer electronics evolved to demand increasingly more innovative products at highly competitive prices, Sony struggled to cope. It had been ill prepared for the increase in the pace of change in its business sector and the constant challenge required to meet the needs of the consumer.

We, as the HR team, were asked to support the transformation effort by re-engineering HR and, as a result, deliver more value to our customers in the business. We were tasked with rethinking the way we managed HR and were challenged to contribute more to the future of the business than we had done in the past.

All good transformation efforts have a strong methodology and in many instances this would be brought in by the team of external consultants tasked with assisting with the change effort. Sony was no different and used one of the world's top consulting firms to assist with their business strategy and transformation planning. However, Sony also wanted to use tools and approaches that they were familiar with, so agreed upon a modified version of the Six Sigma tool box for their work. Six Sigma[2] is a philosophy that uses a range of tools and techniques first used by the quality management movement that swept through manufacturing businesses in the 1970s and 1980s.

It was whilst using some of these techniques with a workshop full of my colleagues that I had a significant insight into the HR function's main problem. It came as a result of running a flow-charting exercise with the intention of mapping a successful employee lifecycle. What became apparent was that we treated our roles and responsibilities as independent domains and, as such, created barriers to effectiveness where none needed to exist. In many elements of our work we created Chinese Walls[3] to separate responsibility and create demarcation lines over work. Whereas some were the result of historic accident, others were related to individual's egos and assorted status issues.

What the flow-charting process revealed was a mash up of old procedures, historic ways of doing things and mismatched supply and demand. Without an overarching guiding strategy for talent, people had done what they had always done. The picture across the rest of the European organisation was no better, with any attempts to coordinate the deployment of talent being thwarted as the result of country-level HR managers paying lip service to headquarters' requests, whilst fulfilling their managing director's more parochial requirements. The result was wasted time, wasted effort and wasted opportunity. In short, it was a criminal waste of talent.

When we used flow-charting methods to model a young talent entering the business and tracked their career to the point of becoming CEO (Chief Executive Officer) of the European business, it quickly became apparent that the route was not clear, and certainly was not a smooth process from an HR perspective. There were so many contradictions about what was expected, different definitions of success, different competency requirements, conflicting levels of experience and problems with salary cost centres, and obvious across it all was complete lack of transparency. So much of what constituted our HR process was illogical, disconnected and ineffective. Something needed to change both at the strategic and local implementation levels.

What was abundantly clear was that if a senior group of HR managers could not understand it, how on earth could our customers, line managers and department leaders? We needed a simpler and more effective way to manage the talent that Sony so desperately needed if it was to be successful in its transformation efforts. What was needed at that point in time, and what any new HR organisation model needed to provide, was ETM.

The organisation needed a process that the managers could easily understand, that delivered high-quality talent development and that supported a successful business. The new approach would need to be designed from the business's point of view. It would need to create a pipeline of talent that directly impacted on the future business strategy. The whole process would need to be designed to support the business from the start, rather than use a mosaic of pre-existing HR tools and try to force them to do something they were not created to do.

To give some idea of the scale of the problem the following vignette describes an actual discussion and the resulting scenario.

Helping HR count

Whilst on a flight with the Sony CEO and the Vice President Human Resources (VP HR) to a business school development programme, an interesting issue arose. The recently appointed CEO asked the VP HR 'How many people do I employ?' The response was less than satisfactory, as the VP HR could only estimate: 'It's more than 15,000 but less than 15,500, I'm fairly sure of that.' You can imagine the CEO was more than a little surprised at his uncertainty. As a result we, the HR team, were tasked with giving a 100 per cent accurate answer as a priority and to make headcount a standing reporting issue at the monthly European board meeting.

What that simple question generated was a project to define and measure something that spanned 23 countries, 40 different payroll systems (not one of which interacted with another), numerous definitions of what constituted an employee, legal issues with contractors and historical issues with software, and revealed a distinct lack of capability in our combined HR systems.

To provide an accurate answer required the development of so called 'middleware', a bespoke software package designed to interact and speak to each of the different legacy payroll systems. It then took 18 months of re-negotiating, auditing and redefining role descriptions to give an accurate answer. This question was just one example of a situation that existed across the whole of the HR function in Europe. What was clear at this point was the HR team needed something better to manage talent in the future. We needed something that was simple, robust and effective.

Beware what you ask for

The result of our workshop, and a little additional research into what other large organisations were trying to achieve, was presented to my boss, the newly appointed VP HR Europe. Whilst trying to present a robust case for change I was also aware that as a relative newcomer to Sony, with less than two years of service, that direct criticism of the past and present ways of working might not be openly welcomed. What I had not expected, nor planned for, was the impact that the presentation would have. The charts I had produced summarised the significant problems that we faced as a function. They painted a bleak picture, that of an organisation that didn't know what talent it had or how to manage it, and certainly not one well placed to profit from it.

I unexpectedly left that meeting with a new role, a newly created team made up of a range of incumbent, geographically dispersed generalists and a clear mandate to 'make it so'. What started out as a genuine attempt to try to understand how, as an organisation, we managed talent became my new responsibility and role covering the whole European business. Designing the approach to what I now know as ETM was the result of that project.

It was at this point that my reading and research became more focused and urgent. I didn't want to make the same mistakes that other large organisations had made, nor repeat the ones that my own had made in the past. It was important that any major redesign in the processes could be backed with robust rationale and that there would be an agreed implementation plan. In my experience, both as a talent professional and as a consultant, too many grand ideas and impressive strategies fail because the planning to implement is weak.

What was also obvious from this early research was that we were not alone. This has subsequently been confirmed by a 2009 review of the state of strategic talent management[4] that concluded, although the term was popular within HR functions, the concept of talent management still remained unclear. It seems the idea of creating a specific focus on talent was, and still is, popular but the level of understanding of how it contributes to business success, and what the core elements are that need to be undertaken to be effective, are still not widely appreciated.

The way many large organisations dealt with the critical issue of talent management was less than professional. In many it was rebranded 'training and development' with little systemic impact, and in others it was to create a new role with no power, budget or influence. What was needed at that point in time in my own organisation, and it seemed in many other large organisations, was a better way to manage talent, one that made a positive impact on results.

What is talent management

The term talent management emerged into the mainstream business lexicon around the mid-1990s. Before this time there were clear specialisms within the HR function designed to manage the organisation's various people needs. There were recruiters, assessment specialists, training staff, management development practitioners, managers whose responsibility was succession planning and manpower plans, and then, of course, there were those whose role it was to determine the compensation packages for the workforce. In addition there were many generalist HR managers, who in small businesses did all of the above.

Around this time, with the publication of the influential article and book *War for Talent*[5] by two McKinsey consultants, HR woke up to the fact that there were no good reasons to sub-divide much of the process and responsibility for managing people within the business. As a result many forward thinking organisations reshaped their HR teams to deal with the newly defined problem, that of acquiring and retaining good people. The rise of the importance of knowledge workers and an increasing demand for more creative and independent staff meant that HR teams were required to treat their businesses more like a core customer, and their talented staff more like valued clients.

These new models encouraged individual managers, and small HR teams, to take full responsibility for the whole lifecycle of people in the business – or at least those that met the criteria for being talent. The definition issue is discussed later in the book and has a critical role to play in understanding what is effective and what is not.

ETM is an integrated approach to ensure that the right people are within the organisation in order to deliver on its strategic aims. Therefore any talent strategy must be intrinsically linked to the organisation's strategy in such a way that it drives success, not follows behind the needs of the business.

Collings and Mellahia's study of talent management is revealing.[6] Having looked at both academic sources and practitioner surveys they define strategic talent management as:

> activities and processes that involve the systematic identification of key positions which differentially contribute to the organisation's sustainable competitive advantage, the development of a talent pool of high potential and high performing incumbents to fill these roles, and the development of a differentiated human resource architecture to facilitate filling these positions.

Whilst it's a little wordy, as befits an academic definition, it does capture most of the elements that are the hallmark of an ETM approach.

It doesn't always have to be sequential; however, there is a natural flow to the process of managing talent across an organisation. It is represented here in Figure 1.1 as a simple schematic diagram.

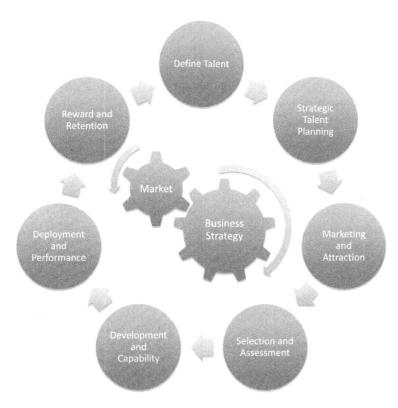

Figure 1.1 ETM – a diagrammatic representation

ETM is a systematic approach starting with the business aims. It moves from this to the initial definition of talent and finishes with a review of the means of rewarding and retaining those people whom the organisation believes really add value. All of these activities are dependent on, and therefore must take account of, two other variables: the businesses strategy and the conditions of the wider market. Without reference and actions to adjust to these two factors the talent management approach will neither be effective nor strategic.

Best practice v good practice

There is a popular saying that the best is the enemy of the good. Whilst it is always admirable to be striving for excellence it is not always practical. However, the search for best practice is one that it seems is an evergreen mantra for many business leaders. There is no doubt that some organisations are better at some things than their competitors or counterparts. There is no doubt that some things can be transferred into other organisations and as a result there will be some tangible benefit. There is also no doubt that the source of that best practice will evolve and develop something new and more effective over time. Copying other people's ideas and expecting the same results is an attractive proposition, but one that ultimately regresses the industry to the mean, and something that at one point in time gave a strategic advantage merely becomes the entry ticket to play. If you want an entertaining view on the dangers of copycat strategy read the 2004 classic *Karaoke Capitalism*.[7] Whilst systematically copying others is a sure route to mediocrity, taking what is good from another business and using it to fast track your own plan is an approach I wholeheartedly advocate. It is rare for individual practitioners to come up with something truly unique – but it's good practice to learn from others and adapt a suite of approaches to achieve the specific effects that make your business more successful. What the best practitioners do is learn fast and add value by customising approaches using their depth of understanding of their organisation.

Good practice exists in many organisations: things that work well and add value. You do not need to always do what is industry leading to add value – sometimes it the cumulative effect of a collection of good practices that ensure an effective talent strategy. I am a strong advocate of 'stealing' ideas from anywhere and learning from the mistakes and success of others. Never be too proud to admit others do things better than you do.

What follows in this book is the collected good practice of over 30 years in business working for some of the world's biggest and best organisations, either in a role with direct responsibility for talent, or, whilst as a consultant, advising client organisations on their talent strategy. It is a mixture of the pragmatic approaches of a consultant practitioner, backed by the academic rigour that many years of studying organisational psychology brings, blended with a business acumen that completing a business master's instils.

Almost all of what follows has already been seen in a variety of contexts and applied in many different ways with employers or client organisations. That means there is a generality of application; the approach will work across many situations. What has made the approach effective in the past is the blend of initiatives and interconnected nature of them. How you blend and apply the elements of the approach will determine how effective it is within your own organisational context. As a result of taking this approach, you will have a deeper understanding of what sort of capability drives the business and how as a talent professional you can have direct impact on the organisation's success.

The case for effective talent management

In the last few years there has been an increase in the number of articles in HR journals and blogs complaining that senior HR managers are not represented on boards or as present as they should be in executive committees. Making the case for HR to be a strategic partner has become an ongoing battle for many it seems. The wide adoption and implementation of the title HR Business partner from Ulrich's model of the discipline,[8] has been an attempt to reposition the role and increase its importance. What is a surprise, given the results of many surveys into what CEOs spend their time on,[9] is that talent is not more popular as a lever for power and influence with these same undervalued HR professionals. If CEOs are reportedly spending around 20 per cent of their time thinking about talent, then what are talent professionals doing to address and support these thoughts?

The rest of this chapter will address the case for ETM and why there is currently so much focus on talent. In addition it will highlight how each of the subsequent chapters explores a specific element of the ETM approach.

What readers should discover as they progress is a clear understanding of why talent is currently so high on corporate agendas and what they can do, practically, to design and implement an ETM approach in their own organisation as a response.

Whilst this is not meant to be an academic text, however, where there is further reading that will help, or alternatively sources for interesting ideas, the reader will be directed to them via the endnotes. The main aim of this book is to stimulate and inform the reader, whom I expect to be in the main HR and talent management professionals, to think differently about talent and ensure that they create talent strategies for their own organisations that really add value.

Business strategy and talent

It seems from reading the current business press,[10] and looking at the agendas for management conferences across the globe, that talent management has come of age. It appears that the time has come for organisations to really understand and think strategically about their people and the talent they need to succeed in their business endeavours.

When you consider how a business competes, that is gain competitive advantage over its rivals, and then think about the technological changes that almost all businesses have seen in the last 20 years, the strong case for attracting and employing the best people becomes clear. When any major disruptive technology arrives in an industry the advantage the innovator has ensures its competitiveness. Whether the innovation is product based, such as Apple's industry-leading smart phone, or service based, such as Airbnb, the initial idea can soon copied or improved upon. Technologies that challenge an existing paradigm will eventually be copied, replicated and sometimes significantly improved upon by the competition. What enables a company to have a temporary monopoly, and therefore a short-term competitive advantage, is often easy to replicate and it's just a matter of time before someone in the less regulated developing markets reverse-engineers it. Success and market dominance creates professional envy and that almost always leads to new entrants coming into the market. Over time the dominance is reduced as competitors take some of the market share and prices are reduced to reflect an increase in consumer choice. Paradoxically it's sometimes the second to market that becomes the dominant player.[11] So what we need to understand as intelligent business people is that technology and innovation used to drive business success is always open to replication and sincere imitation.

What is much more difficult to replicate and re-engineer is the way people work and develop ideas within your organisations. Replicating your organisation's culture, the source of those ideas and creativity is almost impossible. This is why getting the right people and building an environment that they thrive in is the key to sustainable competitive advantage. It is for this reason that talent management is becoming recognised as the key to developing a sustainable strategic advantage. Google,[12] recognised across the globe as a talent magnet, hires people who they believe are passionate about their work and who demonstrate insight, not people who just fit a specific technical profile or vacant post. They understand getting really good people is not a question of filling roles, but hiring talent that will grow with them, regardless of what they do next. Having an abundance of the right sort of talent ensures that Google remains relevant, as their talented people drive the innovation that makes the company revenue.

A recent survey by Hay,[13] for the Chartered Institute of Personnel and Development (CIPD), suggested that over 80 per cent of the HR managers surveyed agreed that competition for their key skilled workers was increasing; it is becoming harder to find candidates for some highly skilled roles. The same survey suggests that to compensate for this increase in competition half have increased their salary offer and also the amount they spend on learning and development. Clearly the current situation for talent is highly competitive and requires some sort of strategic response. Whilst increasing the salary for roles will have some immediate short-term effect, a better way to ensure you have the talent you need is to look at the problem in relation to who adds the most value and then find ways to attract and secure just these specific individuals.

Any talent manager needs to understand what their organisation's core business strategy is, and how this translates into specific people capability. As outlined above, technology plays a part in most businesses but what lies behind that application of technology is the people in the organisation and their capability. These core capabilities are the things that separate your organisation from others in the same industry and should therefore be at the very centre of any talent strategy.

People can be strategic contributors or supporting employees. It is for some a hard fact to accept that, even in the most egalitarian of organisations, not all employees add the same value. Some capabilities impact more than others on the success of the organisation; people with these capabilities are harder to recruit and replace, and the value they contribute is often higher, by a factor of 10–15, than the average employee. In this instance I am not describing hierarchy or status of role, but a capability that impacts on the business strategy.

For example, two of the core capabilities of grocery retailers is buying and supply chain management. These roles, if carried out well, determine how much profit the retailers make, and can be measured in real time. A similar case can be made for the people who manage the utility of container shipping and who negotiate the unloading schedule with the world's major ports. Where turnaround and efficiency are the major profit levers in a commodity industry, managing the utilisation of a cargo vessel and its time in port makes or breaks the business model. It is considered a core capability in these organisations.

In other industries the critical capability is not analytical, but creative. When advertising agencies pitch their ideas to their clients it's the ideas of their people that determine their success. A similar case can be made for the fashion and apparel industry. Knowing what will sell and what will be popular is not a pure analytical process but one based on other competencies and experiences.

In the examples above, the roles highlighted are not necessarily the most senior, but those where there are clear capabilities in place; these are the ones that an organisation needs to thrive. Any talent management strategy must look at the market at any given time and assess where those capabilities lie and where they are absent, and how they can be grown or developed. We will explore in Chapter 3 how to analyse the roles in an organisational structure and determine which of them are truly critical.

Once the critical capabilities have been determined, finding the right talent to deliver and develop them is the challenge. Not every role will make the same contribution and the talent strategy needs to recognise this and respond appropriately.

Differentiation of talent is now becoming widely recognised as the most effective way to generate the most value from people in organisations. There was a phase when the idea of hiring only the very best in the market for every single role was dominant, often referred to as 'top grading'.[14] However, experience has shown that for many organisations this approach filled the organisation with expensive, over-qualified, ambitious people who could not always fill their potential in non-pivotal roles. This clearly impacted on retention and didn't always produce business success.

In the diagrammatic representation of talent shown in Figure 1.1 you see both the business strategy and the markets in the centre. Whilst the business strategy drives the organisation's definition of talent, the markets may determine some of the tactics for attracting and retaining it.

What is essential for any talent practitioner to understand is that their strategy is a response to the other two conditions: the strategic aims of the business and the state of the wider employment market.

A more strategic approach to talent

Collings and Mellahi[15] conducted a wide-ranging review of the current thinking on talent management and found that there were very few organisations really linking talent management and business success. Their work, based on research and discussions with practitioners, suggested that the whole area of talent management was lacking a strong theoretical model. HR journals and more academic papers had not really come to a consensus on what talent management added that previous incarnations of HR practices didn't provide. A result of their work was a theoretical model, which is adapted here and shown in Figure 1.2. It illustrates the components of the HR system or architecture on the left and the expected business and talent outcomes on the right.

Collins and Mellahi considered the market as being both the existing internal employee group and the wider external recruitment arena, both of which should feed a talent pool. Figure 1.2 suggests multiple pools to represent the different levels of talent required in a large organisation. They also identify what they refer to as pivotal positions, referred to in this adaption as strategic talent. It is these relatively small number of roles, not individuals, that their model suggests talent practitioners focus on. We discuss how their model works, and some of the theory and research behind it, in later chapters.

Their conclusion is an important one: that focused and differentiated talent practices drive better business outcomes by concentrating on those people who contribute most to the success of the organisation. The business outcomes they see as a result of strategic talent management practices are: higher work motivation; high organisational commitment and extra role behaviour, which in the adaption is re-labelled as discretionary effort.

In later chapters we will explore how the models and assumptions that organisations adopt either support or refute this view, but in their opinion only when talent management is differentiated is it truly strategic.

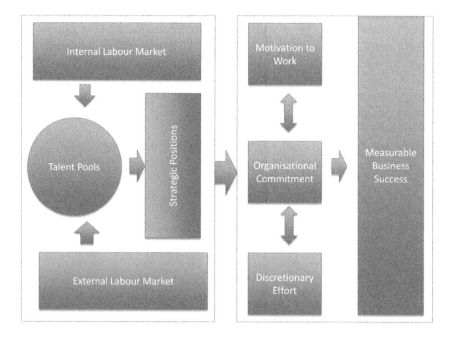

Figure 1.2 Strategic talent, a theoretical model

Source: Adapted from D.G. Collings and K. Mellahi (2009) Strategic Talent Management: a review and research agenda *Human Resources Management Review*, 19.4, 304–13.

The market influence

When an organisation recruits it does so in an open market place – regardless of its position in the industry – be it a global goliath such as Google or a small boutique software house, it's an open market. Any business plan that requires growth and therefore a likely increase in people, must take into account the current and, even more critical, the future state of the employment market. Failure to do so will result in frustration and wasted resources.

As with any market, a mechanism for trading based on supply and demand, there are times when things are expensive or elusive and there are times when there is surplus. As talent professionals we cannot accurately predict the future, but in the case of capabilities we can, if we understand the business's strategy, determine what sort of skills and abilities we might need more of and then shape our plans accordingly.

Some of these insights are based on emerging socioeconomic trends. For example the increase in the use of 'Big Data' in many organisations to gain customer insights, drive innovation based on individual consumer behaviours and schedule processes based on the analysis of huge databases suggests that there will be an increasing demand for certain types of people. Those that can do the maths and coding that this type of work requires will be at a premium.

As a result, this specific type of talent, those that have what is often referred to as STEM skills – science, technology, engineering and mathematics – will have more choice of where they can work, making an attractive employee value proposition a more important issue for many organisations. Great talent has choices where it wants to work. Scare talent has even more choice.

This situation is not lost on the big recruiters, such as the consultancy houses who specifically target this type of talent as they expect recruitment across their industry to increase 16 per cent in 2015 alone.[16]

Other insights to future market conditions are more prosaic. As the UK economy becomes more stable and shows signs of growth, an increase in demand from both public and private sources for construction creates a market supply issue with skilled builders. Whilst this can be seen as predictable, many large construction firms are suffering from a short sighted 'fire and forget' mentality that means skilled workers are currently demanding premiums of 100 per cent on their daily rate as a result of the shortage.[17] A response by the government to increase their support for apprenticeships in construction seems to be a little late and a case of bolting empty stable doors.

The entry-level positions in many talent pipelines have traditionally been the annual graduate recruitment schemes. Again the market dictates the way organisations need to address this section of the potential employee pool. There has been a lot of discussion in recent years about how this generation need treating differently, believing that somehow there is a magic formula for enticing 'Millennials' or more recent graduates. To a large extent the need to adopt a different approach to their recruitment or treatment in the workplace is based on anecdotal evidence, and driven by management guru fads rather than any substantial research-based evidence.[18] Young talent wants a chance to develop, grow and contribute, and that hasn't changed significantly in decades of graduate recruitment.

What has changed in the past few years is the market conditions,which suggest that graduate recruitment is increasing and that organisations are once again looking to invest heavily in young talents.[19] The annual review of the UK Graduate Market[20] suggests that, at the time of writing, the demand for graduate recruits would exceed that of the years preceding the financial crisis of 2008. What is also clear during this recovery is that overseas graduates aiming for global careers will contest a much higher number of these vacancies.

The market is global for almost everything. With the transparency and opportunity that the Internet has provided recruiters can be on any continent and time zone. This means for talent that is mobile they can be poached by competitors many organisations didn't even know existed. This same fact means that good talent professionals also need to be aware of market conditions across the globe, not just their own employment market.

Janus – the god of talent

The Roman god Janus was depicted as having two faces, one looking to the past and one looking to the future. Whilst not being blessed with godly powers, the talent management professional does need to have their focus on the present needs of the business and yet still be able to anticipate the future requirements of the organisation.

It is the ability to understand, and meet, the specific, strategic, capability needs of the organisation, whilst being aware of the potential impact of any emerging trends in the employment market, that makes an effective talent manager.

Talent management professionals should be concerned with the long-term success of their organisation and therefore be thinking of timelines of 10–15 years. Their role is, in practice, more strategic than many board-level executives, who are primarily concerned with a time horizon that is the next quarter's reported results. Whilst the talent professional's role is to provide the talent needed to meet a particular quarter's market expectations, it is also necessary to look to the future to ensure that there is a pipeline of capability for two, five and 15 years' time. It is for this reason that talent professionals who are building an ETM approach need to start with acquiring a deep understanding of their business strategy and only then can they determine how to build the necessary people capability to deliver it.

Structure and content

The following nine chapters explore all the elements that make up an ETM approach. It is not intended to be a prescription for every business, but a guide to the key elements that, if addressed, ensure the talent professional's work contributes to business success. It will of course require customisation and adaption, but the underlying fundamentals are generic to most industries and business sectors.

Chapter 2 starts by examining the fundamentals of business strategy and explores how the talent practitioner should align the talent strategy to have maximum impact. The chapter content is illustrated by examples of generic strategy models and mini-cases, to show how businesses can compete and what effect their strategic choices have on the way people need to be managed. This in turn influences the specific definition of talent for each organisation.

This chapter also examines the concept of strategic capabilities, and how to understand and define these in a way appropriate to a specific organisation. Strategic capabilities are the core elements of the organisation's business model that differentiate it in a crowded market. By understanding this concept and building their talent strategy around it, the talent professional will be making a significant contribution to the organisation's success. Finally, in this chapter, the reader will understand the basic principles and everyday practices that help create a direct line of sight from each integrated HR practice to the overall results of the business.

Most HR practitioners strive to have an influence on the business's success but sometime struggle to link their day-to-day work to some direct business impact. This is a fundamental tenet of ETM: the direct and explicit linking of talent and business strategy.

Chapter 3 explores how you begin to define talent in any organisation. At the core of any ETM practice is a precise and transparent understanding of who the right people are. What does talent mean in any specific organisation? How could talent be defined in such a way that everyone within the organisation understands what it means? What are the factors that make some roles more important than others? What sort of people would make the organisation more successful now and will that be different in the future? How many talented people are needed and in which areas of the employee lifecycle? The tools and techniques in this chapter should help the talent professional answer these questions for their business.

In addition, the chapter outlines a simple method for identifying the core capabilities in any organisation and how to involve the critical stakeholders in the definition process. In order to have an ETM approach you need to understand what makes someone a talent in the organisation you work for, and how this specific definition links to business success. The link between the two is the critical capability of each organisation.

Finally, this chapter explores the spectrum of talent management models, from the all inclusive at one extreme to the fully differentiated approach at the other, and examines the implications of each approach on effectiveness. Some models are certainly more inclusive at the expense of effectiveness, and the content of this chapter tests the arguments in favour of each.

Having crafted a clear definition of talent, the next stage is to use this in some form of strategic plan. Chapter 4 outlines a means of mapping all of the key roles in the organisation, so that the talent professional can assess the size of the challenge and the current and future talent gaps.

The core capabilities are not necessarily evenly distributed and therefore some roles in the organisation will have more strategic impact than others. The concept of 'role mapping' shows where these core capabilities meet delivery of strategic goals. There is an example of a robust method to define what is strategic and what is not and this will be illustrated with a real example from industry.

Following a clear understanding of which roles are genuinely strategic the next step is to establish what talent already exists within the organisation and what sort of pipeline and talent pools are going to be required. This is part audit and part talent planning. The outcome is a fully thought through, strategic talent plan with clearly defined goals for each talent pool and the steps necessary to achieving them.

The combination of the output of role mapping and a talent audit gives a scale and focus to the design of an effective talent strategy. Any gaps in the talent requirements will be quantified and any bench strength issues identified. As result of applying the practice and principles of this chapter, the organisation will know what it needs to do to either develop or attract talent, both in the near term and in the future. Ensuring you attract the right people is both a marketing and a public relations (PR) responsibility but needs to be part of the overall talent strategy.

Chapter 5 looks at ways of marketing the organisation and ensuring you have a positive presence in the employment market. The traditional way of sourcing talent will be examined, as well as some of the newer approaches driven by social media and other digital relationships. Regardless of the media used and the employee value proposition, the attractiveness of working for your organisation needs to be managed. A laissez-faire approach to your employer profile will allow other people to tell a story about the organisation and it may not be the story that you want, accurate or not.

This chapter also explores how the 'employee value proposition' needs to be consistent with the values of the organisation but differentiated enough to appeal to the different talent groups in the business. What is attractive for one age range and functional speciality is not necessarily seen as 'sexy' to another. It then explores three different generic segments of talent and examines the range of tactics available to the talent professional that affect each group, from executive search at one end of a continuum, to the use of internships at the other.

Chapter 6 deals with the process of selection and assessment. The focus should be on finding the right people both from those that have been attracted to apply and from those who already work in the organisation and who may be considered as having higher potential. If there is no selection process, every employee is considered a talent or, alternatively, the organisation doesn't have criteria for talent. It is essential to be able to define talent clearly and then sift the existing pool of employees to find it. Selection processes help us do this.

However, if the philosophy of the organisation is one where everyone is considered a talent then there are other considerations that the talent professional needs to address. Without any selection criteria and selection process, the whole population would need to treated as though they are high performers with potential for development. This lack of differentiation would create a considerable resource requirement, with little economic value creation in return. For some people, this altruistic approach is one that they feel very comfortable with. However, a significant investment deserves a proportional return and some people as well as some roles don't provide that return. As with any business investment there has to be cost–benefit analysis that shows the value of investing. Selection processes ensure you are investing in the right people and therefore increase the probability of getting a reasonable return.

This chapter explores the fundamentals of good selection process, from the initial process of designing some self-selection into the application, through to making tough decisions for appointments between highly talented people.

Whilst entry-level selection tools, such as those used in graduate programmes, are generally well understood, the chapter also explores how to assess and evaluate senior incumbent roles as part of a strategic review of talent. Evaluating top executives can be a both daunting and career limiting process if carried out badly.

An effective talent strategy must include all levels of the organisation but find an appropriate and acceptable way of managing the need for assessment. Assessment methods for external applications and internal development needs are explored in some depth. The core tools of assessment can be applied in both cases whilst their outcomes are often different.

The aim of Chapter 6 is for HR professionals to understand the choices they have in carrying out selection and assessment as part of a strategic approach to talent. By the end of this chapter they should understand a range of different methods that are fair, robust and inclusive.

Chapter 7 is all about building the capability of individuals and the overall business. It is primarily concerned with what happens once you have identified your talent. Whilst employee development has been part of the remit of HR for many years, targeting this process on specific talents with the clear intent of building increased organisational capability has not always been the primary focus.

Talent development should be focused on building the specific capabilities that help the organisation succeed. In many cases the ambitions of the individual and the needs of the organisation overlap significantly and everyone wins. In others this is not the case. To ensure that development is really about building individual *and* organisational capability there needs to be an open and candid discussion about the expectations from both parties. This chapter also explores the many ways that specific capability development can be tailored to different individuals.

A number of approaches are reviewed in areas such as executive education, 'on the job' skills training, coaching and mentoring, stretch assignments and networking events. The chapter will also explore how to link these approaches into the day-to-day work of talents and how to ensure that coaching and mentoring become embedded within the overall talent strategy.

Chapter 8 discusses the single element of any ETM strategy that has the most impact on business results: the process of deployment. The whole purpose of any ETM strategy is to support the organisation's achievement of its strategic goals. The deployment of the right people, into the right roles, at the right time is the most critical part of talent management.

For the organisation to ensure the right deployment, the talent professional must have complete visibility of the whole organisation's performance and be central to, or very influential in, the decision-making process. In this chapter we explore how to design this process and then how the talent professional can build the influence they need to implement ETM.

When deployed into the organisation the individual talent also needs to perform well, so approaches to performance management are also explored here. Deployment without a supporting mechanism to help the individual succeed in the new position is a waste of resources, which may lead to unrest, possibly creating future retention issues.

In Chapter 9 the dual issues of reward and retention are explored. Building a great talent pool and developing great potential is necessary for success but not sufficient. In addition you must retain them in the organisation. Losing the wrong people at the wrong time can be both expensive and a significant business risk. The content of this section examines the various issues that link reward and retention to the rest of the ETM approach.

The chapter starts by exploring what motivation models inform us about reward and how we can use these insights to craft approaches that retain the best people, whilst not ignoring others in the organisation. This is not a book about reward and compensation; however, this chapter will link the core practices of reward to those of developing a strategic talent.

Retention is an important issue and one that can become business critical when it becomes a one-way street out of the business. Losing the wrong people can be costly, but the organisation must also look to refresh its view of talent and therefore the content of its talent pools. In some cases exiting individuals from a talent pool is a necessary step to allow others to take advantage of the attention and focus that membership brings. In addition, a refresh may be necessary as the market demands change and the profile of the pool no longer makes sense.

Chapter 10 is where we summarise the case of ETM and review what really makes this approach strategic. This final part of the book will bring together the threads that have run through each chapter and summarise how talent is a critical part of business success.

In addition, the chapter will review some of the current issues in talent management, guiding the reader to think more strategically about each.

Finally, we will reflect on some of the fundamental mistakes that organisations make when thinking about people, strategy and performance and try to build a simple check-list for any talent professional to use as a 'quick and dirty' audit of their situation. It will not solve their organisation's talent issues but it will help guide them to some of the more effective approaches.

How to get the best from the book

This book was written with the intention it would be read sequentially, as many of the concepts in each chapter build on, or are derived from, the content in the preceding text. However, like all good practical books the way to get the most value from it is to scan it first to understand the overall layout and structure. Then read it in full to see how much of its content you agree or disagree with. Not every element of the approach will resonate with your own beliefs or organisational situation. Finally, use the specific chapters that focus on the issues you need to address to guide and inform on any changes you may want to make in your organisation's current talent strategy.

This book is aimed at practitioners in all areas of managing talent, from the proactive line manager through to the full-time professional talent specialist, rather than HR student, but the need to be academically robust still remains. Good practice always follows good theory and where appropriate the models and principles are discussed in the text. Where they are more suitably read in the original source the reference is provided in the endnotes, which may be a website, a research paper or a journal article. There is no monopoly on good ideas and it is important to find inspiration from a wide range of sources.

Key review questions

Does your organisation have a documented business strategy?
Does your organisation have a documented talent management strategy?
Is the talent management strategy explicitly linked to the organisation's strategic goals?
Does every manager know what defines talent in the organisation?

Notes

1 Michaels, E., Handfield-Jones, H. and Azelrod, B. (2001) *The War for Talent*, Harvard Business School Press, Boston, MA.

2 Six Sigma is a set of techniques and tools for process improvement. It was developed by Motorola in 1986. Jack Welch made it central to his business strategy at General Electric in 1995. Today, it is used in many industrial sectors. Six Sigma seeks to improve the quality output of process by identifying and removing the causes of defects (errors) and minimising variability in manufacturing and business processes. It uses a set of quality management methods, mainly empirical, statistical methods, and creates a special infrastructure of people within the organisation ('Champions', 'Black Belts', 'Green Belts', 'Yellow Belts', etc.) who are experts in these methods. Each Six Sigma project carried out within an organisation follows a defined sequence of steps and has quantified value targets, for example: reduce process cycle time, reduce pollution, reduce costs, increase customer satisfaction, and increase profits. (Source: Wikipedia, https://en.wikipedia.org/wiki/Six_Sigma.)

3 Chinese Walls are artificial dividers to separate aspects of work. It is a business term used to describe an information barrier within an organization that was erected in order to prevent exchanges or communication that could lead to conflicts of interests. It has specific uses in banks and law firms where client confidentiality is important or a regulatory requirement.

4 Collings, D.G. and Mellahi, K. (2009) Strategic Talent Management: a review and research agenda, *Human Resources Management Review*, 19.4, 304–13.

5 Michaels, E., Handfield-Jones, H. and Alexrod, B. (1997) *The War for Talent*, Harvard Business School Press, Boston, MA.

6 Collings, D.G. and Mellahi, K. (2009) Strategic Talent Management: a review and research agenda, *Human Resources Management Review*, 19.4, 305.

7 Ridderstråle, J. and Nordström, K. (2004) *Karaoke Capitalism, Management for Mankind*, Pearson, London.

8 Ulrich, D. (1997) *Human Resource Champions*, Harvard Business School Press, Boston, MA.

9 Schleckser, Jim (2012) How Effective CEO's spend their time, 27 Aug, http://www.inc.com/john-mcdermott/jim-schleckser-ceo-project-where-effective-ceos-spend-their-time.html; Economist Intelligence Unit (2006) *The CEO's role in talent management*, Economist Intelligence Unit, London.

10 Lawler, Edward E. III (2014) What should HR leaders Focus on in 2014? *Forbes online*, 15 Jan; Ready, D., Hill, L. and Thomas, R. (2014) Building a Game Changing Talent Strategy, *Harvard Business Review*, Jan, http://www.forbes.com/sites/edwardlawler/2014/01/15/what-should-hr-leaders-focus-on-in-2014/; Growler, Rebecca (2015) Talent shortages a 'major challenge' for UK companies, *HR Magazine*, 26 Jan, http://www.hrmagazine.co.uk/hr/news/1149351/talent-shortages-major-challenge-uk-companies.

11 Facebook is currently by far the dominant player in social media with an estimated user base of close to 1.5 billion people per month. It was founded in 2004. It was not the first significant player in the social media space with MySpace predating it by a good 12 months or more. However, being first is not a guarantee of enduring success: MySpace now has an active user base of just 50 million. Selling the platform to News Corporation in 2008, however, netted its founders a cool $580 million.

12 Green, Sarah (2015) How Google Manages Talent, interview with Eric Schmidt and Jonathon Rosenburg, Sep, *Harvard Business Review*.

13 2015 CIPD Hay Resourcing and Talent Planning Survey, http://www.cipd.co.uk.

14 Smart, B.D. (1999) *Topgrading: How Companies Win by Hiring, Coaching and Keeping the Best People*, Prentice Hall Press, Paramus NJ.

15 Collings, D.G. and Mellahi, K. (2009) Strategic Talent Management: a review and research agenda, *Human Resources Management Review*, 19.4, 304–13.

16 Balshaw, Liz (2014) Engaging the next generation of talent is the big challenge for consultancy firms, *Financial Times*, 10 Nov.
17 Tovey, Alan (2015) Want a job? Construction's going to add a quarter of a million of them, *Daily Telegraph*, 27 Jan, http://www.telegraph.co.uk/finance/newsbysector/constructionand property/11370839/Want-a-job-Constructions-going-to-add-a-quarter-of-a-million-of-them.html.
18 Furnham, Adrian (2015) On Your Head: Talkin' 'bout my generation . . . just the same as the others, *Sunday Times*, 25 Jan.
19 Richardson, Hannah (Education Reporter) (2015) UK graduate recruitment prospects 'at 10-year high', BBC News, 12 Jan, http://www.bbc.co.uk/news/education-30745839.
20 High Flyers Research Limited (2015) *The Graduate Market in 2015, Annual review of graduate vacancies and starting salaries at Britain's leading employers*, http://www.highflyer.co.uk.

Chapter 2

How does my organisation compete?

Introduction

You cannot design an effective talent management process if you do not fully understand the long-term aims of the organisation. Without a clear understanding of the specific business strategy for your organisation you could be doing things that are unwittingly undermining the business's performance, or at best be busy doing something that is not adding any significant value. The key to having an effective talent management approach is strategic alignment: ensuring that everything you deliver within the talent management process directly links to the strategy that the business is pursuing. It is this visible line of sight that ensures your talent strategy gets senior management support and that enables employees to understand the link between the way they are being managed and the wider business plans.

Many practitioners struggle with the ideal of business strategy, wishing to be involved but sometimes not having the confidence or understanding to challenge what is proposed in the boardroom. Others are at times guilty of taking the senior management's vague statements of intent and growth targets as a coherent strategy. By having a better understanding of the fundamental elements of any business strategy it allows a practitioner to challenge and therefore shape the organisation's future. There is little point in agreeing to some future that is incapable of being realised with the current workforce. However, if you are clear what the strategy demands and believe it to be credible, it immediately creates a strong case for an effective talent strategy, one that is designed to achieve the strategic aims of the organisation.

Strategy is simply the process of making focused choices. Professor Michael Porter,[1] one of the world's most respected authorities on competitive strategy, an academic who advises not only global industry but also governments on their economic strategies, says the fundamental process is one of saying 'no' to things. When the senior team is discussing what is your organisation's purpose, ask of every major proposal, 'is this something that we should be focusing on?' When you have stopped saying no, the things that are left are the things that the organisation should place its focus on, and then endeavour to do better than its competitors and thereby build a competitive advantage.

When we discuss specific talent strategy in this chapter, we use this approach to focus the activities of the organisation on attracting, selecting, recruiting, developing and deploying only those talents that help the business meet its strategic goals. Focus is one of the fundamental principles of an ETM approach and one that helps deliver measurable results.

A more recent publication on strategy, and one of the best for many years, is *Good Strategy, Bad Strategy* by Richard Rumelt.[2] He puts forward, very concisely, what the core of good strategy is;

> A good strategy includes a set of coherent actions. They are not 'implementation' details; they are the punch in the strategy. A strategy that fails to define a variety of plausible and feasible immediate actions is missing a critical component.

Strategy is not just about having numbers extrapolated from today's results into the future and given a 'sexy' project title, as some senior managers seem to think. Good strategy is about the creation, and implementation, of plans that play to your organisation's strengths relative to its competitors in a market. It's then about using these strengths to exploit your competitors' weaknesses or gaps. Implementing a strategic plan requires the right sort of workforce and therefore a strategically aligned talent management approach. Understanding your organisation's strength is therefore crucial, and understanding how people contribute to this potential differentiator becomes a core element of the talent strategy.

This chapter will help you understand the basics of generic business strategies, in order that you can compare your own organisation's plans against a core framework. A number of examples will show a range of organisational strategies and highlight how different business scenarios require quite different talent responses. Each of the examples will offer insight into a generic business strategy and then illustrate a specific talent response to show how that a particular HR and Talent Management team supported the organisation.

The examples are based on real organisations and real business needs, but have been made anonymous to protect the commercially sensitive nature of their business and to respect the individual talent professional's cooperation.

Hopefully these examples will give you, the reader, a clear insight into what may need to be considered in different industries, varying sizes of organisations and different competitive market positions. This should inspire you to shape your own strategic responses to the challenges your organisation faces, based on a clear understanding of how the business plan impacts on people and talent.

Generic models of competitive strategy

Without doubt the most influential thinker in the field of strategy is the Harvard Professor Michael Porter.[3] His quite weighty books have unfortunately remained the domain of the business student rather than mainstream managers. However, his ideas have undoubtedly shaped how many professionals now think about corporate strategy.

Porter's research and private consulting work centres around what factors create a sustainable competitive advantage and then how to maximise these through sound strategic choices. He has a number of models in his armoury but one that stands the test of time is the idea of generic competitive strategies.

The basic concept is that there are only a limited number of ways for any organisation to compete successfully. Although there may be thousands of organisations in the same industry and many countless industry sectors, there really are only a few different ways to distinguish yourself from other players in the market. You can be better in only one of three ways: be more efficient at doing things and therefore less expensive than competitors; be better at the product or service so have a loyal brand or product following allowing you to charge more; or be so responsive to the customer, giving them such outstanding personal service that they choose you more than competitors at a similar price.

The best explanation of how this generic competitive strategy model works is given not by Porter but by two of his consulting contemporaries Michael Treacy and Fred Wiersema.[4] Their very accessible book, *The Discipline of Market Leaders*, simplified Porter's ideas and gives some excellent examples of different organisational approaches to market dominance.

The model shown in Figure 2.1 shows three axes, each one representing a potential generic competitive strategy. The axis has three significant points, the extreme outer end represents where the organisation leads the market. The mid-point on any axis determines the industry average performance on that axis discipline. The central point, close to where the three axes meet, shows performance below industry average, or signifies worst in class performance.

We'll start with the upper axis, product leadership, and explain the way the model works. Porter, and therefore Treacy and Wiersema, contend that to dominate or create a significant advantage within a market, the organisation needs to be structured to compete along a single discipline. So with a generic strategy of product leadership the structure of the organisation would need to be designed to create value from unique products that are leading in terms of design or technology. A good example is found with pharmaceutical companies, who invest heavily in expensive research programmes; hire the very best scientists in their fields; provide leading edge facilities; and locate in desirable locations with clusters of related activities nearby. Their products are industry leading in their chosen field and demand very high returns

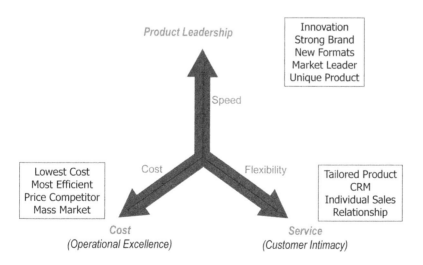

Figure 2.1 Competitive choice diagram

Source: Adapted from M. Treacy and F. Wiersema (1995) *The Discipline of Market Leaders*, Perseus Books, Cambridge, MA.

to justify the years of research by their unique and expensive workforce. However, their competitive model is not easily replicated because of the requirement for high investment and the relatively long-term nature of research before a product becomes commercially viable. They are not trying to lead the market by being lowest cost, nor are they trying to tailor every product to specific individuals or very small groups of users. The strategic choice they have made is to develop a capability for world-class research into groups of products and therapies that demand very high returns to justify the investment.

Another good example of a similar product leadership strategy is that of Apple, which leads on design and innovation, not production costs or individualisation of products. This is a different market altogether, but a shared generic strategy that proves very profitable when the structure of the organisation and its talent strategy are aligned.

The second axis, going clockwise, is labelled customer intimacy. To dominate a market in this discipline the organisation must offer a service or product that matches the expectations of the customer better than that of its competitors, it must almost be a bespoke service. Examples of organisations that offer customer intimacy are architectural practices, law firms and other professional services where the client is core to the business. Many small or niche consultancy firms are operating on this dimension: giving their customer a personal bespoke service to meet their specific needs. Once the relationship is formed, and the provider is seen to listen and meet all the particular needs of the client, the issue of cost is secondary, and the need to be part of an established big brand or have an innovative product to offer is much less important.

Customer intimacy can be used by large organisations to differentiate their standard offering, by adding choices and personalisation to a core activity. It's here that airlines such as Singapore Airlines and Emirates are leading the way: giving touches of individual care to business class passengers; allowing privileged customers a concierge service; larger variations in the menu selections; personal chauffeured cars and other attractive, additional features to their paying customers. The concept here is to give customers a personal, unique and positive experience with industry-level costs on standard offerings. So a flight from London to Singapore is always going to be on a large wide-body jet that meets aviation standards. It will always take around 14 hours direct and business class tickets are always going to be within 10 per cent of each other. This is the standard offer; however, some things make the customer more likely to select a ticket with a specific airline and that is about customer intimacy.

The final leg of the model and the easiest to understand is called operational excellence. The idea is simple, if your business can give better value, the lowest cost for a similar quality product as your competitors, then more people will buy from you enabling you to dominate the market. This strategy is currently being played out in the European grocery sector, with low-cost supermarket retailers such as Aldi, Lidl and Netto taking significant market share from more established retailers across a price-sensitive consumer market. The recent difficulties in the economy have made consumers more sensitive to the price of food and other regular home purchases and the big European players such as Tesco and Carrefour have not really responded quickly enough to the changes in the market. Aldi, the German low-cost retailer, recently reported 65 per cent growth whilst its traditional retail model rival Tesco had to deal with share price collapse, rethink its growth plans in Europe and announce the closure of a large number of its stores in the UK.[5]

Being a low-cost producer, retailer or manufacturer relies on efficiency designed into the business model in every aspect of operation. There is no room for waste in any part of the business, as it leaves room for competition. Famously Sam Walton,[6] the founder and CEO of the largest retail organisation in the world, the classic discount store, stayed in 3-star motels when on business trips. To do otherwise would be wasteful and give a bad example to others.

Whilst it can be a very successful strategy it is the one that drives many companies who attempt it out of business as they race for the lowest possible price.

Aligning business strategy and talent

The model outlined above is a great starting point for looking at your own organisation's declared strategy. Using the three-legged Treacy diagram (Figure 2.1) as a guide, you can map your own business on the three legs. You will find that it's relatively easy to declare what your core strategy is, whether that is concentration on customer intimacy or focus on cost control and efficiency. More difficult is to determine where you sit on the other axis. Beware people who demand that all three are equally important. These people do not understand strategy, which, as Michael Porter has taught us, is as much about saying no to something as it is about deciding to do something.

I presented this model in a UK National Health Service master class I was asked to run a few years ago. I was challenged in a post-presentation question session by one participant, a senior health service administrator, who said that their main stakeholder, the government, wanted all three: lowest cost, world-class surgery outcomes and patient care with 100 per cent satisfaction. What I carefully explained to the participant is this expectation was unreasonable and would break the laws of economics. The best surgical outcomes come from the best facilities being worked in by the world's best surgeons. Those two factors prohibit the third element, which is to be the most operationally efficient operator. An organisation can aim for whatever outcome it likes but its achievement is determined by competitive forces and some things are just not economically possible.

Low-cost operators do not hire the best in the world; they get, at best, industry standard and make do. They do not invest in personalisation of services, as variation in any of the process increases the standard cost. The generic competition model and the economic theory that supports it suggests designing your organisation's structure to compete on one dimension, develop a clear dominance in that area and then stretch to a second dimension; to become better but not the best is possible. It is simply impossible to compete effectively on all three – the economics do not compute.

Defining where you compete

To determine what dimension your organisation competes on, ask yourself a simple question: why do people do business with us?

If the answer is that you offer something they value that they cannot get elsewhere – a product that you have patented, a service that is unique to your organisation or a brand that is perceived to demonstrate quality – then your organisation is product leading. Your investment in the brand may offer people the quality and experience they aspire to. Think about organisations such as Apple, Nike, BMW, Chanel, Gucci, Pfizer and any brand that is globally recognised.

If the answer is that you are very good value for the customer – no one beats you on price – then the obvious answer is you are competing on operational efficiency. It may not make you a discounter but your organisation is prepared to offer price matches or uses price as primary promotion tool. Think about organisations such as Aldi, Ryanair, Ibis hotels and any business that uses the phrase, 'won't be beaten on price' in its marketing.

If the answer is all about relationships and how your organisation understands and offers unique tailored services or products to your customer then the competitive strategy is one of customer intimacy. In addition customer intimate organisations make the experience of doing business with them easy and enjoyable. Not all customer intimate businesses are providing luxury, but the cost of personalisation can be significant in a large organisation and this affects the price. Think about organisations such as Four Seasons Hotels, Singapore Airlines, Kuoni Travel, Gieves & Hawkes and your local, favourite hairdresser.

It is possible that different parts of the business operate different strategies, either because as separate business units there is a clear need to, or as a result of historical growth by acquisition and subsequent misalignment. If this is the case any talent strategy needs to be multifaceted to meet the differing business unit needs.

Right people, right place, right time

Understanding the generic competitive strategy is a great starting point. To support your businesses strategic aims you must now understand what the key goals of the organisation are and their timeframe for completion. With these two additional facts you can start to determine what an effective talent management strategy might look like.

Many organisations' goals, as demanded by the shareholders, are related to growth of market share and/or profit. It is not uncommon for a business to have a strategic target to increase market share by 5 per cent and profit by a similar figure within three years. For some organisations these targets are much more ambitious. However, for the purposes of illustration let's take 5 per cent market share growth and 5 per cent profit growth within three years, a common timeframe.

Any talent strategy must recognise how the business intends to achieve the market share, so that the right decisions can be made to support this tactic with the right people. To highlight the point, let's take the same targets in the same business, a food manufacturing business, with two different possibilities:

- **Scenario A – 5 per cent market share increase, 5 per cent profit increase, three-year timeframe**
  The market share increase will result from aggressive price promotions in the current countries of operation, mainly mature markets with little new business. This increase will come from undercutting competitors for similar products and aggressive promotions in retail stores supported using a digital media campaign. Reducing price has cost implication and requires higher levels of productivity in the manufacturing units to maintain the expected profits and increased volumes. The larger market share will account for the increase in profit overall.
- **Scenario B – 5 per cent market share increase, 5 per cent profit increase, three-year timeframe**

The market share will result from extension of the product ranges successful in the mature markets to the growing markets of Eastern Europe. There is a requirement to build new partnerships with existing Eastern European retailers and potentially adapt some products to regional tastes. Existing business units will need to expand to cope with volume and transportation and supply chain management will become key elements of the profitability of the expansion. There will be a need for some new production sites in the new markets.

In each scenario the implications for any talent management strategies are quite different.

In scenario A, there is a likelihood of a need for excellent operations managers in the production units, to maximise productivity of existing plant. In the same case the capability of the sales and marketing people needs to be high calibre, as the growth is expected from taking consumers from competitors – a difficult thing to do. Key talents implied in scenario A are production management and planning, and sales and marketing. These are short-term needs that may be met through recruitment, intensive development or internal transfer. Of course there will also be longer-term implications after the three-year target is achieved.

Scenario B is significantly different in the way it achieves its target. Eastern European expansion requires some degree of cultural awareness, an understanding of the local market and excellent language ability. The plan to expand the manufacturing units in the new territories requires skills in start-up or commissioning of plants. The strategy also calls for more focus on supply chain management, inbound and outbound as some of the product is going to be shipped to Eastern Europe. The main talent management implications are for local hiring and training of Eastern Europeans; potential expatriation of senior managers to oversee the business growth; an increase in the capability for supply chain management and the sourcing of project managers able to commission new plant for manufacturing.

Understanding the key elements of the business strategy allows the talent professional to craft a supporting and enabling response, rather than a 'one size fits all' best practice talent plan. Without this understanding it would be difficult to determine what talent is critical, where it needs to sit in the business and what would be required in terms of performance management to achieve the organisation's goals.

Ultimately, we need to provide the right people in the right place and at the right time. The numbers offered in any business strategy do not always tell the full story. Talent professionals need to dig deeper and gain a better understanding of how the strategy will affect capability and whether the goals are achievable with the current people.

Aligning business goals and talent strategies

In order to explore strategy and alignment in more depth, as they are key to success, let's look at a case study of one business. From the outline it will be possible to see what its generic competitive strategy is, what its key targets are and therefore what sort of talent management response might work. From this we can define some of the challenges that talent professionals typically face and explore ways to overcome them.

Fast Fashions

Fast Fashions (FF) was a subsidiary division of a global apparel and luxury goods business based in Paris. The division was a group of branded mail order apparel, sports clothing and soft, home furnishing businesses, with strong local brands in 11 countries in both Europe and North America. Its headquarters was in France, where its largest business was based, but local businesses had significant autonomy. The turnover was over €3 billion. The portfolio of businesses had grown by acquisition, but all shared a mature mail order business model with the vast majority of the orders still being taken over the phone, in contrast to web orders at just 20 per cent of revenues.

Much of the sales activity was derived from special offers, discounts and bundled offers, so it was expected that revenues would be linked to new promotions and end of season sales. Banners advertising 20 per cent discount were commonplace on the brand's web pages and in leaflet shots to existing mail order customers.

The group of businesses shared a resource in Asia for sourcing suppliers, and for the brands operating in France there was a shared transportation and home delivery network.

Most of the brands operated on a two catalogue a year model: Spring–Summer and Autumn–Winter. This required that fashion collections span two seasons and relied on staff trying to predict the customer demand weeks in advance of production of the hard copy catalogues. The skills of collection creation were critical to the business's overall profitability and were carried out by designers and buyers who had already gained extensive experience in the retail fashion industry.

The other critical capability was the use of databases to create bespoke, mail order lists in order to initiate the distribution of flyers and marketing leaflets to supplement the seasonal catalogues. Target mailing the right promotions to the right people could dramatically increase the sales. Finally, the logistics of inbound product and outbound distribution of millions of Stock Keeping Units (SKUs), was a determining factor in selling out a product. The inbound supply chain required 12 weeks' lead time for goods to arrive in the European warehouses.

The organisation's corporate team, the executive board, created a strategy that they hoped would transform the business within three years. The strategy's stated aim was based on the ambition of becoming the 'Amazon of Fashion' and replacing mail order with a web portal that allowed cross-selling from all the brands and also taking on their high street competitors at the game of 'fast fashion'.[7] The target for turnover for the group in three years was € 4.2 B. In addition, it expected more than 80 per cent of its sales to be via the web across all brands. In both cases these were very ambitious goals.

This business strategy posed a number of significant challenges. Growth was expected to come from new markets, such as China, where currently there was no organisational presence. Additional profit was expected to come from the reduced cost of doing business via the web rather than the labour-intensive mail order model. The logistics and supply chain capability was also going to have to significantly change to meet the higher speed of response required from a web-based sales model.

Two of the most significant challenges the new strategy implied was a reduction in product to customer cycle time and overall agility of marketing. A twice a year catalogue model of business gave cycle times of around 24 weeks. Fast fashion online typically required refresh rates of around 10 days. Additionally, FF's current web presence merely mirrored the catalogue's content with occasional offers added. A fully web-based catalogue with real-time stock data and inventory refreshed every 10 days, was not possible on the current infrastructure, nor with the limited number of support staff in the existing Information Systems department.

Reading the case above you find a business with a great sense of ambition but also with significant challenges that its declared strategy posed. For the strategy to work, the talent actions that support it need to be perfectly aligned and adequately resourced. By examining the core strategy of FF it's possible to determine the new capabilities that the talent management process will need to provide.

In this specific case, the executive group believed the generic business model they were following was that of product leadership. This matched with their collective view that they offered great fashion via their catalogue. In this niche market they were brand leader. However, research suggested that many of their customers bought based on price, waiting for the inevitable discounts that the organisation offered. The business, across its brands, was historically quick to discount apparel very early in the current season, being keen to sell stock it had already purchased some weeks earlier due to the use of Far East-based suppliers. This created a customer expectation of lower prices for the savvy buyer who was prepared to order late.

In reality the business was already competing with the high street fast fashion retailers, such as Zara and H&M, as well as the thousands of small web-based retailers. To succeed now, and in the future, they needed to adopt a more operational efficient model that the web could help them enable.

The talent challenges only become apparent when you recognise this fact. To be operationally efficient you need a fast, reliable supply chain that can respond to new information on sales to refresh and reorder in smaller more flexible batches. FF needed to develop the skills of running an agile business. This would challenge how they had traditionally operated and require new mindsets and new capabilities. Any ETM strategy would need to be focused on acquiring the new capabilities whilst still enabling the business to operate as usual during the transformation.

This business model change would mean different skill sets for the operations people across the whole business. The first skill challenge sat in the design office where collections were created in the traditional model of two cycles per year. The new strategy demanded collections refreshed every 10 days to compete with the fast fashion retailer on the high streets and in shopping malls. This much more reactive buying approach, following trends rather than trying to predict them, was already in huge demand. Finding people who were skilled in this was going to be both difficult and expensive. Given FF was not considered a particularly cool brand, it meant any initiative to attract skilled, fast fashion buyers from other more established players would be need to be very creative. An alternative approach, and one that would be taken in parallel, was to develop the talent in-house from existing employees who demonstrated potential. The drawback of this tactic was that it required a significant time to develop the required expertise.

A similar challenge was faced with building the capability to move to a web-enabled business. FF had a web infrastructure that could not be scaled up to a full e-tailing business model. To build or commission a platform that could deal with the proposed new business model was beyond the skills and experience of the current team. In addition the existing resources in their central Information Technology team were busy maintaining legacy systems across 11 business brands. Switching their attention to development rather than maintenance may impact on the revenue from current business streams.

The CEO's ambition was to be a destination of choice for fashion conscious consumers on the web searching for apparel, and as such wanted a premium online shopping experience. This put FF in competition with the major web retailers for creative web talent. FF wanted the same skill sets as sought by Google and eBay. Again, the challenge for the talent team was to be creative to overcome the difficulty of building a new capability in the business whilst maintaining their current systems and profits.

A final element of the strategy that impacted on talent was the aim to launch the business in China. Given that there were currently no Chinese employees in sales, marketing or design and only a small number based in Hong Kong in supplier management, it was a significant challenge. Whilst the business logic of expansion into the rapidly growing market of China was sound, it was not clear that the executive team had appreciated the resource requirement needed to execute their plans.

The outlined business strategy of FF created some infrastructure challenges, some change management problems and some cultural issues. All could be positively supported in some way by the right talent strategy and the right level of resource investment. Table 2.1 outlines some of these issues and how they impact on what a talent strategy should focus on. Every strategic aim creates choices and therefore some form of consequence and many of these goals impacted on how talent should be managed in the future.

Table 2.1 Strategic aims and implications

Strategic aim	Business implication	Talent implication
Entry to Chinese Market	New territory to establish, new culture to understand, new logistical demands. Rapidly growing affluent market.	No current Chinese speakers in head office. No fashion buyers with insight into market demands in China. Need to establish office staffed by local talents in China.
Web-driven sales model	Expand web sales infrastructure to meet expected demand of 70 per cent of sales. Innovation in online sales to distinguish their business. Create new marketing model based on web and social media.	Need to recruit high-calibre technical talent to build web infrastructure. Need to attract creative technical talent to low-brand recognition fashion business, instead of high tech competition. Build capability in social media management and marketing.

Compete with fast fashion high street retailers	Demand driven supply chain with increased responsiveness. Web inventory to be updated in 10-day cycles rather than 4–6-month cycles.	Specialists supply chain experts required to rebuild logistics model. Change to more local sourcing expertise and buyers with experience of fast fashion.

To make a positive impact on business, any talent strategy needs to recognise the implications that the business strategic goals have on people, both now and in the future. Only then can the talent professional create a meaningful response. Linking the business aims with the impact on people is the key element of any successful response.

In the case outlined above, the organisation was trying to compete in three completely new areas of talent, all of which were already in high demand on the open market. The technical expertise that they required to build a fully scalable web sales platform, able to innovate and distinguish their business from the other online retailers, placed FF in competition for talent with the likes of Google, Amazon, eBay and all the other existing web-based sales platforms. Social media-based marketing was emerging as a key way to establish real conversations with customers, and had already become a core skill of the multimedia marketing professional, a highly competitive field. Finally, the expertise required to take an existing logistics system and dramatically increase its responsiveness by a factor of 15–20 was not easy to find. Most of the large retailers in Europe were responding to the on-demand expectations of society and the rise of Internet sales by building more responsive supply chains. Again this meant FF was competing with Carrefour, Tesco and DHL for talent in this area of need.

FF's talent strategy had to respond to this gap in a way that meant it could acquire and retain the talent it needed in spite of attractive alternatives in the market. There are a number of tactics available:

- Pay above the market rate.
- Make the role of a higher responsibility than that available in more attractive, bigger brand employers.
- Significantly increase the development budget available to new hires.
- Bonus people for high performance – attracting high achievers
- Create a culture that is attractive to this target group – work–life balance or desirable working environment.
- Bring in new talent from outside the current labour market – India, China, Eastern Europe.
- Take a risk on young talent with less proven experience but high potential.

In FF's case its response was a mixture of the above, with each element tailored to attract interest from the targeted talent groups.

The most important element of any talent strategy is how closely aligned it is to the overall business strategy. If the organisation gets this right, then every euro invested in talent will positively impact on the overall goals of the business. If the organisation, and the talent professional responsible, gets it wrong, then at best the investment is helping employees learn and develop additional skills. At worst the investment could be unintentionally working against the future success of the organisation.

Line of sight

When the organisation determines that it wishes to expand into a new market, as in the FF case above, then there are clear implications for the talent plans that result from this decision. Hiring, developing and performance managing people to support the opening of a new market can all be planned and quantified in terms of cost and time to achieve, and how much impact it will likely have on the revenue can be estimated. When these plans are proposed it is important to undergo a line of sight test.

The plans outlined to support the new market expansion should be tracked forwards to the end goal. If the plan's outputs all positively impact on the revenue, there is a positive line of sight between the plan's and the organisation's goals. If there is not, then some of the planned actions need to be adjusted or omitted.

Using the example of expansion in the Chinese market in the FF case outlined above, one of the goals in the larger organisational strategy was to have 200 million euros of revenue in the market within three years. To achieve this level of revenue, the organisation had agreed milestones for the start-up to be achieved within 12 months and these then had implications for the talent strategy.

Initially an office was to be established in one of the major cities of mainland China; this was to be achieved within the first six months of the strategy timeframe. The expectation was that the office would be 90 per cent staffed by locally recruited people. It was also expected to grow from fewer than 10 employees in year 1, to over 40 people in year 3.

All of these milestones seemed rational and connected to the organisational aim. However, in terms of the talent response, the critical business factor was the hire of a local country manager who would lead the start-up process. This single act, the search for and selection of a highly experienced manager willing to locate to China, was the crux of the expansion plan. The skill mix was crucial: Chinese national; excellent English language; desirable French language; significant, fashion retail, buying experience; proven leadership and excellent business acumen. The successful candidate would not be easy to find.

Putting significant resources and time into this activity gave a straight line of sight to the goals of the organisation, which was to achieve 200 million euros of sales within three years. Spending time and money on this activity was directly linked to success and therefore was an urgent priority.

The right country head appointment would make the start-up of the new office location, recruitment of local staff, gaining market insight and capability building more effective. In this case, the line of sight is clear. If the organisation spends more time and effort here, there will be a significant positive impact on future goals. This post became a critical and urgent appointment and the first priority of the HR team.

Given that the talent management strategy also needed to deal with an expansion of web sales, technical platform development, social media marketing capability and fast fashion skills, being able to scale the actions to the potential impact on goals is both critical and helpful to the talent manager. Priority should always be given to those actions that have most impact on the end goals and have a clear line of sight to them. Expanding the web capability became the second priority for FF.

A good strategy, including all effective talent strategies, should have clear lines of sight between actions taken and their impact on the future performance of the organisation. Where that impact is not evident, questions need to be asked as to whether the action is absolutely necessary and, if not, should the investment of resources be transferred to something more effective.

Reflections on strategy

Strategy is about focus and therefore saying no to things that the organisation cannot do well. For the things that the organisation decides it can do well, it should create the structure to do it better than all of its competition. That structure relies on the right type of employee, and disproportionally relies on some talent that has already proven strategic capability.

Aligning the goals of the talent and the business strategy is at the heart of ETM. As a talent management professional or HR manager responsible for talent, it is important that you understand the range of approaches to attracting, developing, deploying, rewarding and retaining the right people. However, to be really successful you also need to understand how the business strategy impacts on talent and as a result can craft a talent management strategy that is truly effective.

By applying some of the basic analytical frameworks discussed so far, such as those for generic strategies, it is possible to unpick the implications for talent in your own organisation. With this deeper insight, talent and HR professionals can then craft a more meaningful response, confident that when their plans are implemented they are going to have a positive impact on the success of the business.

This chapter has introduced you to some of the basic frameworks for thinking about business strategy. Particularly, the work of Richard Rumelt, Michael Porter, and Michael Treacy and Fred Wiersema are great resources for developing your understanding of the foundations of strategy. In order to earn a place in the decision-making forum of your organisation, it is first necessary to understand, and speak, the language of business and then discuss talent. Increasing your own understanding of what good strategy is will enable you to create specific plans to support your business in achieving its goals. As a result you will have significantly more credibility and influence with your senior team.

Key review questions

Which generic strategy is the organisation pursuing?

What is the organisation's current key capability or strength?

Is the strategy coherent with the current capabilities?

What capabilities or capacity will need to change to achieve the strategic goals of this organisation?

Notes

1 Michael Porter addressed the CIPD conference a number of years ago, stressing that saying no to activities and focusing on those few, that if done well, create a difference is the key to all strategy. In the late 1990s in his role as a consultant he was reputed to have been paid $1 million for three days of workshops for the Singapore Port Authority. He is one of the world's most influential voices on strategy.

2 Rumelt. R. (2011) *Good Strategy, Bad Strategy: The difference and why it matters*, Profile Books, London. Quote from p. 6.

3 Porter, M. (1998) *On Competition*, Harvard Business School Press, Boston, MA.

4 Treacy, M. and Wierseama, F. (1995) *The Discipline of Market Leaders*, Perseus Books, Cambridge, MA.

5 Spary, Sara (2014) Aldi reports 65% surge in pre-tax profits, *Marketing*, 29 Sept, http://www.marketingmagazine.co.uk/article/1314560/aldi-reports-65-surge-pre-tax-profits; Khan, Mehreen (2015)Tesco closures: is your local store getting the chop? *The Daily Telegraph*, 28 Jan, http://www.telegraph.co.uk/finance/newsbysector/retailandconsumer/11333964/Tesco-closures-is-your-local-store-getting-the-chop.html.

6 An extract from the book by Vance Trimble, *Sam Walton: The Inside Story of America's Richest Man*, highlights the operational efficiency concept taken to heart by Sam Walton:

> 'To the despair of the nation's decorators, he lives in a modest house in a small town in Arkansas a few blocks from one of his warehouses. He keeps a dusty pickup truck in the driveway, a dusty Chevy sedan in the garage and a couple of muddy bird dogs in the yard. Each weekday, after breakfast at a local Days Inn, he drives the pickup, missing two hubcaps, to his office, a cubicle 8 by 12 feet. There, beside the secretarial pool, amid stacks of papers, he settles in at his desk, furniture that one visitor describes as having an 'early Holiday Inn' look.

> His lifestyle was in complete congruence with his business philosophy and therefore strategic choice (see Trimble, Vance (1990) *Sam Walton: The Inside Story of America's Richest Man*, Dutton, New York, quoted in Anderson, Jon (1990) The Frugal Lifestyle of the King of Thrift, *Chicago Tribune*, 17 Dec, http://articles.chicagotribune.com/1990-12-17/features/9004140388_1_sam-walton-wal-mart-discount-stores-vance-h-trimble).

7 'Fast fashion' is a contemporary term used by fashion retailers to express that designs move from catwalk quickly in order to capture current fashion trends. Fast fashion clothing collections are based on the most recent fashion trends presented at Fashion Week in both the spring and the autumn of every year. These trends are designed and manufactured quickly and cheaply to allow the mainstream consumer to buy current clothing styles at a lower price. This philosophy of quick manufacturing at an affordable price is used in large retailers such as H&M, Zara, Peacocks and Topshop (Source: http://en.wikipedia.org/wiki/Fast_fashion).

Chapter 3

What sort of talent do we need?

Introduction

Any talent management approach will be primarily shaped by the definition of talent that the organisation agrees upon. This definition must be congruent with the strategic direction of the business, so that successful implementation of a talent management process will positively impact on the organisation's goals.

Talent is an ethereal concept, something that we all know when we see it, but few can really claim to understand what its component parts are. However, if the organisation fails to agree upon a clear definition of talent then its strategy for resourcing, development and deployment may be at odds with the real strategic goals of the business. Without a consensus on what sort of people make a disproportionate difference to organisational performance, a talent professional could quite easily be very busy on activities that are considered to be great HR initiatives, but are ineffective in terms of driving business success.

This chapter will explore how to create a clear and transparent definition of talent that is intrinsically linked to the business strategy. It will also examine the different ways that talent can be defined, and guide the reader through the various frameworks for thinking about performance and potential.

This crafting of a meaningful talent definition underpins the next stage in the process of an ETM approach, that of strategic talent planning, which is covered in Chapter 4.

The definition is the foundation that talent strategy is built upon. However, as discussed in Chapter 2, the talent strategy should only be created as a response to the demands of the business strategy; this is its only rationale. Different business strategies will therefore require different supporting talent responses, ones that meet the specific challenge of that set of strategic choices. Also within this chapter we link the idea of generic, competitive strategies, explored previously, to the variety of different talent management responses that each of these approaches demands.

Defining talent – What really matters?

We have been spotting talent within commercial and public organisations for decades using a cornucopia of approaches. Some are based on widely agreed logic, but many more are related to the personal bias of senior executives within the business, or even the falsely held belief that all talent shares some unique visible trait or habit. It is not unusual to hear that some managers believe that they can 'spot potential a mile away', but when asked, the same people can't articulate what it is that they are looking for. Again, their belief is 'they know it when they see it'.

What we know from research and experience is that a more effective and productive approach is to first determine what sort of specific talent matters in each organisation, then undertake some form of job analysis that will inform you of what specific factors indicate when someone would meet the criteria for success in each role. These are more often than not described in some form of competence language. It's more systematic and reliable than just taking the opinion of managers unable to rationalise their choices. A shared definition allows a more consistent approach that all managers can use: the ones who believe they know what talent looks like and also the ones who are more open to learning what talent means.

Masters of the universe

Whilst in my early career, running the graduate scheme for a global fast-moving consumer goods (FMCG) business, I was approached by a London-based merchant bank, now absorbed into another banking entity, to discuss becoming the head of its graduate recruitment and development team. During an extended informal interview I explained to the HR Director how I would approach the task of defining exactly what would differentiate talent in the organisation and how to design a rigorous assessment process aligned with that definition, so that the organisation could easily select the best fit for its business. It was at this point he explained how the organisation currently operated.

I was shocked to hear that the organisation already had a tried and tested process it was happy with. It consisted of two things: a basic approach to sorting applications resulting in a long list of potentials, who were then required to attend an evening cocktail party at the head office in London. It was here that the CEO and one other of his senior team would circulate and engage in small talk. There was no structured interview or competence question in sight. From this informal chat they would be able to spot 'talent'. Hastily updated pro forma contracts were presented to the lucky few that same evening. Apparently the CEO was gifted with some deep insightful intuition, which was never questioned and required nothing as vulgar as the candidate meeting a written person specification.

The organisation and I mutually agreed that we were probably not a going to pursue this any further, even though the salary and bonus attached were very generous for a role more akin to a dating agency manager than a graduate recruiter.

Given the current state of the investment banking industry, and the way that people behaved within it during, and subsequent to, the crash of 2008, maybe my horror was justified. If I reflect on the timing it is plausible that some of the people making decisions and trading during the time leading up to the crash would be the same graduate talents hired through intuition and senior executives' personal 'gifts' alone. Even with these serious failures of selection, which across many financial institutions led to hiring people who would literally do anything to succeed, there have been few, if any, that have been successfully brought to account.[1]

As discussed in Chapter 2 talent and business strategies must be aligned. To do this effectively the talent practitioner must understand what drives success in their business and therefore what makes someone a talent within it.

Just as copying a business strategy verbatim is both naïve and unproductive, mimicking some other organisation's definition of talent, and hoping it will work for your own situation, is also flawed logic. Whilst many organisations will have a talent strategy, many of these are still based on imprecise criteria and vague understandings of how these factors drive business success. A recent survey[2] of HR practitioners by the CIPD found that whilst over 50 per cent were involved in some element of talent management, only 20 per cent had a formal definition of talent in their organisation.

The reason some organisations thrive whilst others struggle to survive is their unique approach to finding the right people, deploying them in the right place and developing their latent potential whilst they are in role. What makes it unique is that successful organisations have a very close match between what the organisation is trying to achieve, its business strategy, and what sort of people the business focuses on finding and retaining. The focus should be on the *right* people for their strategy, not just good people.

The talent continuum – a tale of two philosophies

Over the many years I have been responsible for or advising clients about their talent management strategies I have become aware that there is a wide range of beliefs about talent; a real philosophical continuum.

At one extreme, within the staff of the HR or Talent Management function, there exists a belief that all employees are talented and that equality and fairness requires that their purpose as a function is to bring that latent talent out in everyone. Holding this philosophical position, everyone within the organisation is considered to be a talent. It is clearly driven by a strong personal belief in fairness and openness of opportunity. However, there are significant implications with taking this position regarding its impact on business performance. To support the ubiquitous talent belief there needs to be significant investment in development budgets and other associated HR resources.

At the other end of the continuum, there are organisations that apply the more meritocratic approach that defines talent as people who are meeting, or could with development meet, a strictly defined criteria. These people are then deemed worthy of some additional special treatment and associated investment. With this dominant philosophy it is clear that not everyone in the organisation is considered as talented. This position is one where differentiation of treatment is embraced and those considered to contribute more to the business's success have more invested in them and in their development. This is sometimes referred to as a human capital approach, but regardless of the label it is simply a more strategic approach to talent management.

Other organisations place themselves somewhere along the continuum. I have always characterised it as a choice between a 'Gandhiesque' approach and, at the other polar extreme, a 'Genghis Khan' approach. I have a clear preference for a working more towards the Genghis end of the continuum, as none of the organisations I have worked for, or advised, have had the unlimited resources that treating every staff member as a genuine, high-potential, talent requires. It may well be a laudable management aspiration and sounds good in a recruitment marketing brochure or a senior executive presentation. However, believing that you can spread the finite resources that an organisation has access to across every single employee, and still gain the same impact on the organisation's success that a more selective approach would bring, is flawed thinking. ETM requires differential treatment of a few critical people who drive more success than most around them.

If this sounds unfair, and somehow elitist, then consider the alternatives whilst reading the rest of the book. If your organisation does not invest where it gets the most return then it is not carrying out the primary objective of a commercial organisation, to maximise the return to the shareholder. For those who work in government institutions or the third sector then the same broad logic applies. The best use of resources is that which will generate the best return in terms of benefit to the stakeholders. Investing in things that reduce that return is poor management.

The harsh truth is that not all roles contribute equally to the organisation's strategic aims. Investing in a few specific roles, and ensuring you have talent in abundance within them, can be linked to measurable business success.

Take a moment to think about the people in the organisation you currently work in. There are definitely people employed in most organisations that, if they left, would have no negative impact on business results. In fact for some, their very absence would have a positive increase beyond the savings in salary and employment costs. There are clearly others that if they resigned would impact on your share price within weeks, or in some high-profile cases, days should they choose to go to a competitor. The status of being a talent is a criteria- and performance-based categorisation, not something given as a reward to hard workers of limited impact on business success. Talent, when clearly defined and nurtured, can have a direct measurable impact on the bottom line. This cannot be said of all roles within an organisation.

If your organisation was selling consumer goods across the globe you would expect it to focus its marketing and sales activity on those products that had the biggest potential market and the highest margins. You would not expect the company's executives to invest in small markets and niche products, where even excellent sales would fail to positively impact on business success. In fact, over investment in areas of the business where there were limited short-term returns and no long-term growth, would be considered bad governance by the shareholders.

Why is it then that some talent management practitioners, HR managers and senior executives like to tell their employees that they are all talents? Clearly the message should be that they can all be valued contributors to the business, but in terms of talent, they are not all equal and not all can be invested in to the same degree. If the organisation wants effective talent management that drives business success, it needs to recognise this fact.

This hard business perspective has at times divided opinions about the purpose of talent management strategies. It is very clear for me, and for many other enlightened practitioners, that the purpose of an effective talent strategy is to support business success. This in itself doesn't exclude organisational wide development or training opportunities for wider groups of employees. This provision of necessary training and development is a local management issue and something that could be provided by a trusted supplier or education partner. However, talent management cannot be left to chance as it is central to the strategic intent of the organisation, and therefore it should prioritise the use of its resources so that its talent is given every possible opportunity to thrive.

What is talent and what makes it strategic?

There are many different definitions of talent, some provided by commercial consultancies offering their services, some from governmental bodies trying to provide frameworks for training and education and others from professional institutions. They share much of their wording and describe the same thing from slightly different perspectives.

The following is the current definition of talent from the UK's CIPD. They offer:

> **Talent** *consists of those individuals who can make a difference to organisational performance either through their immediate contribution or, in the longer-term, by demonstrating the highest levels of potential.*

Whilst it's no more accurate or definitive than any other alternative it does represent the thinking of Europe's largest professional HR body and, as such, enjoys significant support and influence.

In this instance, talent is defined as those individuals that make a difference to the performance of the organisation, either immediately or in the longer term. If we accept this general description we then need to focus on the specific context of the organisation in order to understand how talent might impact and make a difference.

To do this, we need to understand what general activities impact on the performance of any organisation, and then tailor that generic action to the specific situation of the business. It is those roles that have genuine impact on the success of the organisation that should be deemed strategic talents and therefore determine the shape of any talent strategy.

Strategic impact – the generic choices

As we explored in Chapter 2, there are three generic choices that drive success in almost all businesses. They are described in *The Workforce Scorecard*[3] as: customer success, financial success and operational success. All three strategic choices result in a different talent requirement, one that is specific to the competitive focus for that organisation. To deliver against their strategy they need the talent in place in the key roles that epitomise the characteristics of the business

In the same way that there are three generic business strategies, there are three general talent responses. To understand how these three areas of focus impact on business success, we will examine each in some detail with examples of organisations that typify them.

The first group of strategic talent is those whose work positively impacts on sales or the decisions customers make to purchase the organisation's innovative new products or 'must have' service offer. This can include any role that can influence the product design or marketing, or an indirect role that influences changes in the product or service offered. Here the people who create the products or services are key talents as they design solutions that keep the organisation at the leading edge of their industry.

The second, distinct group of strategic talent, is those whose role can save costs – directly, or indirectly. So, many purchasing department roles where the buyer's decision, or their negotiation skills, can influence the costs incurred by an organisation. These are the roles that optimise production processes, or impact on the cycle time in order to achieve the same level of quality of product or service. Regardless of the industry, these roles focus on reducing the cost; increasing utilisation and reducing cycle time and therefore maximise the profit of any organisation.

Third, is any role that can create strong relationships with specific customers, and provide personalised or bespoke solutions. Customisation, or the implementation of real customer intimacy, is a way to build loyalty and relationships with buyers in a market with lots of available choices. Here the emphasis of the role is to understand the differences in each customer and provide a tailored solution.

The generic business strategies explored in Chapter 2, shown in the Treacy and Wiersema diagram (Figure 2.1), are dependent on the business structuring itself to support the strategic choice it has made. One critical element of the structure is the way it recruits and retains the talent it needs to achieve its business aims. For example, structuring your business to enable it to compete in a market by optimising its costs and being a low price competitor requires you to take talent decisions that are congruent with that choice.

Fresh food focus

Whilst working as a consultant advising the board of a large UK fresh food business whose products were own label, commodity ingredients supplied to global fast food companies and the big four grocery retailers, I was asked to facilitate a meeting focused on its strategy. Their business was built on selling large quantities of cut and washed vegetables, fresh cut salad and mixed salad leaves to some of the most cost-conscious buyers in the fast food and grocery industry. The margins were wafer thin, as winning business was almost always a price-related decision.

During the meeting the Managing Director expressed her desire to build a high-value gourmet brand, in the category of convenience salads. This would be competing with her customer's own label on their salad shelves. She wished to do this within the same manufacturing facility, with the same staff and at the same time provide the same volume of commodity business to her existing customers, still at competitive prices.

What this request led to was a debate by the board about strategic choice and structure. It is incredibly difficult, if not impossible, to compete with two opposing competitive strategies at the same time. The prevailing logic and experience suggests that the structure of your business needs to be designed and focused to support each strategy.

Low cost can only really be achieved by setting low pay, having low overheads and achieving high levels of productivity through the optimisation of the plant. There is little justification for marketing spend and very little invested in research or product development. High-value gourmet offers would demand investment in research, investment of time and money on brand building and would require lower volume production runs that create productivity problems. In addition, from a talent perspective, it would require an increase in the cost of marketing and recruiting staff with expertise in food product innovation. The two approaches required completely different organisational structures and distinctly different talents to achieve success.

The result of this heated debate was a review of the long-term strategy of the organisation and the decision to research the possibility of spinning off part of the company to build a gourmet brand, using a focused business structure. In business, structure always follows strategy and this organisation had neither the structure nor the talent to achieve its ambitions.

The result of this boardroom debate was a decision to source and attract a talented branded food specialist to head up the new venture. The organisation needed talent it did not possess to start the new venture.

An effective talent strategy needs to align to and support the overall business aims. However, in order for this to be possible the business strategy needs to be coherent in the first instance. It is surprising how many businesses have incongruent business/talent strategies, yet plough on thinking one is helping the other.

David Ulrich and Dick Beatty, two highly respected American business professors have written extensively about the need to align the generic competitive strategies with a coherent talent response.[4] Their research into HR strategy and what sort of HR initiatives drive business success have informed them about what sort of talent management approaches work in different industries and with different generic competitive strategies. Table 3.1 shows how they have interpreted strategic fit and talent needs.

It would be foolish for an organisation to take a strategic position of competing on low cost and then have talent strategies that sought out the very best marketing and research talent who are best able to develop new innovative approaches. These types of talents would be too expensive and too difficult to attract. Importantly, they would also be frustrated if they joined such a cost-focused organisation where resources to explore and research alternatives were scarce. When the strategy depends on people who enjoy, and are skilled in, incremental improvement and the optimisation of systems, the best tactic is to maximise the profile of the company to attract exactly these types of people. Then, when they are recruited, ensure they are retained with the appropriate mix of rewards and benefits. Finding great people is important but retaining them is critical to success. Reward and retention tactics and how they support the overall ETM approach are discussed in some detail in Chapter 9.

Components of a strategic talent definition

A good talent definition reflects the different levels in the organisation, or career stages of talents, from entry-level young professionals through to the top executive team. It would also be a combination of factors, some describing the experience required, others reflecting the international or global mobility that some roles demand. What must be achieved is a clear and transparent definition. Vague notions of what talent looks and smells like are not good in terms of building an ETm strategy.

Table 3.1 Talent strategic fit

Operational excellence – cost-based competition	Product leadership – innovation and building brands	Customer intimacy – solutions and customisation
Core talents – skills and mindsets		
Identifies with the process	Identifies with brand/product	Identifies with customers
High concern for quality	Interested in discovery	Open and sharing
High concern for output	Challenges status quo	Seeks out customer insight
Systems thinking	Long-term focus	Makes things happen
Short-term focused	Learning is important	Customer champions
Incremental improvement	Tolerant of ambiguity	Quick to learn what works
Low level of risk taking	Open to risk taking	Customer success matters
Stability is key	Curious about what might be	Flexible
Not free spirits/ostentatious	**Not** structured/optimisers	**Not** clones, very individual
Typical work behaviour		
Teamwork	Problem solving	Shares ideas
Reliable	Challenge people/ideas	Develops broad skills
Predicable	Collaborative cross-functional	Networks effectively
See themselves as part of a system	Creative	Customer relationships work
Example organisations		
Dell, Ryanair, Aldi, Ikea, McDonalds,	Sony, Glaxo, Microsoft, Nike, Nestlé, Intel	Four Seasons, Singapore Airlines, Coutts, Kuoni.

Adapted from David Ulrich and Dick Beatty (2001) From Partners to Players: Extending the HR playing field, *Human Resources Management* 40.4, 293–307.

A common and agreed definition of what constitutes talent already puts the organisation at a distinct advantage over its competitors, as many businesses have yet to really understand what strategic talent is and how it can drive success.

When talking about talent, the organisation should also focus its definition on those that contribute most, not the whole population. As discussed earlier, the notion that everyone is a talent is laudable, but neither realistic nor sustainable in most organisations. This means any definition must reflect what makes those people in this smaller sample of the whole work population special, in regard to the organisation's goals and strategic intent.

Whilst there is no perfect framework, Table 3.2 shows some of the key components that may feature in a large organisation's talent definition. It would, of course, be tailored to each level in the organisation, to reflect the different seniority of talent pools.

Determining potential

The nature of talent management is to create long-term success of the organisation, by finding and retaining the best fit of people to the strategic goals of the business. Doing this requires the talent professional to be able to identify future potential in people, some of who already work for the organisation and in many more who don't.

The concept of potential generates a lot of debate, particularly in the field of organisational and occupational psychology. The key questions are: can future potential really be measured and if so what determines who has it and who does not?

Some organisations have attempted to define potential in terms of promotion and readiness for promotion. This has a reasonable amount of support as it seems on face value to be easy to understand. Typical ratings for potential in these organisations are:

- High Potential – someone able to move two positions above current level within 36 months.
- Promising – someone who may be able to move two positions within 36–60 months.
- Promotable – someone who may be able to move one position higher.
- No potential currently – should stay in role and concentrate on performance.

Table 3.2 Example components of talent definition

Component	Requirement	Comments
Experience	Are there levels of experience required to be a talent at this level? Some organisations require specific previous experience in order to qualify as a talent and/or technical qualifications .	Talent pools should be built from people with the ability to take on a number of roles, but some generic experience may be needed to be credible or effective.
Mobility	Does the individual have a mobility mindset, which could involve regular business travel, secondments, relocation short-term work assignments requiring a weekly/monthly commute.	Talent should be considered an asset of the organisation, and so be ready to be deployed wherever necessary for best effect. Is the individual prepared to travel or relocate as required?
Languages/ cultural sensitivity	Are there language requirements to be successful? Local cultural sensitivity may be an issue affecting success. Working in English at business fluency is normally a standard in global companies.	If the market opportunities are in countries such as China or India, some cultural sensitivity may dramatically impact on success.
Competencies	These describe what factors the organisation believes are important in determining potential. Competency frameworks for talent try to describe immediate and future abilities.	Competencies are key to the whole talent management process, as they form part of the definition, assessment, development and performance management.
Performance	What level of performance does the individual need to display in their current role/situation to be considered talent? This can be measured from current appraisal, bonus results or assessment processes.	Many individuals may be high performers, but still lack the potential for qualification of talent. Some high-potential individuals may not be currently high performers, but could be with help.

Different organisations may have slightly different timescales for moves or different words to describe the rankings, but a notion of 'promotability' pervades this approach.

The underlying weakness in this approach is that the evaluation of promotion potential is not really defined in most organisations by criteria that can be measureable or validated. It is generally the opinion of the individual's line manager, or a consensus of a small number of reviewing managers. Whilst this is not particularly objective, the discussion to reach a consensus should contain evidence or supporting arguments for the ranking.

This approach, sometimes linked to succession planning reviews, works reasonably well where the roles are very similar and the business stable over time. Therefore, predicting someone's ability to move to the next most senior role over a specified time period, where there is little organisational change, is possible. However, where the talent management system employs a wide pool of talent and the roles are evolving and changing, this approach to determining potential is less useful.

What is needed is a more measurable and more objective determination of potential. There is no perfect solution, and some real debate about whether measuring potential is possible; however, rating, based on a wider range of factors that are more transferable, seems to be a more effective and acceptable approach. This is where competency frameworks have some real utility.

Competencies are discussed again in Chapter 6 in relation to assessment methodologies. In terms of identifying potential they are useful in describing the characteristics that are most often applied when people are working successfully in roles. All competencies are definitions of the abilities, attitudes and skills that when applied seem to create success in roles.

To determine which competencies matter most in the roles or talent pools within a specific organisation, it is necessary to undertake a basic job analysis. This would focus on key roles and then, in addition, some analysis of individual high performers, so that a template can be built linking the two. The objective is to find out which roles require which competencies and which of those competencies influence high performance. There will be a few critical competencies in each role that differentiates between high and average performance. It is these few that can form the core of the definition of potential.

Three is the magic number

There has been a lot of research into which competencies predict or measure potential in management roles. Some of the more recent meta-studies,[5] have concluded that there seem to be clusters of competence that correlate with high performance in future roles. These are represented in various ways in different organisations' competence models, but all seem to share the same three underlying dimensions. For talent managers who are finding leaders of the future, as well as meeting the current managerial needs, these three dimensions are very useful as a benchmark for defining potential.

The first dimension is based on applied intellectual ability. The cognitive ability to think strategically; use pattern recognition skills; apply the big picture thinking and then focus on the long-term impact is considered important. It is also contrasting the ability to dig down into the detail and think operationally where necessary. The capacity to balance these two at the same time seems to be a feature of people who have the cognitive ability to understand the complexity of business and be successful at a senior management level.

The second dimension is focused on what is now commonly referred to as emotional intelligence. This is the combination of skills and abilities that allows others to work well with you, and you with others. It also encompasses the confidence that is needed for people to influence others and also to be comfortable being challenged by those around them. This dimension is more than just deep self-confidence, often called self-efficacy by psychologists, it's also about inspiring confidence in people who work with them.

The final dimension that emerges in most competence frameworks is about personal drive and organisation. A high degree of intrinsic motivation and personal ambition to achieve success is present in high achievers. They also have a frustration with inaction, which manifests itself as a drive to make things happen. Again the dimension has many labels but seems to cover the aspects of taking personal responsibility for actions and their own performance.

Whilst these three dimensions may not cover all the specifics required in a definition of potential for every organisation, they do provide a good starting point for a detailed discussion about which competencies seem to make a difference to high performance. It is essential to have the discussion on specifics in each organisation, if not to discover something new, then at least to assimilate the ideas into the language and thinking of each organisation.

When Sony Europe developed its own model for potential it used a similar set of three dimensions but aligned these to its existing competence framework. In this case each dimension was made up of two or more management competencies. In Sony's case the three dimensions were labelled Competence, Confidence and Courage:

Competence – Strategic Thinking, Analytical Skills

Confidence – Influence, Negotiation, Building People Capability, Communication

Courage – Change Leadership, Personal Responsibility

These three dimensions are examples of factors that seemed to determine success in management roles at all levels within Sony Europe. They were arrived at as a result of comprehensive job analysis and a full review of performance of individuals across the European business. Not all three dimensions, or individual competences that made each dimension, had equal predictive effect. The assessment process for the most senior managers suggested that the single most predictive factor for success in a role was demonstrating a high score on the competence 'Building People Capability'. Being a good manager of other people seemed to ensure business results were achieved more than any of the other factors in the potential definition.

Candidates for all of the four talent pools that existed in Sony were measured for potential using these three dimensions. In addition they were expected to have a 'good' or 'excellent' rating in their performance management appraisals in at least two of the previous three years.

Evaluating performance

Another key aspect of any talent definition is that of individual performance. It is now very common for organisations to plot their talent against the dimensions of performance and potential. If potential can be defined in terms of competencies, and assessed using well-established tools and techniques which will be explored in Chapter 6, then performance must also be quantified in some defined way. Chapter 8 will look in some detail at the various approaches that organisations take to performance management and the assumptions that lie behind them.

Existing employees will already have some record of their on-the-job performance, regardless of the type of system employed. This can be used as one input and integrated with other elements of any talent definition to arrive at a decision as to whether this individual meets the criteria.

It is more difficult to measure performance of individuals who are not yet employed, as you either need to rely on third-party information, often provided by the candidate, or substitute some other performance indicator. Again in Chapter 6 the discussion on assessment will highlight some opportunities for measuring performance of candidates rather than incumbents.

Senior talent in the organisation has more historic performance available to assist decisions. Over their career it will be possible to measure success against targets, use bonus payments as a guide and also get feedback on specifics behaviours from peers and managers.

The more junior employees may have much less historical performance data so alternative assessment methods must be used as a substitute. Again this will be expanded upon in Chapter 6.

Key review questions

Does a talent definition exist in the organisation?

How does the organisation currently measure potential and performance?

What are the key capabilities that this organisation needs to succeed?

How would these capabilities translate into a talent definition?

Notes

1 Eisinger, Jesse (2014) Why Only One Top Banker Went to Jail for the Financial Crisis, *The New York Times Magazine*, 30 Apr, http://www.nytimes.com/2014/05/04/magazine/only-one-top-banker-jail-financial-crisis.html?_r=0.
2 CIPD (2006) Talent *Management: Understanding the Dimensions*, CIPD, London. Over the nine years since this survey the evidence for significant change in their findings, at least in the UK, is hard to find, with many organisations still having no formal definition of talent nor a strategic link between talent activities and business success.
3 Huselid, M., Becker, B. and Beatty, R. (2005) *The Workforce Scorecard: Managing Human Capital to Execute Strategy*, Harvard Business School Press, Boston, MA.
4 Ulrich, David and Beatty, Dick (2001) From Partners to Players: Extending the HR playing field, *Human Resources Management* 40.4, 293–307.
5 A useful paper covering competence models from both public and private sector, related to leadership talent, is Bolden, R., Gosling, J., Marturano, A. and Dennison, P. (2003) *A Review of Leadership Theory and Competency Frameworks*, Centre for Leadership Studies, University of Exeter, http://www2.fcsh.unl.pt/docentes/luisrodrigues/textos/Lideran%C3%A7a.pdf.

Chapter 4

Which roles are strategically important and require top talent?

Introduction

Defining talent for the organisation in a clear and transparent way is the starting point for creating a strategic plan. The next step that needs to be taken is the clarification and agreement of the organisation's strategic roles.

The principle that underpins ETM is that you do not invest in all people in the same way. It's not a 'sheep dip' approach, but a focused investment in the specific talents that return the best performance for the business. It is therefore critical that those roles that offer greatest returns are identified and agreed amongst the senior executive team. This agreement initiates the construction of a strategic plan for people.

It is important the talent professional, and the rest of the management team, know which roles have greater impact on success than others. Sometimes these roles are strategically important regardless of their place in the organisational hierarchy. A relatively junior role that is customer facing and significantly affects sales revenue, can be considered strategic. By focusing the talent strategy primarily on these types of role there is an exponential impact on the organisation's success.

An ETM strategy should provide the right quality and quantity of talent to populate all of the business's strategically important roles. It is therefore important to understand how to map an organisation, and determine how many of the roles are genuinely critical and what sort of skills and experiences are required to carry the role well. This will influence the type and size of talent pool required. Mapping the organisation requires a representative senior management group to agree and define the key roles across the organisation, from its entry-level talent through to executive incumbents.

These strategic roles are sometimes called different things in different organisations, depending on the consultancy offering advice or the national culture of the organisation. In the next section we will define some of the generic categories of talent typically required by an organisation.

There are two distinct tasks in strategic talent planning: first define the strategic roles and then define the strategic players. The first task is clearly about structure and how the organisation faces its customer, the second is about evaluating who within the organisation is already performing well and shows potential for the future.

As in the case for strategic roles, organisations apply a range of different labels for talented people. In most it's a mix of performance and potential that defines someone as talent. As you will have come to realise, the fundamental aim of ETM is to have the best match of strategic role with the very best performer available.

Finally in this chapter we will examine the concept of the talent lifecycle, in order that the talent professional can understand how the organisation's strategic response may need to evolve and adapt to emerging individual needs as well as the changing business environment.

Talent mapping – strategy, places and positions

As clearly stated in Chapter 2, strategy is about creating a focus and that requires specific choices to be made. In terms of roles this means focusing resources and HR support on those roles that add the most value to the success of the organisation.

In many organisations there is widely held belief that all the roles above a certain pay grade or level will be strategic. Therefore any role with the title Senior, Head of, Director or Vice President would automatically be thought of as strategic, by nature of their seniority in the hierarchy. Whilst this approach initially seems logical, as most roles in the senior ranks of an organisation are managing people and resources, it doesn't always demonstrate a direct link between investment and outcome. When each role is tested for its outputs, relative to the organisation's goals, things can appear quite different and as result a more focused approach can be taken.

The core requirement of any commercial business is to maximise profitability. It is a legal and ethical requirement of the management to maximise the profit of the organisation for the benefit of the investors, the shareholders.

In publically owned organisations the basic requirement is to maximise the efficiency and effectiveness of the organisation to deliver the very best value to the tax-payer. Success in both private and publically owned organisations therefore requires the management to make decisions to maximise productivity. This means that the management's investment in any talent process, be it skill development or individual reward, should be linked to the specific individual's impact on the overall productivity of the organisation. Sometimes this sounds like a very clinical decision-making approach, but the logic behind it is indisputable.

Not all roles in an organisation contribute equally to the productivity and effectiveness of the business. Some roles have a direct significant impact, others support strategic goals and some, even when carried out to the highest possible standard, still have no impact. The mix in any organisation is always different and what constitutes a support role in one organisation may well be a significant impacting role in another.

To determine which roles in the organisation are strategically important and should be the real focus of any talent strategy, the senior team needs to invest significant time mapping the roles against a talent template. This requires the right mix of senior team members to examine their own organisation, often using organograms (hierarchical maps of the organisation), and try to build a consensus on which roles impact directly on profit, costs or customer satisfaction. The group should be senior enough to make decisions, and representative enough that no part of the business can say it had no voice. By default, divisional boards make good groups to carry out this task as they represent the whole of the business unit and most of the heads of functions.

The mapping process is often quite revealing, bringing out many issues that do not always get discussed but are raised to help the executives start to clarify what the organisation really values. It is not unusual for this process to take two to three days in a complex organisation and involve a range of groups to achieve the overall end result.

These roles are then indicated on the organogram as strategic important roles. An example of such a diagram is shown in Figure 4.1. This definition suggests that the role, when carried out well, directly reduces costs in the organisation, or directly increases profit, or directly impacts on customer satisfaction. Not all roles have a direct line of sight to these three strategic outcomes. A good example would be a senior supply chain role in a large retailer where the efficiency of the supply chain can significantly impact on the sales of the organisation and therefore directly impact on profits.

In working with clients we tend to refer to these roles as 'strategic roles'. In some publications or organisational cultures they are called 'pivotal roles', in others 'A positions'. The name is not that important but the concept of a role that has more direct impact on the success of the strategy is.

Many roles support others in the organisation that then have an impact on cost, profit or customers, but not directly by themselves. These roles are indicated as supporting roles on the same diagram. They are necessary, as they indirectly impact on business success by supporting wider business aims and others in strategic roles. Many HR roles fall into this category. Sourcing and providing support for the organisation's people is important work, but unless the customer is affected, or it affects the price they pay, the role is mainly supporting others whose work does.

For our purpose, we will refer to these roles with an apt label, 'supporting roles'. Again, some consultancies or organisations use the term 'B positions' or 'marginal roles'. All three terms describe the same sort of role, necessary and supporting of the main strategy but with limited direct impact.

Figure 4.1 shows the roles marked as A for strategic importance, B as supporting roles and C as roles with no strategic impact. For clarity, these charts are commonly colour coded, with the traditional traffic light coding of green for strategic, amber for supporting and red for non-strategic roles.

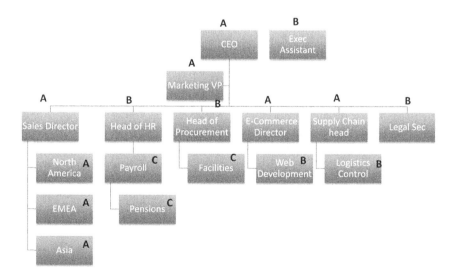

Figure 4.1 Strategic roles – an example organisation chart

The third categories of roles shown in Figure 4.1 are those with no strategic impact and very little supporting contribution. These may be roles that are necessary for an organisation to operate, but if carried out to world-class standards would not add any benefit. In many instances identifying these roles can lead to some of them being outsourced, as they do not impact on the strategic aims of the organisation but are a service that the organisation requires in order to function.

An example would be a role that manages the building's facilities in a large organisation. The role is required to enable the effective running of the office building and ensure maintenance and cleaning is carried out. However, even if the role were carried out to a standard of excellence it would have no impact on overall business costs, customer satisfaction or profit. In fact, for many large organisations, the most cost-effective way is to have the building managed by a contractor whose sole focus is market-leading services provision and whose business is structured to do this to a high standard. Provision of these outsourced services to other companies has built the business of global giants such as Serco, Initial and Sodexo

If your business model was to provide serviced office space, such as Serco, the facilities manager in that building would then be in a direct customer-facing role and it would in that case be a strategic role, directly impacting on revenue and costs.

A second example, closer to home for many talent professionals, is the role of payroll in an HR department. It is clear that pay and salary needs managing effectively, and that enquires from staff need timely answers, but in many cases it can be handled better by an outsourced supplier. There is no added value in it being carried out to any standard better than satisfactory. Being more responsive is not going to impact on business results. Having a reputation for in-house world-class payroll admin is not a strategic advantage, unless that is the core service you provide for other business clients, as do companies such as Ceridian. They do nothing but software and payroll services for clients so can invest in doing it to world-class standards.

For our purposes these roles are termed non-strategic, showing that they do not impact on the core goals of the business, but may, for another business, be their considered core work; hence the propensity for these roles to be outsourced or contracted out to more focused organisations who want to manage the work well. Again in some other models these roles are referred to as 'C positions' or 'requisite roles'.

This mapping process can be quite demanding of the management team. It requires them to step back from an individual's performance in the role and also to think about the organisation's aims, not about their departmental priorities. The process demands that they examine the outcome of a role if carried out well and link this to one of the three generic strategic impacts.

In some cases, the categorisation of a role as supporting or non-strategic, particularly in the domain of expertise of the incumbent, is seen as a challenge to its position and the individual manager personally. In order that some level of objectivity can be maintained in the discussion, and that all the roles are genuinely examined, it may be necessary to use some skilled external, or at least independent, facilitation. If the managers cannot discuss and agree what really matters in terms of each role's impact on overall business performance, it will be difficult for them to really commit to the talent strategy that derives from this analysis process.

Again the focus here is on roles, not the current people incumbent within them. To enable the team tasked with this action to be clear on their decisions, they should be provided with a common definition of what determines a strategic role within their organisation.

This is effectively stage 1 of the mapping process, defining and agreeing what is really important in order to compete. One real example of an organisation's definition of strategic roles is shown in Table 4.1. In this case, Fast Fashions, they have focused on certain core capabilities that matter to their industry and specifically their niche. They determined that this set of criteria contributed more to success than any other area of work:

- Marketing
- E-store development
- Product planning
- Leadership and people development
- Supply chain

Table 4.1 Fast Fashions' definition of strategic roles

'A' positions	'B' positions	'C' positions
Work directly linked to strategic imperatives. Almost all of this work has strategic impact.	Work indirectly linked to strategic imperatives. Helps/supports strategic impact.	Not linked to strategic imperatives Required for company to function, but has little strategic impact.
Wealth creating: substantially enhances revenue and/or substantially reduces cost.	Provides support to wealth creating positions.	Has little economic impact/ if not done wouldn't be missed.
Has significant impact on customer success.	May have some customer interface but not necessarily impact on revenue or cost reduction.	Unknown by external customers.
Output is highly valued by external customers.	Output is valued by external customers.	Possibly non-value added work.
Usually requires unique skills.	May in some cases require unique skills.	General skills usually required – not expertise.
If started all over again, this position would be always recreated.	If started all over again, this position could be recreated.	If started all over again, this position would not be recreated or would be outsourced.
High impact on the business when something goes wrong.	Some impact on the business when something goes wrong.	Barely any impact on the business when something goes wrong.
Autonomous decision making.	Specific processing/ procedures must be followed.	Little discretion in work and procedures may be driven by regulation.
Interfaces with 'A' level/ stretch customers.	Interfaces with 'B' level/ profitable core customers.	May deal with customers, but not in transactions.
Is core strategically important work.	Is aligned to support core work.	Is often discretionary work, not necessary aligned with strategic focus or wealth creating efforts.
Work is continually changing and dependent on understanding the emergent customer needs.	Work is more standardised, part of a process contributing input to 'A' position or 'B' customer success.	Work driven by routine requirements requiring little adaptation.

As a retailer, marketing was considered a given, particularly as they were selling both via mail order and through e-tailing. Their 'E-store' development was a new capability, one that was not currently present in the organisation, but that needed to be created to compete in their new business model. Product planning was concerned with the building and selecting of collections of apparel. Poor choices within this discipline directly impacted on overall profitability. In terms of leadership and people development there was a clear recognition that the organisation had in the past concentrated so much on profitability and revenue generation that it had not invested at all in leadership development. The executive team's reflection was that if they had done so, maybe they would have adapted more rapidly to the new business environment that the Internet retailers had created. This capability, the means to develop people and lead them, was considered to be core to their future business model. Finally, any retailer who wishes to compete effectively on the Internet needs to have a world-class global supply chain capability.

The 'A' roles were those that they determined had the strategic impact necessary to drive success in one or more of the agreed capabilities. Debating this out with the group of business heads built a consensus of what talent meant in their organisation. It also raised an expectation about what investment would be required in talent to achieve their strategic business goals. Table 4.1 was a guide to mapping their own business against the corporate blueprint for strategic roles.

It is not unusual for this process to be contentious and create a lot of debate over relative worth of some roles and as some functional managers defend their own people. However, the result of the process is a clear map of the roles, not the people, that impact on business success directly, and a clear understanding of those that do not.

Matching people, performance and potential

Just as defining exactly what talent you need requires a map of the critical positions, highlighting those that are strategic, supporting and non-strategic, the organisation also needs to know the levels of performance and potential required to fill these roles. This is where the second element of the talent strategy comes into play. Who, which individuals have the performance and potential required to be successful in these strategic roles?

Defining the requirement is sometimes difficult, as it asks the senior team to differentiate which roles are more important in the organisation. Their next task is even more difficult, which is to decide which people are best placed to work in their most important roles. Then they need to decide who needs to be replaced by higher performers or those with more potential.

The ability for a senior manager to differentiate an individual's ability and potential is not only important for their career but also for their role in the organisation. If they cannot do this consistently and effectively it will negatively impact on all their deployment decisions.

This is, for some managers, one of more controversial areas of HR and talent management. It requires the organisation to identify some individuals for more focused support and benefits than others, based on an agreed definition of performance and potential. In order to reduce some of the anxiety managers may experience judging their colleagues and direct reports, it is necessary to use simple but effective assessment tools to support their decisions.

A reliable assessment process will provide consistency. Reliable in this sense means it will be accurate when repeated with a range of people. It also needs to be valid, meaning it measures what the organisation intends to measure. There will be more about these two important concepts in Chapter 6 when we cover assessment.

The approach to defining performance is relatively simple, particularly if a performance management system already exists within the organisation. However, a range of approaches will be discussed in Chapter 8, with some suggestions for which may be effective in different organisations and cultures. If there is no reliable performance measurement already in place then creating one must be considered a priority. Without a performance measurement system in place it is difficult for the organisation to create a meaningful assessment of individual talent.

Potential is the other dimension that organisations must attempt to measure and make career decisions about. The mix of performance and potential can then be used to make up a talent management grid showing the two dimensions on the axis of a four, or in some cases a nine, box grid. The purpose of such a grid is to assist the senior team plan for the future deployment of talent. This is helpful for the immediate future but also useful to guide any succession decisions they need to make for the longer term.

Figure 4.2 shows one company's grid, using their business disciplines (based on their core competencies) mapped against performance (based on objective achievement). This grid was later populated with the names of individuals for each division or business unit. This enabled the organisation to map or audit their current management talent in a simple graphic way.

These grids are powerful communication tools, as they highlight the degree of confidence the organisation has in the current talent pool and also indicate where future investment may need to be made.

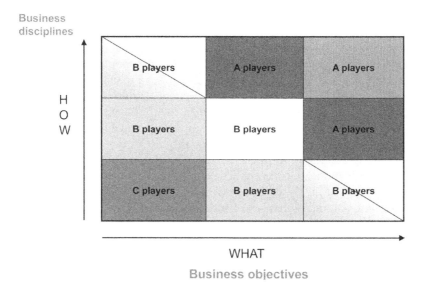

Figure 4.2 Talent mapping Fast Fashions – example performance/potential grid

There are not set quotas for talent in any level, but the principle of identifying 'A' players is to ensure you have enough to fill your strategic roles. Without some form of mapping the roles the organisation cannot quantify the demand, and without mapping the available talent it cannot assess the capability gap

So what is meant by performance? In most organisations this is measured by some assessment of results in the role, which is easier to carry out in some positions than others. The measurement of a sales professional's performance is relatively quantifiable in terms of revenue and sales booked. In other roles the defined output of a successful role is less visible and not as easy to quantify. In some roles the output is more qualitative by nature. This is where the performance management system the organisation chooses will significantly influence the way talent is managed. What is not debatable is that there are many different ways to measure people's performance in a business. Whatever method is chosen should be able to differentiate between, poor, average and excellent performance in all roles in the organisation.

Statistics and research studies show that the top performers in many organisations can generate results some 10–15 times greater in impact than the lowest performers in a similar role.[1] This fact alone suggests a failure to measure the difference in performance across similar roles could be significantly under rewarding some talent and over rewarding others who barely contribute.

It is of paramount importance that any definition of performance is transparent for the staff being measured and that the approach chosen is easy for managers to understand and implement. A simple system that is applied well will be much more effective in managing performance than a more complex data capture tool that is barely understood and applied sporadically.

Potential is a much more ethereal concept and has at times been the subject of vigorous debate. The currently accepted view is that there are some specific indicators of future success that are measurable. These are not always so specific to the organisation, and yet still have some predictive ability. These relatively generic indicators show success at selecting people who have the ability to take on more complex roles, more senior positions or more challenging assignments within a short period of time.

By measuring the two constructs, current results and future ability, it is possible for an organisation to audit its talent pools and find the 'sweet spot' of those talents that have high performance and high potential across a range of management levels.

The example in Table 4.2, an actual company talent definition, shows a match of each of the levels of talent, here labelled A, B and C, with the expected behaviours as determined by the organisation's existing leadership competence framework. Whilst it is not faultless, it does have the hallmarks of a quality definition. Each level is clearly shown against an agreed definition of expected behaviours, relevant to the specific organisational culture and leadership challenges.

To achieve this level of fit, the end stage of a comprehensive process, the organisation's senior team of HR and global board started with the generic descriptions of the three levels of potential and performance given here in Table 4.3.
Through a series of facilitated discussions based on the three generic descriptions of qualities of strategic players the definitions morphed into the more specific behaviours shown in Table 4.3. In the process, the senior team and all the most senior HR professionals built a clear consensus of what talent looked like, how important is was and how it might be best used to build more success for the organisation. The end result

Table 4.2 Fast Fashions – an example of defining players

	'A' player	'B' player	'C' player
Responsive to customers	Is sensitive to and anticipates breadth of customer needs (internal and/or external). Builds relationships and builds customer loyalty.	Responds to current customer needs but not pro-active in defining future needs.	Demonstrates limited awareness of any external/internal customer needs.
Entrepreneurial	Seeks out ways to develop the business and new opportunities to grow profit. Open to different and creative ways of doing business. Takes measured risks to get things done. Learns quickly from mistakes.	Is able to develop existing opportunities and supports ideas. Accepts their mistakes, learns from mistakes. Looks for business improvements.	Comfortable with the status quo. Rarely take risks. Slow to learn from mistakes, may even blame others for their mistakes.
Delivers	Makes things happen. Produces exceptional results, even in tough situations. Maintains their ethics and integrity throughout. Balances business unit focus with FF overall success. Has a strong reputation across the group.	Prioritises plans in order to focus on essential objectives, but may lack regular follow-up. Accomplishes majority of objectives on time, mainly focused on their business unit. Is trusted within their business.	Results are currently below expectations. Complies with policy and plays by the rules.
Courageous	Willing to stand alone based upon convictions. Faces and resolves problems or issues. Is decisive, even in tough situations. Not afraid to hire people who are high performers.	Tends to avoid confronting problems. Makes sound decisions, yet leans towards uncontroversial decisions. Makes safe hiring decisions.	Is often passive, withholds opinions, where there is potential for conflict. Hires people who will not be a challenge.
Ambitious	Highly adaptive and able to 'sell' the organisation on change. Extremely high energy level, fast paced, tenacious. Pursues high standards.	Initiates incremental change and continuous improvement. Motivated, energetic and pursues acceptable standards.	Accepts currents standards but does not drive change. Objectives lack stretch.
Talent developer	Coaches others to significantly improve performance. Recruits and promotes based on capability and diversity. Creates focused, collaborative, results-driven teams across FF. Gets people out of their comfort zone, but supports their development. Sees talent as a group resource.	Uses coaching on occasions. Tends to limit conversations regarding development to annual performance/development reviews. Generally recruits and promotes on merit. Promotes teamwork primarily within own business.	Career discussions a low priority. Talent-related decisions sometimes less than objective. Rarely uses feedback to develop people or capability.
Strategic	High level of understanding of the industry, the market and their business situation. Translates vision into action. Balances long-term and short-term needs of FF and their own business unit.	Priorities tend to be tactical, some may be strategic or long term. Able to translate vision into business unit plans. Cultivates knowledge within own area of expertise.	Perspective is generally short term and remains within their own work area.

Table 4.3 Generic definitions of performance and potential

Strategic player levels	Displayed qualities
'A' player	Talented people who have strong potential and constantly over perform in role. High learning agility, high achievement needs, drive business forward. Usually evaluated with an exceptional performance (E) or a performance over the expected level (O).
'B' player	Good solid performers. Meet expectations regularly and occasionally exceed. Seen by peers as strong company people. Usually evaluated with a performance in line with expected level (IL) or even over the expected level (O).
'C' player	Currently meeting most expectations, occasionally fail on some. Could be a low performer or someone having difficulty in a new position. Usually evaluated with a performance below expected level (B).

was something that built on their understanding of the leadership challenges, as outlined in their competence framework.

Some organisations have chosen to use an even more specific definition. In the example shown in Figure 4.3, a division of a European technology business, the definition of senior talent detailed the likely cognitive range of an 'A' player and also the specific way they would influence in different situations.

How specific and detailed the definitions of players becomes, is a product of the culture of the company and the confidence of the talent professional involved in being able to evaluate the different elements. What is clear from the example in Figure 4.3 is that there is absolute clarity about what it takes to be senior talent in that organisation.

From plans to pools and pipelines

For many years the method of choice for securing future management capability was a succession plan. In larger organisations it was common for these complex tile puzzles to be reviewed annually, even when there was little real change in the senior ranks, acting as metaphorical stoppers in the system. Charles Handy,[2] talks about his amusement at seeing his life mapped out in detail for the next 20 years when in his early career he was a young high-potential manager with the oil company Royal Dutch Shell. They were renowned for having a comprehensive succession and career planning system that dictated your country, role and expected last level of appointment years in advance.

Whilst succession plans are a good start, they tend to assume that individual roles will endure over years and that talent will remain within the organisation over time in order to mature into the roles mapped out for them. In the past, the psychological contract we had with our employers meant that loyalty and patience were often rewarded for the talented with promotion and career progression. We no longer live in a world where that same psychological contract can be honoured. Even the largest and most successful organisations, such as HSBC (the second largest bank in the world), are at the mercy of the market and can no longer offer careers for life.[3] It seems now career-minded talents are more likely to remain within the company if the boss is motivating

ISSUE	A players	B players	C players
Vision	Facilitates and communicates sound vision	Vision lacks credibility, can be unrealistic	Embraces tradition rather than the future
Intelligence	130 IQ or higher, Quick to learn, complexity is overcome rapidly	120–129 IQ, smart but not as insightful as A players	110–120 IQ, has some difficulty with complexity, new issues
Leadership	Initiates needed change, highly adaptive.	Favours modest incremental change	Prefers status quo
Drive	Passionate, high energy levels	Motivated, energetic at times	Dedicated.
Resourceful	Impressive ways to overcome obstacles	Open minded and can find new solutions	Requires direction
Customer Focus	Sensitive to customer needs, unstated and stated	Knows customer is king, does not always act as if..	Too inwardly focused
Coaching	Successfully coaches others, performance and development focus	Performs annual reviews, sporadic coaching	Lacking praise, inconsistent, shallow feedback
Teams	Hires A players, confident with them, demand performance	Hires other B players, willing to compromise performance	Hires people like them, crisis occur due to talent deficit.
Performance	Exceeds expectations	Meets most expectations	Sometimes meets expectations.

Figure 4.3 Example player definitions – European technology business

them and the work interesting. In this new career reality, succession plans are not flexible or dynamic enough.

Over the last decade the concept of talent pools has emerged and gained wide acceptance as a better way to think about talent in an organisation. The key feature of a talent pool is that there is a wider range of skills within it and that the diversity of the pool can feed a number of roles, not just the next most senior rank indicated in the traditional succession planning approach. In the pool approach, instead of having succession plans for the top 100 positions, each showing the next three possible candidates with various levels of readiness for promotion, only 80–100 high-potential and broadly skilled talents may well cover the same number of roles.

An additional feature of talent pools is the way they are fed and refreshed. In the past succession was about finding talent from within the ranks of the organisation. With the more dynamic, talent pool concept, talent can enter from within or outside the current organisation to strengthen the bench or bring in new capabilities. This approach is considered to reduce the risk of the organisation being too low on specific talent or alternatively oversupplied, whilst also allowing a wider career path for those within the pools.[4]

Talent pools have changed the way organisations think about succession and future appointments. Being criteria based, having people join resulting from some form of assessment against agreed criteria for being talented, means that they are more robust and reliable. They can also be more dynamic and able to respond to changing capability needs. As future needs change, the criteria change and the pools can morph to include more of the emerging skills requirements.

We have explored the idea that talents will be defined to some extent by the strategic choices that the organisation pursues. This means that the talent pools will reflect specific talent congruent with that strategic choice.

Pools can, and should, exist at different levels within the organisation. If the organisation is large and complex the idea of a series of more senior and increasingly experienced pools of talent shared across the divisions and geography of the business is gaining wide acceptance. Talent is a resource, an asset and as such should not be owned by a single business unit or division. The use of talent pools at different levels across the organisation reduces this parochial thinking and opens opportunities for essential resources to the smaller business units.

Defining talent must be thought of as a multi-layered approach covering the generic levels of entry and immediate need, core managerial capability and current and future executive stock. Of all the functional HR roles in an organisation, that of the talent professional is one of the most strategic and therefore must, by nature, be focused on the long term. Whilst working to deliver the immediate talent needs of the organisation, to be considered effective, they must also think about the impact of their current decisions on the long-term need for senior management and executive potential. A typical time horizon for a talent pipeline is around 10–15 years. This is the time it might typically take for a new hire, if consistently successful, to reach a senior executive role in the future. It is important that this perspective is covered in any talent strategy. The organisation may only plan its business in three-year horizons, but this is insufficient for long-term talent development.

The difficulty for talent professionals is that many of the roles that entry-level talents go on to fill in their future careers are unlikely to currently exist and therefore the competencies required to be successful are almost definitely going to be different from the ones currently exhibited. However, this is the ongoing challenge for talent managers: to have the right people in the right place at the right time for current needs and, in addition, to consider the potential future needs.

It is useful to think of the talent pipeline as a flow of leadership and functional talent gaining experience and seniority over time. With the right development, job experience and the right level of personal effort, an individual talent should be able to move from entry level through to a mid-level manager with high potential, and on into the pool of executive successors, ready to take on senior management roles as they become vacant, or changes in the organisation's requirements create new opportunity.

This pipeline is a helpful concept to shape the organisation's approach to talent. For the last decade, the most popular analogy for HR professionals has been that of the talent pool. Where pools suggest reservoirs of potential waiting to be appointed or deployed, the concept of a pipeline is more dynamic. Pipelines have direction and to some extent pressure to push talent upwards. They also have leaks – parts of the organisation where talent leaves, or where there is a need to increase the flow by recruitment. Pipes also have blockages: obstructions where intervention is required to reinstate the flow.

Whilst not wishing to delve too deep into analogies, there is a real benefit to having a clear picture, or mental image, to share with others about how talent works in the organisation. It is easier to communicate the concept of how talent management flows in a diagram, particularly when discussing the concept with managers whose day-to-day focus is not always people. Figure 4.4 is a simple representation of the concept of the talent pipeline, showing the transition from entry-level employee to a current incumbent executive.

Below, the arrows representing the flow of the four talent pools show the common elements of any effective talent management approach. It is the consistent application of common processes, regardless of seniority of the talent that makes the pipeline work. The key supporting processes are objective assessment, performance management and coaching or/and mentoring.

Whilst we will cover each of these processes in some depth later in the book, Figure 4.4 shows them as integral to the pipeline approach

The concept of flow strengthens and underpins the idea of a talent pipeline. For some organisations there may be a number of parallel pipelines, some creating managerial and leadership talent flows and others specifically concentrating on functional talents. This is often the case where the success of the organisation depends on two different, but essential competency sets.

For example, most global pharmaceutical companies require genuinely world-renowned research talent and in addition highly competent commercial talents to enable them to compete in a very aggressive global marketplace. If there are two parallel career tracks by design, the organisation avoids the common problem of promoting their best functional talent into senior management roles, away from their expertise, to meet the career ambitions of the individual. Having parallel pipelines for talent allows real expertise to be recognised and world-renowned specialists to be developed without compromising any long-term career ambitions. Alongside the functional talent pipeline, a management and leadership track allows the promotion and development of more commercial and operational talents. What transpires from such an approach is a win for the talented individuals and a win for the company. It is a much more comprehensive, pragmatic but still strategic approach to talent management.

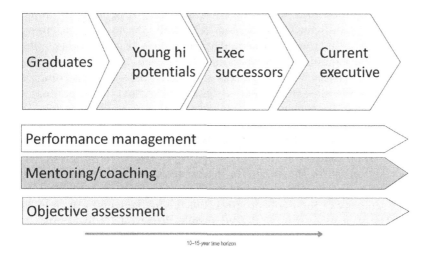

Figure 4.4 The talent pipeline – four connected pools

Figure 4.3 shows four talent pools within the leadership pipeline. Each represents a different career stage and specific organisational need. Whilst the diagram suggests people flowing from the previous stage to the next in some form of hierarchical and chronological way, there is also a need for people to be able to enter the business at each level. Not all of an organisation's entry-level talent, often focused on graduate schemes, will make it to the next high-potential pool. To enable this pool to meet the overall demand of the organisation it may need topping up from internal candidates who meet the criteria for membership and also external applicants recruited for vacant positions.

There are many reasons why some people's early talent potential doesn't develop. Life is not all about careers and many young talents start families and don't maintain their mobility or ambition to continue in a fast track career. Others leave if their talent is not rewarded with the right level of responsibility or visibility. Some just plateau, and never move beyond the level of responsibility that they came into the talent pool with. What this means is the talent professional needs to regard the talent pipeline as a flow, some coming in, topping up pools, and some leaking out, meaning the pool requires constant monitoring and, if necessary, filling.

The same, just different

Figure 4.3 also shows the common processes that ETM demands. Whilst the different pools in the pipeline may require different roles, rewards, development and deployment, they share the same need for three core HR support processes: performance management, objective assessment, and coaching or mentoring.

Entry-level talent can be assessed in groups typically in assessment centres when applying for young professional roles or graduate schemes. It's normal that groups are assessed against the company's requirements, and attending an event and finding others in the same process is considered as normal and has little in the way of career or confidentiality problems. The same cannot be said for entry into an organisation later in the individual's career lifecycle. In this case applying for a role may put you in competition with people from the organisation you already work in, or from competitor organisations who also know you. This can be both embarrassing and commercially difficult for applicants who really do not want to arrive at a recruitment process to find their confidential application is visible to other colleagues who they meet in the candidate waiting room. This is even more of an issue as roles become more senior. That is why the process of objective assessment is common, but the methods need not be the same. What is considered acceptable for graduate entry level cannot also be used for executive hires who would expect a more individual and confidential approach.

The various approaches and methods for delivering objective assessment are discussed in detail within Chapter 6.

Without exception, all of the talents in the organisation will require and benefit from an effective performance management system. Again there may be necessary differences as the seniority of the pools progress, but the fundamental principles should be the same. The vast majority of talented people thrive on feedback and a well-constructed performance management system will ensure they are working at their potential and identify issues that are preventing them from realising their own potential. Performance management is discussed in more detail in Chapter 8.

Finally, the third core process that spans across the whole pipeline is coaching or mentoring. These are not the same processes, although in some organisations the terms are interchangeable. It is clear to me that coaching is provided by someone independent to the line relationship of the individual talent to help them make choices focused on their performance and achievement of their goals. This is often linked to a new role or development of new skills. Whereas mentoring is often a more political relationship based on advice, guidance and long-term support, which may involve the mentor using their network to aid the protégé (the person being mentored). This relationship may span a number of roles, whereas coaching is generally shorter term in nature.

Again the type of coaching or mentoring required is quite different for a newly appointed graduate from that of a finance director hired to fill a difficult divisional role, but the need for the process is common. Coaching and mentoring, as support processes for talent, are fully explored in Chapter 7.

Talent strategy – it's about people, strategy and performance

This chapter has explored the key themes that need to be addressed in any ETM response. The sometimes contentious issue of differentiation has been explored in relation to strategic roles and also its impact on the talent groups that need to fill those roles.

There are only a few roles in management that can claim to have such a direct impact, either positive or negative, on the results of the organisation, but that of the talent professional really does. Earlier in this chapter the concept of strategic roles and how to identify them was illustrated with the help of the case of Fast Fashions. In the following chapters we will explore how to find the talent to potentially fill these roles and how to select those that are best placed to perform well within them. The success of any ETM strategy is a result of putting the right people in the right place to drive performance. Strategically important 'A' roles require talented people to fill them.

Finding and recruiting the right sort of talent requires the talent professional to understand what really drives business success. To understand this requires them to understand the strategic aims of the organisation they work for. Linking the two should be a performance management process that ensures the right talent delivers as expected. All three factors, finding people, understanding strategy and driving performance, sit right at the heart of ETM.

Key review questions

What are the strategic roles within the organisation? Is there a map?

Which organisation capabilities are currently most difficult to fill?

Is every strategic role filled with an 'A' player or alternatively a 'B' player with potential?

How confident is the organisation in its bench strength – the current talent pool?

Notes

1 Becker B.E., Huselid M. A. and Beatty R.W. (2009) *The Differentiated Workforce*, Harvard Business Press, Boston, MA, p. 61.
2 Charles Handy (born 1932) is an Irish author/philosopher specialising in organisational behaviour and management. Among the ideas he has advanced are the 'portfolio worker' and the 'Shamrock Organisation'. He has been rated among the Thinkers 50, a private list of the most influential living management thinkers. In 2001 he was second on this list, behind Peter Drucker, and in 2005 he was tenth. When the *Harvard Business Review* published a special issue to mark their fiftieth anniversary they asked Handy, Peter Drucker and Henry Mintzberg to write special articles. (Source: Wikipedia, https://en.wikipedia.org/wiki/Charles_Handy.)
3 Ahmed, Kamal (Business Editor) (2015) HSBC plans to cut 8,000 jobs in the UK in savings drive, BBC News, 9 Jun, http://www.bbc.co.uk/news/business-33058957.
4 Cappeli, P. (2008) Talent Management for the Twenty First Century, *Harvard Business Review*, Mar, 74–81.

Chapter 5

How can the organisation attract enough of the right sort of talent?

Introduction

In this chapter we will explore how a business builds a set of 'attraction profiles' to draw attention to the opportunities for talent within the organisation. There is a growing interest and many recently written articles on employer branding. The last few years has seen an increase in the number of conferences whose central theme is the need to communicate what the organisation's offer is in the employment market. The ETM approach advocates crafting this communication effort into a more specific format by creating a range of profiles that target the specific sorts of talent the organisation needs.

This approach to communication, that of crafting roles' profiles, showing the range of careers and opportunities across the organisation, is a way of creating a pull effect without having to market every individual vacant role. The idea of these attraction profiles is to specifically communicate to the target group of talents what the organisation can offer them in terms of opportunity, culture, reward, development and challenge. Most organisations concentrate on the overall company brand, but not all talents are looking for the same thing from an organisation. By having a range of profiles raising awareness of the organisation, but aimed very clearly at the specific target groups, the company can focus its marketing at those that it needs to fill its strategic roles. These attraction profiles need to reflect how a range of different people with a variety of career ambitions can fit into the organisation.

In addition, we will explore the idea of employee value propositions (EVPs). A talent professional needs to understand what the explicit or implicit deal for the employees is. The EVP is one of their key tools to leverage their overall attraction strategy.

The attraction profile suggests what is good about the company in terms of career, opportunities and the sort of challenging work that a talent may be doing – it's mainly about the content and the culture. The EVP needs to add some detail behind this, which may also apply to the wider workforce. Some of the EVP will be concerned with the general benefits of working for the organisation, such as holidays, health insurance cover, travel allowance and staff discounts, but there also needs to be something more specific to highlight what being in a talent group offers them in addition. The element of the talent group's EVP needs to be clearly illustrated within the attraction profile. Examples may be attending some prestigious education institute, opportunities for international business travel or the chance to work with high-profile products or events. Whatever you require your talent to do within the role should be part of the attraction profile and embedded within it should be some of the details of their EVP.

As the competition for talent remains high, it is essential to find the most effective channels to get the right employee brand message out. For prospective talents, those currently outside the organisation, the message should be focused on creating a raised awareness of the career opportunities that exist and building a positive reputation as an employer. For incumbents, those who have already chosen to have a career within the organisation, it's about building a strong employer brand to help re-affirm their career choice. A strong, widely recognised employer brand becomes a positive factor in the retention of talent.

The purpose of most marketing activity is to promote the brand, which could be associated with a product name or the name of a particular service. The brand exists to give wary consumers a short cut to the values and qualities of product or service in a crowded marketplace. A brand is essentially about consumer trust. Where there is a lot of consumer choice there is a tendency for confusion and, potentially, paralysis at the stage of the buying decision. Strong brands help people make quicker choices. Ideally, when consumers think about a brand they should immediately have an understanding of what that name means to them.

A good example is the globally recognised brand Virgin. It encompasses airlines, trains, weddings, mobile phones, broadband, cola drinks and financial services. What remains consistent across Virgin's message is 'fun, simple, on the side of the consumer and slightly anti-establishment'. Given the wide range of industries covered the company has managed to add something consistent and valuable to the consumer with the overall brand message – trust us to be simple and on your side.

Some of the very best brands are aspirational, those that people really aspire to be able to afford and own; think BMW, Bang and Olufson, Apple, Chanel and Jimmy Choo. There is a similar list in the minds of ambitious professionals, the corporate brands that they want on their CV. Think of giants in the world of work such as IBM, Unilever, GE, Apple and the likes of McKinsey. Each of these corporate brands says something about their work culture and expectations. It's not the same sort of list as for consumers, not all commercial brands are the best in their industry for employer reputation, but it exists and is created by the same thinking process. Now think about your own organisation and ask these three questions:

- What does the brand tell any prospective employee?
- Would a prospective talent have any idea what working for the organisation would be like?
- What would you like it to say in the future?

Employees of choice – needles and haystacks

Google is, according to a number of rankings,[1] the number 1 employer brand in the USA, and this is also true for many countries in Europe. They are infamous for their rigorous selection process, with multiple stages, unorthodox interview questions and multi-layered decisions about every potential hire. They initially attract thousands of applications for every role. Finding the right people to trust with their brand is like finding a needle in a haystack, an exhaustive and expensive process.

What would be much more effective is if the number of people who applied was smaller, and they were more realistic about their chances, already suited to the work and easier to select from. It's the holy grail of recruiters, a short list of extremely well-matched applicants.

Achieving a better fit to the talent roles starts with the way the organisation attracts people in the first place. It should start by giving them the sort of information that enables them to self-select out of the application process in the early stages. We will talk about some of the methods that can be designed into the selection process in the next chapter. Selection should really start with the marketing of the role before any application is made. The organisations want the people who fit their attraction profile to be really excited; the message should really grab them. You also want the opposite to happen to those that wouldn't thrive: they should hear the message as asking for too much; not realistic for them; too demanding or some other conclusion that stops them applying. Applications from people who cannot meet the challenges presented in the talent profile are a waste of an organisation's time, money and effort.

The aim of any ETM process is to attract only the 'employee of choice'. This means each organisation should be clearly seen as requiring very specific employees and not be regarded by everyone in the job market as the ultimate 'employer of choice'. The organisation's marketing message needs to be very clear about what it takes to succeed in the organisation. The story it tells should be transparent and demonstrate the real values of the organisation; the expectations on performance; the demands on work–life balance and the real nature of the opportunities. If this is clear, only the people who are excited and motivated to meet this challenge will continue with their interest, others will decide it's not for them and not apply.

We want creativity and determination – now prove it!

An old friend and colleague shared an example of an application process from one of his old clients. The only way an applicant could initially enquire for the fast track graduate scheme was directly via telephone. Those that did were sent a small parcel. The parcel was in a strong plastic mailbag, which resisted tearing open and needed to be cut with scissors or a sharp knife. Inside was a coarse sackcloth mailbag sewn round the edge. This needed to be unpicked by hand to get inside. Within this bag was another similar cover, and inside that another layer of finer ever more frustrating enclosures. After about 9–10 successful unwraps, they found a small sealed envelope. Inside this was a short hand written message –

> If you thought that was hard to get into try getting into . . . [the name of one of the world's most famous advertising agencies]. If you still think you are good enough call this number.

More recently Saatchi and Saatchi invited a group of potential candidates for their business to sell themselves in an elevator pitch: literally in this case. Each candidate was asked to take a numbered slip and join the queue for the lift. As their number came up they would

(continued)

(continued)

ride up the 18 floors with the recruiter and had the 30 seconds of the journey to pitch themselves for the role.

These stories are fantastic examples of clarity of message. If the organisation is a creative advertising agency then it needs to demonstrate this in its attraction profile: the marketing of positions it wishes to attract people to. The implicit message in this example is all about creativity, tenacity and not giving up, but executed with a great sense of humour and style. The same agency only reacted to phone call enquiries; it did not take postal applications. It wanted a more human touch and to attract people who would make whatever effort they needed to, in order to be noticed. It also generated a lot of interesting and free PR for its brand.

Marketing fundamentals

To prospective talents, your organisation's career paths are considered products. Their decision to join you is an investment in their career, and they are potentially buying into the organisation offering an opportunity. In just the same way as the services and products your organisation delivers to its customers, these careers need selling. In the talent marketplace, good products will move quicker and be in more demand than average or poor offers. However, the quality of the product is not something that can be sold without awareness. Marketing professionals know that their first objective in any brand building process is to raise awareness, get the brand offer into the minds of people, regardless of their immediate intent. There have been some spectacular success stories in this regard where the default name for the category are actual product names; think Hoover – now superseded by Dyson – iPod – now the generic term for any portable music device – and Jacuzzi – the default name for any spa hot tub. Does the same brand value exist for employers in the minds of talents? Well, we know from the countless media articles written about them, that employees of IBM refer to themselves as 'IBMers' and Google staff as 'Googlers'. People are identifying themselves as part of the business and work culture. If a strong brand can bleed over into the lexicon of how employees refer to themselves, then it has become an effective concept to create loyalty, and therefore retention, to the organisation.

The reverse can also be true, just as CEO Jeff Bezos is finding,[2] as he now has to spend time defending his Amazon work culture. It took a severe blow to its employer brand image when staff complained of its expectation of long working hours and its aggressive culture in a report in the *New York Times*. It will require a lot of work and some executive time to reverse this unexpected negative PR.

There are brands that attract a disproportionate amount of applications given their real career opportunities, as career-searching applicants equate corporate brand visibility with a great career. This is not always true. Whilst heading the talent management team within Sony, I was told by at least two different European business school professors that, as a company, we were their number 2 and 3, respectively, in terms of preferred career destination for their MBA graduates. As the Head of Talent at the time, I was surprised to hear this, as we had no specific MBA hiring process, nor any history for hiring them over the previous five years. We were becoming an employer of choice for this profile without any expressed need.

Creative advertising[3] can attract the right people, but there is more to getting the employee of choice than just a creative image and clever copy. The need to build a brand with a reputation as a career destination for the right talent is a priority on the to do list of all talent professionals. Having a profile that is attractive for too many people is almost as bad as having one that attracts too few. The organisation's marketing needs to be focused on the right niche, enabling the HR and Talent team to spend their time and resources sifting from a more qualified list for the very best candidates.

Historically there have been many indexes or rankings of the most valuable global brands.[4] In fact there is now a small industry grown up in sites for rankings[5] of the most desirable brands or companies to work for. Some of these rankings are part of the publishing media's attempts to get us to buy their newspapers. In other cases the tables are driven by consultancies needing to express their expertise in a particular sector or industry. What is clear is that ranking is here to stay and offers prospective talents another perspective on employers; a form of benchmark.

With access to a search engine, they have in one place some sort of independent sense check and a means to compare the company's offer – a career opportunity – with others in the same industry or similar market. Some of these indexes are heavily influenced by meeting criteria to become a better employer, such as providing health insurance, crèche facilities or a free canteen. Others are more reflective of the employee's own ratings, giving a user's view of the culture, work–life balance and management style. These annual indexing sites, mainly rated as a result of an annual survey, are also supplemented by real-time, user-generated data on employers. These social media sites, such as LinkedIn[6] and Glassdoor,[7] use current employees to share information about companies. What is evident in the current marketplace is that information is freely available and increasingly transparent. An organisation cannot completely control the message that the employment market hears, but it can influence it and hold an open conversation within it. The implication of this is that talent management professionals need to be aware of the fundamentals of marketing and relate these to the message they want to share about their organisation. To do this effectively means becoming savvy about social media, not just the traditional marketing that is controlled by the organisation, but also the conversations that are being held about it but are not under its control.

The four Ps of talent

Most general business courses contain some reference to the four Ps framework as a tool for thinking about marketing. The Ps in the framework refer to the four aspects needing attention from the marketer: Price, Place, Promotion and Product. If you take this marketing mix as a framework and apply it to the organisation's talent pools, you can generate a more comprehensive approach to employee branding. Using this concept to explore the employment proposition, the organisation will, out of necessity, need to think about its strengths in the market and what its competition is offering similar candidates. It takes time and effort to build a brand; however, once established it has an enduring value in the recruitment marketplace.

Price

Price refers to the percentage of the market rate you are willing to pay to get the talent your organisation requires now, and wishes to retain in the future. Some organisations can only thrive with the very best talent that is available in the global market and must pay accordingly.

If your business is about pharmaceutical research and development, world-class researchers are a finite resource and will attract a lot of competitive attention and a commensurate salary. However, as a niche group of scientific talents they are not entirely motivated by pay, but more likely to be highly motivated by the right facilities, collegiate workplace and the resources to do great work. Paying upper quartile, the top 25 per cent, is probably appropriate, but it may not be necessary to pay the highest in the market. Other elements of the EVP may compensate for pay.

On the other hand, hiring the best fund managers in a thriving financial market, such as the City of London, may require top of the market salary and bonus packages to attract interest from talents with plenty of options. Having a package that is not competitive with the upper decile, the top 10 per cent of salaries in the market, may be considered a negative message about the organisation by the potential talents.

If you search for the current highest paid salaried roles in the USA in 2015, you find they are dominated by high-tech and consulting firms. The social network site Glassdoor's chief economist Dr Andrew Chamberlin commented:[8]

> Salaries are high largely because of shortages of the highest skilled employees needed to advance business into new realms. Booming demand for software engineers, database administrators and data scientists has far outpaced the supply of these skilled, hard-to-find employees. With tech companies scrambling to poach these valuable workers from competitors, a bidding war has pushed tech salaries to unprecedented heights in recent years.

The need to set the right price, and its ability to shape the candidate pool, has not been missed by the UK Government. Their flagship initiative, Teach First,[9] is the largest of all graduate recruiters in the UK. Successful applicants in difficult to source subjects, Maths and Sciences, get an enhancement in their overall employee package. Some subjects command a higher price in a market with a high turnover of staff.

Regardless of the organisation's stated ambitions in the talent marketplace, the salary package it is willing to pay says something about the organisation. If you state in your marketing that you wish to hire the very best people but pitch the price at the average level in the market, the message will be confusing to the very candidates you wish to attract. You cannot control what conversations are held in the social media spaces, but you can understand the implications of the choices you make and make those choices consciously. Be aware that your salary offer is already a factor in the organisation's attraction profile, whether you have chosen to make it so or not.

Place

Place influences many recruitment decisions for talented candidates. For many organisations and career seekers, it's about location, location, location. Where your organisation is based has a massive impact on the talent it can attract and retain and this varies significantly depending on the career stage of the candidate.

Whether the site is a city centre head office with the buzz of a metropolis, a leafy suburban business park block or a manufacturing site in an industrial complex, it will have an effect on the potential employee's decision. Many of the young engineering graduates that one of my clients recruits each year are very excited by joining their excellent graduate scheme with a true industry leader. However, when the offers go out, many are less excited about signing up for a life based at a manufacturing site in a small town in Hungary or the Czech republic. This is particularly difficult to sell when they are in contact with college friends and colleagues with offers in Berlin, London or Madrid.

Place also means the places of business that the career may take the successful talent. The same graduate scheme cited above gives the opportunity to work during their career in any one of the 28 countries and 80 production sites that it operates. For many the chance to travel with their career is an attractive, if not essential, part of the offer. It is essential for a marketing message to share the range of possible work places within a career, not just the starting point.

Where your organisation resides can be both an asset and a curse. Your location may be handicapping your access to talent regardless of the product you have on offer. In a recent blog article[10] this issue was highlighted. It has become increasingly difficult to find digital marketing talent outside of the hub of London. The writer's conclusion is that applicants are just not aware of the great brands that need talent but reside in Scotland, Manchester and the North of England, and that these companies are not doing enough to promote their locations, their products and opportunities. Brands need to sell their offers and raise awareness of the opportunities outside the large, capital city, talent magnets.

The recent 2015 graduate market survey[11] reports that of the top 100 employers recruiting, 80 per cent are hiring with positions based in London, and over half of all the vacancies available are in the south-east of England. Whilst this report focuses on just the entry level of talent, it is a significant factor in early career choice. In at least two recent recruitment interviews for clients I have heard this very sentiment expressed: 'I just love London and wouldn't consider working anywhere else, at least for the next 10 years.'

Finally the place element of the mix must also take into account the culture of the organisation. This is naturally affected by the national culture of the location, the site's core purpose, but also much more by the values of the organisation. A city centre head office is going to be a radically different culture from that of a small-town manufacturing site. The nature of the business could be the same, but the place determines what the day-to-day experience would be like.

Whilst your organisation's talent requirements may span a whole range of places, the need to market them in a way that maximises their attraction to the right sort of candidate remains constant. An ETM strategy should find ways to make less attractive places more appealing, both in the short and medium term. In the same way, there are deployment tactics that use the more appealing locations as ways of rewarding the more difficult to retain talent and ensure retention.

Promotion

In pure marketing terms this is the way the product is offered, sometimes with an incentive to build consumer loyalty, or to instigate a buying decision. The same concept can be used to explore the options and propositions that affect an organisation's position in the talent market.

The rise in importance of the Internet channel and the increase in the use of social media-based marketing, has made promotion in the talent market a more aggressive and sophisticated activity. Without spending too much money, it is possible to gain a higher profile for your organisation's brand within your target market, be they a job-seeking graduate talent or career-minded executives looking for a new challenge. Facebook is omnipresent in many people's lives, yet is extremely cheap to use as an awareness-raising tool. Some of the biggest recruiters use this channel extensively for promotion of their opportunities. Dell has over 350,000 likes just ahead of the British Army at around 300,000 – completely different talent needs, but a shared understanding of the power of social media in generating awareness.

Whereas only two decades ago promoting awareness of opportunities for new talent was primarily based on print advertising, career fairs and the use of third-party search agencies, there is now a growing reliance on web and other digital media channels. The network effect of social networks such as LinkedIn has changed recruitment, both for the professional talent manager and the individual career seeker. In the first quarter of 2015, the site had over 364 million registered users with their profiles uploaded. That's the equivalent of being able to search CVs of the whole of the US and the UK working populations, and more, on one site.

Talent professionals must have a personal presence on LinkedIn. To not do so is limiting both your, and your organisation's, effectiveness in the recruitment market. At the very least it gives you a door to be knocked on by prospective talents from other organisations or those new to the talent market. A well-designed corporate or business-specific page allowing members to follow and get news and updates on opportunities should be used to enhance this online presence. This can then be supplemented and strengthened further by joining appropriate industry or special interest groups.

Social network sites allow organisations the opportunity to build a profile that they can direct or shape, and that becomes visible when someone's search criteria match. An organisation that considers itself a world leader in its field of engineering cannot have this verified easily by others if it is not present in the many groups shaping and sharing opinions on engineering practice. What social networks enable is the ability to build an attraction profile that can positively influence talent in the short term and also those who are thinking about a career move in the future.

Promotion is also something that takes place in other settings or channels. For many new, entry-level talents, organisations' reputations are first encountered in their university or college. It is still very effective, and not too difficult a task, to build strong relationships with a respected faculty at specific universities. Again the choice of this relationship will say something about the profile of the employer brand. This is why McKinsey, considered one of the most prestigious management consultancies, has such a strong presence at many of the world's best business schools. Its intention is to reinforce its brand; whether you apply to work for it or not it has an association established with top business thinking. Even if you work for another company, your belief in the McKinsey brand has already been established and you may consider it as a supplier in future.

An ETM strategy should encourage the building of strong relationships with feeder universities and other core education establishments. This can be achieved by face-to-face activities such as alumni talks, faculty site visits and HR's regular attendance at career fairs.

A recent survey suggested that the average number of university special relationships amongst UK graduate recruiters is between 10 and 25. Most recruiters, it seems, wish to build relationships with a few universities that have great reputations in their preferred subject areas. However, having said that, they target for specific subjects. Of the top 100 recruiters, almost all target the same top five universities in the UK. It seems, in the UK, the same recruiters are all chasing the same new talent.

Talent has no boundaries and is a truly global phenomenon. It has therefore become necessary to compete at this global level. Some of the most gifted graduates, particularly in the STEM skills areas, are coming from Asia. There needs to be a promotion presence of some sort for these potential applicants. This is where digital channels have the advantage of being cost effective and scalable; even if the approach is missing the depth of relationship that some form of face-to-face activity can establish, it can still raise awareness of the brand.

However, there are other tactics that build reputation and awareness over time that do not require an immediate presence. Sponsoring events such as technical challenges, design competitions and sports teams makes the employee brand stand out from its competitors at an important stage in many young talents' careers.

We will examine a few of these tactics later in the chapter, when we look at practical actions to build an attraction profile.

Product

Essentially the product is the career package you are offering the talent in your organisation. What is the role, career or track your organisation is providing? To a young entry-level talent this may be the opportunity to be part of the graduate development programme. The product, in this case, is a chance to work in a large organisation with a specific fast track for developing its talent as a young professional. To an external mid-level candidate it may be the chance to manage a team for the first time in their career or being involved in a start-up project. Either could be a reason to consider joining a new organisation. To the more seasoned executive it may be the opportunity to enter a new market not possible in their current role, or to take on the responsibility for a business unit. Whatever the offer, if it is considered as a product, it can be compared alongside what else is available in the market. The task is then to make the offer as unique and attractive, relative to the competition, as possible.

The same thinking is useful when considering the other primary source for talent: existing employees. Here the issue is slightly different. What would attract them to apply for the high-potential scheme or make them interested in specific new appointments, relative to their status quo, and other opportunities outside the organisation? By viewing the talent opportunities as products, it allows you to think about their features and how attractive they might be to different talent segments.

In too many cases talent professionals focus almost entirely on the external market and its perception of the organisation. In doing so, they fail to understand that the internal candidate also needs to see an attractive and meaningful employee value proposition, if not to push for promotion, at least to remain settled and stay in the organisation. Retaining those you already have is still an important consideration.

Talent segments

It is useful to follow the marketing disciplines a little further and segment the talent requirement of the organisation into meaningful groups. In order to illustrate how each segment may require a different approach to attraction, I have taken three generic levels that would appear in almost all organisations. In larger and more complex organisations, you may need to address several different profiles dependant on the structure and demands of the business.

Entry-level talent

Every organisation needs new blood to stimulate creativity, refresh ideas and in many cases fill specific needs driven by growth. In this case we are not concerned with the normal day-to-day recruitment process to fill regular vacancies, as this falls out of the definition of talent as covered in this book. What we are focusing on is bringing in talent: young people with potential, who should be seen as future leaders or who could over time develop into senior-level, functional professionals.

For many organisations, the graduate recruitment process has provided entry-level talent. This is still the main gateway into many organisations for young talented people who want more than just a job. It has been a traditional source of future managers and executives for many global companies who have a long history of operating in this market.

Companies such as Nestlé, Unilever, Procter & Gamble, HSBC, PWC and Accenture have well-respected graduate schemes that most university careers advisors are aware of and that require little effort in terms of maintaining their brand awareness. Some exploit this brand status very effectively, by passing some of the initial pre-selection and marketing to the university faculty. Sony's Japanese graduate applicants were normally recommended by respected professors at the engineering and design schools that the organisation had established links with. A recommendation by your professor to meet a recruiter from Sony was an honour and one that ensured you had a fast track interview and also one that if you ignored would be seen as discourteous by your tutor.

Less well-known corporate brands need to work at their graduate and first-entry profiles to ensure that they are at least considered by the sort of graduate talents that apply to the Champions' League of global corporations. Younger talent in particular are highly influenced by the corporate brand, at times far more than the actual job content.

Awareness is the important issue in any profile. How can a smaller engineering business compete against the large defence and global infrastructure companies? This is where good marketing helps, by not competing head on, but by finding space in the market for clever branded activities and events to raise the profile of the employer.

Given that most students are in college for at least four years, building awareness should not start in their final year as they start selecting organisations to apply to. A more proactive approach should be taken that could include any or all of the initiatives shown in Table 5.1. This table is not meant to be exhaustive, but hopefully inspiring and illustrative, suggesting things that organisations have used successfully in the past to promote their brand with younger talents.

Table 5.1 Entry-level talent specific attraction initiatives

Initiative	Rationale	Issues raised
Individual degree/ course sponsorship/ bursaries	Demonstrates long-term commitment to the company from the individual and from the company to their career.	Large investment in one individual (used by British Army and UK Dept of Education and some large corporates for hard-to-source STEM talents).
Professional qualification sponsorship	To be a professional engineer, accountant or HR professional it is highly desirable to be a member of a professional body/ institute.[12] Membership requires work sponsorship in many cases, qualifications and fees. This is an attractive offer for many young professionals.	Not all functional routes offer a formal professional qualification, whereas others, such as those of the Engineering institutes, are offered by many employers, and therefore are not always able to act as a differentiator in the marketplace. Good PR and kudos for the individual and the business.
Sports team sponsorship/ university society	Good awareness, visibility for sponsors built over time in the university. Good PR for company overall. sometimes at international level.[13]	Would need additional proactive approach to link sponsorship to potential careers in the organisation. Relatively cheap in many institutions.
Branded competitions/ business games/ problem solving events	Awareness and involvement from people with technical skills and motivation to compete and demonstrate skills. Mentoring by managers from the organisations permits deeper understanding of organisational offer. Can be used to target very specific talent groups, such as fashion designers, software developers and engineers. Often finalists get to travel, expenses paid, to somewhere prestigious to present their case.[14]	Business case competitions are used in many business schools and colleges for promotion of consultancies and professional firms. Relatively low investment for a long-term involvement. Gives visibility on potential talent in chosen partner colleges. 25 per cent of the top recruiters in the UK use some form of competition to promote their brand.
Development workshops on campus	Face-to-face influence with students. The organisation is seen as giving something back to a population of students and therefore a more acceptable form of promotion.[15]	Requires resources from the organisation and needs to be of high quality otherwise it will be perceived as low value, which could negatively affect employer brand.
Webinair workshops	Real-time but virtual workshops, less potential impact than face-to-face but scalable and globally accessible. Able to access Asian and North American talents with little additional resources.[16]	Need a mechanism for sign up and pre-selection. The benefit would be greater if the segment signing up matched the talent needed.

(continued)

Table 5.1 (continued)

Initiative	Rationale	Issues raised
Careers web portal	Corporate pages can act as an initial resource but a career portal, a set of role profiles, application forms, guide to company culture, etc., is more effective at maintaining interest once the main corporate site is found. Portals should offer more information and interaction than the corporate web pages.[17]	Can the portal accept CVs and applications for non-vacant positions? Can you build a virtual talent pool/community? Why would people register interest? The best portals have micro-sites for divisions and each specific segment of talent. Some offer general career advice.
Facebook pages	High visibility, good for building some form of relationship, i.e. users following. Easy to get recommendations. A good channel for the corporate story to be heard in a less formal way. Given the large community of users it's an easy win. Quality is important and having material that is fresh and relevant to the target segment.[18]	Needs to be kept relevant and fresh. Old material with no updating is not very often followed. Responsiveness is key, as online communities are fickle. They need constant feeding of relevant content. Needs to be dynamic and linked to other social media channels.
Twitter/other social media	Good for quick news releases and spontaneous reactions. Can be used to keep in contact with candidates in the process. Very Mobile friendly. Ideal for this target segment.	Same issues as above but with a more aggressive timeline for response. Resources need to be focused on the conversations about the organisation.[19] Not controllable.
LinkedIn	A basic requirement for all entry-level recruitment. The minimum is to have a full profile for all talent professionals within the organisation to ensure visibility and the ability to find the brand in a search. Mobile friendly and able to offer notifications and alerts to roles.	Job seekers consider LinkedIn as the default site in the employment market. This makes some individuals lazy assuming that they can be easily found. Groups,[20] corporate pages and blog posting keeps the communication fresh, interesting and targeted to the employees of choice.
Blogs/journals/ ezines	A presence in subject-specific print and online media is a good way of raising awareness. Being an authority on a subject brings reputation to the organisation where the contributor works. A soft way of getting the brand offer into the minds of the entry-level talent.[21]	Finding the right contributors who are willing to publish as part of a brand awareness campaign. It can be made easier if the PR department supports the talent initiative and liaises with the media editors.
Site visits/ collaboration	Bring the individual to the organisation as part of their education. Work with selected faculty and students on business issues. Allows a controlled interaction with a potential employee.[22]	Cost of this can be high, but for local employers with a relationship with a college it can work extremely well. Using the intellectual property of the college requires legal rights to be agreed.

Paid internships	Long-term visibility of a pre-qualified potential employee who has already shown interest in the organisation. Low cost, limited commitment from each side. Ideally a six-month assessment of the intern and potential talent candidate.[23]	Some organisations and some countries use internships very well. They are popular in the USA, Germany and with some large organisations in the UK. To be effective also requires robust selection processes.
Ranking table entry	Times 100 best graduate recruiters list the top jobs, based on research surveys, salaries, etc. Use any opportunity to get placed in similar rankings for specific industries. This raises brand awareness, as the guides with rankings are widely used by careers services and individual job seekers.[24]	Getting a fair ranking takes time and effort but is probably worth it if the organisation takes in a reasonably large intake each year to spread the costs. Most of the large global organisations operating in the UK are listed.
Apprenticeships	Widely supported in the UK and Germany. An increasingly popular option for technical and some professional roles. This requires more investment in raising awareness within schools and tertiary colleges.[25]	A popular option for gaining professional qualifications whilst not increasing debt though university fees and living expenses. Supported by industry leaders such as HSBC, PWC and many engineering companies.
Summer schools	Short duration, subject-specific workshops sponsored by the organisation. These are very popular ways of influencing the graduates before they apply, in their summer breaks in years 2 and 3 of their degrees.	A good way of getting good PR with the target population. Need to focus on very specific profiles to ensure that there is a return on the investment above brand awareness.

All of the above initiatives are being used by different organisations to raise the awareness of their career opportunities and build their attraction profiles to younger talents. Whilst many focus on the well-established and highly competitive graduate market, others are completely independent of universities. What is clear is that the emergence of social media and business networks has changed the way organisations raise awareness of opportunities. It is inconceivable that a talent opportunity for this younger entry-level segment would not try to exploit social media in some way. Advertising on the established recruitment portals, such as Monsterboard, is now almost always supplemented by links or prompts on other organisational channels, be it Twitter feeds, corporate websites, Facebook, LinkedIn or Instagram. Mobile is omnipresent as a channel and one with an incredibly high percentage of smart phone users in this particular segment. Many regard their phone as the default device for all their communication needs, including job search. Pew research[26] reports a specific increase in the use of smart phones in this age group in the USA but the overall trend is considered to be global:

> As in past surveys, smartphone ownership is highest among younger Americans, as well as those with relatively high income and education levels. Some 85% of

Americans ages 18–29 are smartphone owners, as are 78% of college graduates and 84% of those living in households with an annual income of $75,000 or more per year.

For this segment, if your profile is not optimised for mobile then you are not really marketing your talent opportunities to best effect on the device of choice for your target market.

Mid-level talent

This is the population of people who already have some work experience and are looking to develop their career either within their current organisation or in a new company. For many, the desire to change employers is a mixture of limited opportunity in their own organisation and a perceived view that getting different brands on their CV is a good thing for their long-term career. If these people are already high performers and have high potential, their leaving is a significant loss for their organisation. Not only does it not have continued access to their capability, but, in addition, the likelihood is that they are joining and therefore strengthening a competitor.

Finding a way to attract great talent from other companies, and becoming their employer of choice, is a challenge, but one worth taking up. These people are more discerning in their role choice as they are already employed in most cases and need to be confident that any move is a good one.

If it is your organisation's talent who is considering moving, then there also needs to be a compelling reason to stay. The talent professional needs to consider the internal marketing message about careers, expectations and opportunities as much as the external one. With the typical cost of hiring running between £5,000 – 15,000 for non-executive roles, losing a talent that could have chosen to stay is costly and time consuming. Keeping them onside is much more effective, but requires a clear message to address their career ambitions and, at the same time, share the organisation's expectations. Much of that is expressed in the message to the external market, but talent professionals would be wise to consider how it affects their own people who might be also be thinking of their next move.

Again, the tactics shown in Table 5.2 are not exhaustive, but they are designed to ensure a number of considerations relevant to this particular talent segment, mid-level talent, are made. Some tactics overlap with initiatives for the entry level, but then others are more effective with just within this segment.

Executive-level talent

This segment contains the high-performing, experienced executives that every company wishes it had in its most senior roles. The talent pools should also contain candidates that have grown and developed within the organisation, therefore already gaining an understanding of both the culture and DNA of the business. However, these experienced candidates are also the people who have the most value in the market and are therefore the target for executive search agencies and head-hunters. Table 5.3 illustrates examples of Executive Level Talent Attraction Initiatives.

The core characteristic of the employer of choice for this segment is a place where high performers can thrive. In general, people at this stage in their career leave their

Table 5.2 Mid-level specific talent attraction initiatives

Initiative	Rationale	Issues raised
Facebook	This is something that career movers will research to check out the culture, the way the organisation works, and what it says about itself. They research all channels to build a picture, ensure Facebook reflects the right one for mid careers.[27]	Needs to show people like them, i.e. mid-career talents, achieving goals in their work. The site should also convey the essence of the leadership and culture, work–life balance and other potential decision factors for a career mover.
Glassdoor/Indeed and similar career referral rating sites	Now becoming a real force in career search. If companies use it they acknowledge that people have the right to an opinion of their culture and workplace practices. However, it also demonstrates transparency more than other sites.[28]	Can you use the site if its ratings from ex-employees are not positive? Or can you encourage the right candidate with candid descriptions on the site? The talent professional needs to monitor the site and influence reviews in any way they can.[29]
LinkedIn	The channel of choice for mid-career talents. It now accounts for over 3 million posted vacancies and is regularly used by over 80 per cent of recruiters. To be visible your organisation needs to be present and active. Encourage individual experts to create interest groups linked to brand pages. Build a presence as an authority on your organisation's core capability.	Professional groups on LinkedIn now play a more important role, as they can better demonstrate real employee contributions at work and show their depth of expertise. Many potential talents in the same profession join groups in industry sectors to network and test potential openings and get some information about working at new organisations.[30]
Recruitment agency	Building relationships with sector-specific recruitment agencies is a way to ensure an ability to top up talent pools when the corporate brand has low visibility. A good way to establish a presence in the market when restarting a talent drive.	It is important to have a strong relationship with the preferred provider for your sector, to ensure that only the talent profiles you need are put forward. Potentially this is an expensive option, but for specialist roles, necessary.
Conference speaking/ exhibitions	Getting the brand known for expertise and unique achievement via speakers at sector-specific and professional conferences. Many high-ability talents gain good PR from speaking at conferences. The positive by-product is higher visibility with a target audience for the brand. Similarly exhibitions for the industry are good recruiting grounds and ways to show the brand's strength.	You need to encourage the right people to take the speaker invitations. A poor speaker or poor content will damage the brand. Staff manning exhibition spaces need to be made aware of the value of the event to the recruitment of talent. They should ensure contact details are available for recruiters and that enquiries they receive are followed up. Print their business cards reverse side with 'We are recruiting now, ring . . .'. an effective reminder of who they spoke to.

(continued)

Table 5.2 (continued)

Initiative	Rationale	Issues raised
Careers web portal	To be effective at this level, there needs to be something of perceived value for the candidate over and above listing their interest. Building a micro-site for specific career niches may work for some industries. Offering access to white papers and research will work for others.	Company careers portals are good potential pools, but need to accommodate or respect confidentiality. If someone lists, what do they get? Is there an alert system? Is there preferential treatment for new postings? Why would they list their CV here?
Outplacement agency	Used as a possible source of mid-level talent featured in company mergers and relocations. Talent may not always be able to move or stay within new structures. Outplacement consultancies can be a source of specialists.	You need to trust the consultancy you work with, and also be very clear about the organisation's expectations from talent. A good, often untapped, source for the proactive talent professional.[31]
High-potential scheme open application process	Within any company there will be hidden talent, waiting to be discovered before they leave. Promotion of a high-potential application scheme for internal candidates may draw them out. A specific drive for internal applications can get results for previously overlooked individuals.	Some managers will not wish to promote their best people, preferring to keep hold of the asset. Others will encourage unsuitable candidates to apply as some sort of substitute reward. A robust assessment process will reduce these errors in selection.
Recommendations from current staff	People who have a good network are a great source of new talent. If they are happy to recommend the company they work for, it says a lot about the EVP to others. This works well in filling some technical roles where good professional networks already exist.	Statistics show that recommendations are becoming increasingly important to mid-career job seekers. It is common for employees who make a recommendation or referral to get a reward or gift.[32] What needs to be clear is that the gift is rewarding, the incentive not so large a reward that it becomes an income stream.

employer and seek new opportunities where they can get more responsibility or increased control of people, projects or specific business units. If their ambitions are not being met by their current employer, they will consider moving to one where they think their skills and drive will be more appreciated. If your organisation has built a reputation in the market place as somewhere that values high performers, they will show an interest in your roles.

The most significant difference for this group of talents is that a role will most likely be filled by recommendation or individual approach. The individual approach may be done on the organisation's behalf by a retained executive search firm, but it is also just as likely to come from an executive's personal network. Social networks really do matter

Table 5.3 Executive-level talent attraction initiatives

Initiative	Rationale	Issues raised
Executive search partnership	A contracted relationship with one of the top executive search firms will do two things: give you some protection from them head-hunting your own people, and build a strong relationship with people who have a good network in the marketplace.[33]	Costs can be significant. It's not easy to manage more than one relationship well, so choosing the right partner is critical to success. Good partners will proactively present candidates when they fit but there is no live search.
Professional networks	There are high-level professional networks in many countries, not always industry specific. These should be encouraged and used as sources and a way to build corporate reputations at this level.[34]	National and International professional associations need committee members, sponsors and admin support. Getting this provided from your organisation can create high visibility for relatively low cost.
Alumni events	Use your existing executive talent to attend alumni events on behalf of the organisation. Business schools in Europe and the USA are particularly active in this arena.[35]	Senior-level talent will often have business school, college or professional body contacts. Networks and informal approaches are key to building influence in this segment.
Global opportunities	Use the company's locations to attract talent at this senior level. Many high performers want to expand their control. This means getting their first business unit head experience or country-level role. Large corporates can attract good talent using their global footprint.	It is never cheap to source global talent but giving new international experience to high performers and filling critical roles in developing countries may be a good win–win strategy.[36]

at this level. It is common for a senior executive to explore and build relationships with search firms some years in advance of their actual move. It may not be a head-hunter that they talk to initially, but they may share with some close, professional colleagues about their ambitions and then be contacted by a referral. A very common question when the search executive closes their prospecting call is: 'If this is not for you is there anyone you know in your network who you think would suit this opportunity?'

Not many roles at this level are advertised, or applied for, so having enduring influence in network events is a key to success. This relies much more on the good will of senior-level incumbents acting as corporate ambassadors than just the talent professional themselves.

Choosing to use executive search

For this senior segment of organisational talent, it is necessary for the organisation to explore the use of executive search firms. Your best talent will already have established a relationship with one or more of the top companies, either from past career posts or as a natural way to ensure their future career plans. An ETM strategy should include a carefully chosen provider, or in some cases providers, from the search industry. Most of the big five have practices that cover most industry sectors and their global reach is also similar with offices in most major capital cities. So what are the essential criteria that can be used to select a partner in this very sensitive area of senior talent?

The first question to ask of any firm is, what can they offer you in terms of support for your most difficult to source talent? This is, of course, very specific to your own organisation. However, if the firm has researched your industry and your business objectives, they should be able to give an informed answer to this key question. In this segment your partners should be acting as consultants first and recruiters second. If they do not understand your business model and challenges, they cannot offer good advice on who should join.

The second question to ask is, who will be your contact, account manager, lead consultant? In large firms the reputation is built on their methodology, their database, their size and their track record. However, all consultancy projects are primarily a relationship of trust and, as the talent professional leading any relationship, you need to feel completely comfortable with the primary contact. If as part of any selection process you meet a range of consultants, find out who they would offer as the contact person, and do not just talk to the sales lead, talk to the named individual. Some firms have very senior, credible and confident partners who sell their services and seal the deal with clients, but rarely work on assignments themselves. In others you initially meet the same person who will service the assignments should you select them.

The third, and at this stage final, question is what do they offer you in terms of expertise that can add value to your selection process that currently you pay for or carry out yourself? A good firm can offer services that remove some of the work you do or that your organisation pays someone else for. This could be included within the contract for the service they provide. None of this is important if you cannot trust the individual they offer you, or if their understanding of your need is vague and uninspiring, but added value is something to ask for and evaluate in your decision.

A word of caution, based on personal experience, regarding being given a strong recommendation for a particular executive search firm from one of your senior executives. The enduring model of search is one where a strong personal relationship is built with the individual executive. They are clients as much as the hiring organisation is. If the senior executive X was sourced by firm A, they are likely to have developed a strong affinity and regard for that firm. It would not be unreasonable for them to think that any firm that identified them as a strong candidate for their role was competent and trustworthy. This may be true and it may be also out of date for what the organisation now requires. That executive may also not be professionally qualified or experienced enough to judge their capability. If the firm has already placed senior talents for you which you are happy with then they are a reasonable starting point for a continued discussion. However, it is also wise to test what else the market offers.

As Avis used to say in its famous marketing strap line when it was ranked number 2 in the rental car market: 'we try harder'. Becoming a trusted advisor, as a good executive search consultant should be, is a strong incentive for them to really offer extra services or insight into your organisation's talent needs. A newcomer may offer more, or try harder, than those who already believe they have won your custom.

A more practical reason for having a strong relationship with one of the top firms in your sector is that it becomes more difficult for them to represent or poach people from your own firm, whilst taking a retainer fee from you as a client. It's a matter of ethics that they will not directly approach your own people. It doesn't stop talent leaving but it does slow the process down.

Marketing – attracting the right talent

In this part of the book we have explored how marketing principles can help a talent professional think differently about the candidates they wish to attract. A great brand will always attract people, regardless of the actual employee value proposition, which may be significantly different from that conveyed by the consumer brand image.

A useful approach for talent professionals to keep in mind is that of segmentation, which will allow them to build an attraction profile that minimises the non-runners and attracts a larger proportion of more suitable candidates. The ideal applicants are those that understand the value proposition of the organisation, have self-selected themselves in, and are aware of, the expectations of the organisation. The role then becomes focused on sifting them in or out of the talent pools of the organisation.

In the following chapter we explore the various ways to build a robust assessment and selection process for each for the three segments of talent and, later in the book, how to develop and deploy them to the best effect.

Key review questions

What does your employer brand say about the organisation?

Which is your most difficult segment for securing talent?

Where might you need to build a profile to attract more of this scarce resource?

What does your digital media profile for the organisation look like?

Notes

1 Anders, George (2012) The 20 Most Desired Employers: From Google to Nike, Accenture, *Forbes/Tech*, 11 Oct, http://www.forbes.com/sites/georgeanders/2012/10/11/the-20-most-desired-employers-from-google-to-loreal/.
2 Amazon needed to respond to employee criticism of its work culture after a report published in the *New York Times*. The fall-out in terms of negative PR is covered in an article in the *Guardian* Beningson, David (2015) Brand damage for Amazon and a triumph for old media, *The Guardian*, 19 Aug, http://www.theguardian.com/media-network/2015/aug/19/brand-amazon-media-jeff-bezos-times.
3 A blog that shows some creative images and copy for jobs advertised in print media is Pratt, Sofria (2014) 26 Crazily Creative Recruitment Ads You Need to See, *SocialTalent*, 9 Oct, http://www.socialtalent.co/blog/30-crazily-creative-recruitment-ads.
4 Interbrand publish a ranking of the best global brands by value. See Interbrand (2014) The Best 100 Brands, http://www.bestglobalbrands.com/2014/ranking/.
5 See, for example, http://fortune.com/best-companies/; http://features.thesundaytimes.co.uk/public/best100companies/; http://www.thejobcrowd.com/top-companies-to-work-for.
6 See https://www.LinkedIn.com/home.
7 See http://www.glassdoor.co.uk/index.htm.
8 Glassdoor Team (2015) America's 15 Highest Paying Companies, *Glassdoor Blog*, 10 Apr, http://www.glassdoor.com/blog/americas-15-highest-paying-companies/.

9 See http://graduates.teachfirst.org.uk/application-selection/requirements/teaching-subject-requirements.

10 Denholm, John (2015) The UK's marketing talent shortage is worsening outside London, *The Drum*, 6 Apr, http://www.thedrum.com/opinion/2015/04/06/uk-s-marketing-talent-shortage-worsening-outside-london.

11 High Fliers (2015) *The Graduate Market 2015*, High Fliers Research Limited, London, http://www.highfliers.co.uk/download/2015/graduate_market/GMReport15.pdf.

12 The Chartered Institute of Personnel and Development (CIPD) is a de facto standard for HR managers in the UK and increasingly in EMEA. They require post-graduate level study and examinations to gain full membership and they lobby the UK and EU on workplace issues (http://www.cipd.co.uk). other professions have similar governing bodies.

13 The BNY Mellon Boat race is sponsored by a US merchant bank giving it direct access to two of the oldest and most respected educational institutions in the world and a worldwide TV audience expected to be over 15 million with another 250,000 watching the race live.

14 KPMG flies its finalists to Dubai to present their cases. See http://www.kpmg.com/global/en/careers/whatcanido/careerlevels/students/kicc/pages/default.aspx.

15 The likes of Citi Bank, PWC and AIG use this approach actively with their university partners. See http://www.city.ac.uk/careers/recruiters/get-involved-on-campus/employability-skills-programme.

16 Employers are encouraged to participate on campus and with online content with leading colleges. Supporting the brand with online material after a face-to-face event adds depth to any relationship. See http://www.imperial.ac.uk/careers/services/events/.

17 In the UK the National Health Service has an employment portal, to aggregate the vacancies they have across the organisation. Economies of scale come from combining the demand and talent pool. https://www.oriel.nhs.uk/Web/.

18 Nestlé has a number of country-based Facebook pages focused on careers and employer brand. Each is very highly monitored and must reflect the quality of its brand. https://www.facebook.com/NestleCareersUK.

19 Deloitte uses Twitter to spread a wider message about life in the company. Its site shares charity events it sponsors or that its employees participate in. https://twitter.com/deloitteuk.

20 Large organisations have over time changed their policy on LinkedIn. They initially feared having people poached, but now use it to promote their version of events. https://www.linkedin.com/company/bombardier-transportation.

21 Here, an Npower manager writes as a guest blogger on electric vehicles, a subject interesting but not core to its business. It's part of an agenda for promoting Npower as a thought leader in all things Energy: Energy Live News (2015) Guest Blog: npower's Wayne Mitchell on Solutions for Businesses, *Energy Live News*, 25 Feb, http://www.energylivenews.com/2015/02/24/guest-blog-npowers-wayne-mitchell-on-solutions-for-businesses/.

22 Loughborough, a college specialising in Engineering collaborates with business on projects bringing its students into face-to-face and on-site work with industry. Good PR for both but increasingly a way of promoting the industry to talents with sought after profiles. http://www.lboro.ac.uk/enterprise/collaboration/.

23 There is a myriad of organisations willing to assist students find paid and unpaid internships. Registering your organisation with one would increase it visibility at low or no cost. See http://www.goabroad.com/intern-abroad/search/western-europe/internships-abroad-1.

24 High Fliers publishes a number of surveys, for the talent professional as well as for college career services. High Fliers (2015) *The Graduate Market 2015*, High Fliers Research Limited, London, http://www.highfliers.co.uk/download/2015/graduate_market/GMReport15.pdf.

25 See http://www.pwc.co.uk/government-public-sector/issues/higher-apprenticeships.jhtml.

26 Pew Research conducts an annual survey of mobile use. See Smith, Aaron (2015) U.S. Smartphone Use in 2015, *PewResearchCenter*, 1 Apr, http://www.pewinternet.org/2015/04/01/chapter-one-a-portrait-of-smartphone-ownership/.

27 Bain and Company, a major strategy consultancy, has a Facebook page that shows its commitment to social responsibility as an organisation and demonstrates these values in its posts. It focuses on staff members doing things that are not just work, but demonstrate an aspirational lifestyle for professionals. https://www.facebook.com/bainandcompanyUK?brand_redir=137690650043.

28 Glassdoor leads the pack of employee opinion career sites, but there are many starting up in competition, some without the anonymous reviews, others with other ways to rate companies, see http://www.companyconnector.com/; http://www.glassdoor.co.uk http://realref.com/.

29 Walker, Rob (2015) I'll tell you something, *People Management*, CIPD, Jul, http://www.cipd.co.uk/pm/peoplemanagement/b/weblog/archive/2015/06/18/i-39-ll-tell-you-something-rob-walker.aspx.

30 Bombardier Transportation uses groups in LinkedIn to build virtual talent pools in developing markets. https://www.linkedin.com/groups?gid=3717126&trk=vsrp_groups_res_name&trkInfo=VSRPsearchId%3A58818214341013559222%2CVSRPtargetId%3A3717126%2CVSRPcmpt%3Aprimary.

31 Outplacement agencies and consultancies are proactively trying to place talent, and are used for this mid-level group of professionals. Seek a consultancy with international reach or specialist knowledge of your industry. For listed member firms, see http://acpinternational.org/.

32 There are a number of studies that look at the use of incentives in referrals most suggesting that they work if used in tight employment markets and with clear periods of tenure of the new hire before awards are made. See Society for Human Resource Management Research (2001) *Employee Referral Programs*, Society for Human Resource Management Research, Alexandria, VA, http://www.shrm.org/Research/SurveyFindings/Documents/Employee%20Referral%20Programs.pdf.

   The economic efficiency of referral vs other hiring tactics is discussed in this Stanford paper and shows a number of advantages for employee referals. https://faculty-gsb.stanford.edu/oyer/wp/hire.pdf.

33 The 'big five' executive search firms are Korn Ferry, Heidrick & Struggles, Spencer Stuart, Egon Zehnder and Russell Reynolds. These companies have multiple offices all over the globe.

34 Many of these networks offer speakers, dinners and conferences/seminars for members. See http://www.criticaleye.net/about.cfm.

35 IMD, the globally ranked Swiss business school, is very active in its alumni programme. See http://www.imd.org/alumni/.

36 McKinsey has a good article outlining the issues with attracting top talent. They explore the issues of local vs imported talent as part of a sourcing strategy. Dewhurst, Martin, Pettigrew, Matthew and Srinivasan, Ramesh (2012) How multinationals can attract the talent they need, *McKinsey Quarterly*, Jun, http://www.mckinsey.com/insights/organization/how_multinationals_can_attract_the_talent_they_need.

Chapter 6

How can you make assessment methods reliable and robust?

Introduction

In the previous chapters we have linked the concept of ETM to the business strategy of the organisation. To achieve that required clearly defining what talent would mean in any specific organisation, relative to its business strategy. These two factors, the strategy of the company and the talent definition, create the specification for the roles that are then marketed in a way that attracts the right applicants. In Chapter 5 we explored how the tools of marketing can be used to segment the organisation's talent requirement and suggested a number of different initiatives that might build an attraction profile for each pool. The purpose of this was to attract more of the employees of choice and not just a large random applicant group. If the marketing has been done effectively some of the sifting will have already happened by self-selection as people realise they are not a good fit.

In this chapter we will examine the process of selecting talent. This is dependent on understanding a range of the tools and techniques of assessment. If enough of the employees of choice, the right people, express an interest in joining the organisation, then the primary role of the talent team is to select the very best applicant.

A good pool of candidates, made up of internal, external or a mixture of the two, will still need a reliable and robust process to help select the right ones into the various organisational talent pools. Given the significant amount of investment that an organisation commits to the support and development of talent, it is crucial that it has confidence in its decisions about whom it makes an offer of employment to.

Assessment of performance and potential

There are two dimensions that matter when thinking about talent. Each should be represented in some form in the organisation's talent definition. As discussed in Chapter 3, the clearer the definition, the easier it is to select people who meet it.

There is a range of options available to talent management professionals to help them make the crucial selection decisions that ETM requires. Whilst not every talent management professional will be involved in each assessment they should have a good understanding of the advantages and drawbacks of the various approaches.

Not all the tools will work well in every segment of the talent pipeline. Some are well established and easy to implement whilst others require a degree of expertise to apply effectively. In the following section some of the most common approaches are reviewed, then later in the chapter there is a guide as to which may be the most appropriate choice for each segment of talent. This chapter is not intended to be a full technical review of every possible assessment method but more of a practical guide to selection of some of the more effective approaches. However, for the curious reader the endnotes provide a guide to additional supporting research and other helpful sources of further reading.

Competency frameworks

A clear definition of talent will describe the target profile in terms of skills and attitudes. There may also be other expectations or criteria to meet for the successful talent pool member. Talents are commonly described using a mix of essential technical expertise, any specific pool requirement for mobility, desirable or necessary language capabilities and, finally, any specific competencies. The candidate's curriculum vitae (CV) will allow a recruiting manager to ascertain the past expertise and professed proficiency in languages. If necessary, language can be independently verified using one of the many existing language proficiency ratings such as TOEFL.[1] Mobility and willingness to travel if considered a requirement can also be fairly easily determined in the screening interview, which can be conducted face to face, by telephone or the increasingly popular video link.

The specific skills and attitude required for the candidate to be successful, and the more transferable abilities, are termed competencies. Most organisations that have established a formal talent and performance management system will use a competency framework. It is these frameworks that underpin the majority of talent management definitions.

The original idea of using a form of competencies for selection is attributed to the writing of David McClelland, a Harvard Psychology Professor. He published an influential article in 1973 called 'Testing for Competence Rather Than for Intelligence'.[2] Following his thinking a small army of consultants and practitioners created an approach to defining the competencies present in roles and those that seemed to distinguish superior performance from the average performance. As we explore in Chapter 8, where we discuss performance, the use of competencies was pivotal in developing a number of widely accepted approaches for managing people in the workplace, not just in candidate selection.

Competencies are defined in various ways by different academics and practitioners but a good working definition is as follows;

> *Competency*: The combination of observable and measurable knowledge, skills, abilities and personal attributes that contribute to enhanced employee performance and ultimately result in organisational success.

A typical organisation's competency framework may contain 15–20 defined specific competencies. Wherever possible each should be discrete, so what it describes has little overlap with another competence. When a number of them are carefully selected to represent a role they should be able to describe the behaviours an individual needs to demonstrate that they are successful in that role. A well-constructed framework can be used to define different levels of performance in each competence related to the seniority and complexity of role.

Therefore it's possible to use the competence 'planning and organising' as a consistent element in a number of professional roles within an organisation, but rightly expect a more sophisticated level of ability displayed in a candidate for a senior project management role in comparison to that of a newly recruited graduate. In many organisations this differentiation is achieved by using a range of behavioural indicators for each competence with an incremental level of sophistication related to seniority and/ or complexity of role. Table 6.1 shows one competency example with a connected set of behavioural levels. The subsequent level implies having the ability to fulfil all of the preceding levels.

In many organisations these comprehensive frameworks rarely make it into everyday use by the line managers of the business. However, they are useful tools for HR and talent professionals who wish to employ them in assessment design, the development of effective and focused training and also as a core component of a good performance management system.

The competencies, and any additional criteria of the talent definition, form the blueprint for the type of people you are selecting. It is this profile that then needs to be compared to the evidence collected through the use of various assessment techniques. The two items are intrinsically linked with each specific type of competence defining the choice of selection method: one that best demonstrates that particular mix of skills and attitudes.

Assessors and evaluation

The task of assessment is to find evidence of the competencies and any other criteria that are contained in the talent definition. There is a multitude of exercises and other tools to ascertain the level of match between any individual and the competence profile. These tools create opportunities for observing and evaluating the evidence of each competence. The assessor role is critical to every part of the assessment process. An assessor who is well trained and motivated can still make a badly designed system work. However, the best system in the world cannot work well if the assessors employed in the process are not able to understand their role or are not motivated to do it.

In all of the assessment processes there is an evaluation to make, which should always be based on the examination of firm evidence. A reliable evaluation means the rating has been judged by someone who is trained in the process and whose decisions are made with reference to the competencies. Assessors are increasingly being asked to integrate a much wider and more complex range of evidence on candidates. This means that some form of moderation, calibration and agreed decision-making protocol are required to ensure that the assessors don't get lost in the detail of the evidence. More evidence can mean more complex decision-making, but ultimately it also leads to more reliable results.

There are a wide variety of opinions about who should be involved in the assessor role. The choice of which is most appropriate for any particular organisation is dependent on many factors. The four most common approaches together with some of the pros and cons are set out in Table 6.2.

There is no best ideal model for the type of assessors, just what works best for the organisation at that point in time and with the resources it has to hand. However, each different mix brings with it advantages and disadvantages. The mini case below shows one organisation's choice and its implications.

Table 6.1 Communication – example competency definition and scale

Communication: Expresses thoughts and ideas in a clear and concise way. Effectively conveys ideas and shares information with others. Captures the attention of the audience. Responds in an open, honest and respectful manner when communicating with others. Listens and is listened to by others.

1	2	3	4	5	6
Clearly and appropriately expresses his/her desires and needs.	Understands the importance of and demonstrates good oral, listening, and writing skills.	Adapts communications to audience requirements to optimise understanding.	Actively presents information and ideas to all appropriate levels and leads others to do the same.	Promotes open expression of ideas and encourages communication without retribution.	Is recognised as one who effectively clarifies and communicates key/strategic information.

Table 6.2 Choice of assessors – four common approaches

Who assesses	Pros	Cons	Comments
Line managers	High level of involvement and therefore commitment of hiring manager. Good fit for candidates who meet their potential hiring managers.	Some line managers are not always able to see the bigger organisational need. Danger of just filling roles not hiring best talent. Training time and costs are significant, for people not using the skills so often.	Sometimes needs some strong and credible facilitation at the decision-making meetings following any assessment process to ensure a corporate-wide view.
HR managers	Generally already skilled in interviewing and other assessment methods. The understanding of competencies is relatively high. They can see the overview of organisational talent needs.	Distant from the day-to-day impact of their decisions (or can be perceived as such by line managers). Not always able to interpret the roles in technical areas. Still require training but some skill base normally exists in HR.	When HR hires on behalf of other departments without them given a say in the decision, it can become a reason to blame HR if the talent fails to deliver in role.
HR and line managers	A good balance of expertise in the process with experience of the roles being hired. Brings the HR and line roles together on something of strategic importance. Increases HR's understanding of their customers' needs.	Sometimes difficult getting a common level of evaluation from both groups. Ensuring a balance of evidence is also represented in the decision, so not just a line supported by HR but a joint decision for the organisation.	Pairing up assessors during assessment tasks so there is a line and HR manager working together removes some of the potential difficulties and builds a strong consensus on the decision. It does mean more resources.
External experts	High level of independence, so limited bias to any specific department. High level of expertise, so reliable. Doesn't impact on management time for large assessment projects. No training costs or time involved. Can use a wider range of tools due to qualification and experience.	Lacks understanding of the culture of the organisation, which may be influential in a talent performing. Also delegates responsibility to a third party, which lacks management commitment. Expensive if used extensively to replace management time.	Experts have an important role to play in building systems, training assessors and being part of the integration sessions as moderators. However, they are distant from the organisation unless there is a long association.

Endless training

A global engineering organisation has a talent strategy that is heavily influenced by its annual graduate intake across a number of its divisions and business units globally. The Global HQ, located in Europe, takes responsibility for managing its entry-level talent on behalf of the whole business.

Each business unit or division decides in its annual manpower planning and budgeting review how many graduate roles it requires for the following year. These numbers are aggregated and a marketing plan put together on behalf of the whole business. It competes against the specific engineering market, as most of its hires are expected to have a degree in some area of engineering, and also against the wider STEM (science, technology, engineering and maths) market.

The graduates are selected using assessment centres as part of the process, following reviews of applications, tests and telephone pre-screening interviews. Each assessment centre is dedicated to one business unit's demands, although in cases where these are relatively small, an assessment centre looks after two business units' requirements.

The assessors for each business unit are made up of a mixture of HR and line managers. Typically a 12-candidate assessment centre uses 10 management assessors plus the centre manager and an external expert consultant. The duration of the assessment centre is one-and-a-half days for the candidates and two full days for the assessors.

In this organisation, the decision was made to include the decision-making managers as much as possible to ensure that there was full support for the ongoing development of any hired graduates. The line managers would be part of the selection process and make the final decision, but would be supported by their HR business partners to ensure that the business unit had some consistency across its hiring decisions.

There are clear advantages in this approach. As a necessary step to being an assessor, every line manager is trained in the assessment centre tools and exercises, normally carried out the day before the centre. This training is compulsory and comprehensive. As a result the assessors have a high level of competence, and for line managers, it is often their first real training in selection methods. For HR managers it creates a standard approach, even though some may have many years of experience and their own preferences in interviewing techniques. This blanket training of assessors, experienced or not, ensures as much as possible the reliability of the group's evaluations. Wherever the numbers allow, two assessors work together through the assessment centre, ideally made up of one HR and one line, but it is always a more experienced assessor alongside someone less experienced.

The organisation sees the advantages of this approach as:

high level of commitment to the graduate scheme from hiring managers;

involvement of HR in the final decision, supporting the business unit;

decisions made on the day of the assessment centre by the hiring manager;

(continued)

(continued)

a clear and transparent process for the line manager to observe and take part in;

there are a lot of managers trained in assessment in the organisation.

There are some disadvantages of this approach, which are:

less committed managers delegate to more junior replacements without authority;

it's time-consuming for line managers so they normally only participate in one assessment per year;

training line managers at every centre by external experts is expensive;

due to lack of practice some variation in skill level exists with the managers.

This graduate scheme has run for over eight years, with a typical year training at least 80–90 new assessors. This has built up an understanding of objective assessment across the organisation as an unintended positive consequence of the programme. It has also raised the cost of the process by around 30 per cent over other methods and approaches to assessing the same population.

What follows in the rest of this chapter is a review of some of the more common methods used by assessors to help candidates demonstrate competencies.

Selection interviews

Even in 2015 the majority of hiring decisions are still made using the results from an unstructured interview process. In most organisations this is still a simple two-stage process with the recruiter compiling a short list from reviewing CVs, and possibly telephone interviews, and then presenting these to the hiring manager for the final interview and decision. These interviews take place either with just the hiring manager or, in some cases, the hiring manager with an HR colleague.

What we know from extensive psychological research[3] is that unstructured interviews are known to be unreliable and they are not particularly good predictors of future performance in the role. This situation is often compounded by the lack of training that organisations give to line managers in interviewing techniques. Not only are unstructured interviews poor, but the majority of line managers using them are often not trained in interview techniques.

Interviewer training and the use of carefully designed competency-based interview questions significantly improves the validity of interviews as a single method of assessment, but the process still lacks reliability. This inconsistency is mainly caused by the variation in interviewer skills and the interference of the manager's personal conscious and unconscious biases. It seems that in many instances the interviewer spends too much time exploring topics of little relevance to the selection criteria, and therefore misses the opportunity to gain real evidence of competence. This can be mitigated to some extent by more structure in the interview questions and improving the training.

When a competence profile exists for a role it is possible to create a more effective and reliable interview process. Each competence should be explored using a structured set of questions that require the candidate to recall a specific past experience. Their detailed answer can be evaluated against predetermined criteria and given a rating.

This predetermined competence structure, with its carefully crafted questions, minimises the errors that inexperienced interviewers often make. The use of standard competence-based questions for all assessors significantly reduces the variation a group of interviewers brings to a selection process. It stops inexperienced interviewers asking irrelevant questions and also ensures that any asked remain within the boundaries of employment law. This structured approach also removes some of the more leading questions that seem to be popular with line managers who are not trained in gaining objective, fair and reliable competence evidence.

Research into the increasing use of structured interviews has shown it provides a significant improvement in the validity and reliability of the tool.[4] It is now quite common for job interviews to be either competence based or critical incident based – both are more structured in their approach in comparison to the tradition method of exploring the candidate's CV chronologically.

A typical competence-based question is simple and directly elicits evidence from the past experience of the candidate during the interview. When these are then followed up with appropriate probing questions, it becomes possible to gain a real insight into the candidate's behaviour. The interviewing assessor can then start to evaluate their competence level based on examples from a relevant experience that demanded the specific behaviour to be demonstrated. A well-designed competence question set should be structured to elicit both positive examples and counter-examples. These counter-examples, descriptions of less successful examples of behaviour, are called negative evidence questions. Using both types of competence questions the assessor can gain a more balanced profile of the candidate's ability.

The competence 'communication' is defined below; it's a generic competence for many organisations.

> *Communication*: Expresses thoughts and ideas in a clear and concise way. Effectively conveys ideas and shares information with others. Captures the attention of the audience. Responds in an open, honest and respectful manner when communicating with others. Listens and is listened to by others

An example of a competence-based interview question for this is:

> Describe to me a time when you have had to explain something complex to a group or team?

This would then be followed up with the candidate by eliciting more specific details of the situation, the task required, the actions of the individual and the results of the example. In this way the interviewer can use a structured starter question and then use their experience to dig deeper into the detail and get more comprehensive answers.

STAR questioning

The STAR, process of probing is a common and very effective way of gaining more detail and more effective evidence from a simple opening competence-based question. Following each structured starter question, after listening to the candidate's answer, the interviewer asks questions indicated by the mnemonic STAR:

SITUATION – this is the broad description of the event.

TASK – this is the actual objective or challenge faced, the output required.

ACTIONS – this is the specific action taken by the individual questioned.

RESULTS – this is the measure of success of failure or the overall event.

The following example shows how each subsequent question may reveal more depth and, therefore, better evidence of the competence being examined.

Competence – drive and results orientation

Assessor:	Describe to me a time where you worked under significant pressure over a period of time?
Candidate:	That would be, two years ago, when I was working on my first internship at a shipping company.
Assessor:	So what was the situation and where was there sustained pressure?
Candidate:	Well, when I first started there were supposed to be two interns for six months working in the warehouse planning section. I arrived in the first week of May to be told the other girl was quite sick and had to cancel. That meant there was much more work for our department and no chance to get another intern at so short notice. My boss just asked me to try to do more, to help them out.
Assessor:	And what were you supposed to do during the internship, what was your task?
Candidate:	We were both supposed to update their stock management system with new stock codes that were necessary for their biggest customer. It was a lot of data entry and updating old fashioned databases. They had gained some new customers and their old fashioned systems were not coping very well. Obviously, because the other girl was sick, that was mostly done by me.
Assessor:	So what actions did you take?
Candidate:	Well I was learning about their old systems as fast as I could in the first week, which was hard enough, but I found by week 2 that I could get more than my own work done, just because I was good at spreadsheets and found some automatic ways of doing some things. I started to do a bit more automating things for Dmitri, the team leader, to help out as much as I could. I didn't mind the hours so much, as I was learning a lot about real work and I knew how important it was to them. There were over 20,000 lines of stock to check and update just for the new customer.

Assessor: And what happened, what was the result?

Candidate: Well, after only two months we were getting the system to work really well with the new software. It took a couple of very long weekends of stock taking, as some codes were not recognised and we needed to physically check stock till midnight some nights. But by the end of my internship in November, the new system was working really well. Actually Dmitri offered me a junior role in the stock admin department if I wanted to work in Athens.

The use of the STAR process allows a vague initial answer to be probed with relevant questions to get to the actual core of candidate's performance. In this case the answers all relate to working hard over sustained timescales, and show specific evidence of taking initiatives to improve working methods. The candidate's answers also show a willingness to work long hours if necessary.

The STAR technique works well for all competence-based questions and gives newly trained interviewers a solid framework for getting specifics rather than vague answers.

A negative evidence question based on the same competence definition for communication may ask:

Tell me about a situation where, on reflection, you wish your communication had been carried out differently and better?

Again, this would be followed by questions to elicit more details about the situation, the task required at the time, the actions of the individual and, importantly, the outcomes or results.

A negative evidence question is also an opportunity to get the candidate to share what they have learnt from that reflection or from that incident. Negative evidence can be regarded as positive in terms of its evaluation, if the candidate's answer shows high levels of personal awareness and an ability to learn from their mistakes.

The use of a structured competence-based interview is becoming more common, particularly in talent and high-potential selection. It is these groups that need to be able to demonstrate their wider generic capabilities and the use of competencies helps capture this. Where very specific technical skills are required the approach may need to be supplemented with some testing questions from a subject matter expert, in order to evaluate their subject experience, as well as their behaviour at work.

As with most assessment methods, the weakness in any approach is the variability of the assessor, in this case whoever is carrying out the interviews.

Aptitude and ability tests

As a single technique, a statistically more reliable predictor of success is cognitive testing.[5] The use of these tests, and their associated statistical comparison tables, are very reliable predictors of success in many roles. The cognitive tests allow an organisation to select people who are intellectually strong in specific thinking domains. The underpinning principle is that hiring bright people who are able to learn quickly will enable them to perform in many areas where adapting to changing situations is important. However, used as a single tool to filter talent they are a bit of a blunt instrument. Whilst a bright individual may be able to learn quickly, these tests tell an organisation nothing about the candidate's softer skills, attitudes or motivation, all of which impact on performance in a role. Cognitive tests are very reliable instruments and also have high validity. This means if the same candidate is retested in some other situation the results will almost always be similar. It also means that they measure what they say they are going to measure, making them good for comparing across groups of candidates.

Aptitude tests are more specifically defined as measures of a particular skill set. These are useful in some very precise talent demands but feature less in the identification of high potential. As example might be a test of mechanical aptitude where each test item, or question explores a specific understanding of engineering or physics. The results of such a test give a measure of a very specific domain of knowledge and thinking. Most talent management programmes are looking for wider areas of capability and potential. That is why the most common cognitive tests used are those that give a measure of numerical reasoning, verbal reasoning and abstract reasoning.

Personality questionnaires

The psychometric test or personality questionnaire helps the assessor understand in more depth the motivations, decision-making styles, personality traits and preferences of a candidate. These questionnaires are instruments designed to measure work-based personality traits. Most questionnaires report on a range of scales measuring personality traits, or personality preferences, that are considered most relevant to a variety of working situations. The specific scales vary dependent on the test publisher's approach but most are work-based derivatives of the Big 5 personality factors identified by early researchers into personality. An example of one such personality preference would be 'detail consciousness'. A result showing a strong preference for this trait may be a useful predictor of success in roles where attention to detail was critical, such as performing audits or proofreading legal text. Lower scores on this scale may suggest a person who would be more comfortable in a role with tasks requiring a broad overview rather than attention to specifics.

The results of individuals can be compared to comparison group statistics to get a profile related to the norm – the average score on each scale for a given population. It is possible for a skilled practitioner to build a profile based on a job description that should be useful in predicting the strengths required for success in specific roles.

Whilst their use is widespread, their predictive validity is not as strong when used in isolation, as compared to that of cognitive tests. Their added value comes when they are interpreted by an expert practitioner and provide additional information about the candidate for use in interview or as supporting evidence to other sources, such as assessment exercises.

The purpose of any assessment is to find out if the candidate is suitable for a role now, or shows potential to carry out the role in the future. Tests and questionnaires are well-established ways of gathering useful information about the abilities and preferences of candidates. Interviews are still the most popular method of gaining a deeper understanding of the candidate's experience and motives. What is missing from both approaches is evidence of actual behaviour, and that is where an assessment exercise proves invaluable.

An important consideration for the use of tests is the necessary expertise and qualification of the assessor. Most test use is controlled by the test publisher or by a supervisory body. In the UK, and most of Europe, tests require the user to have been trained and authorised by the publisher, be a chartered occupational psychologist, or trained to a level of test administration approved by the British Psychological Society (BPS). In order to maintain their standards and comply with the code of practice of the BPS, publishers will not sell their tests to unqualified people. In reality, this means there are four real choices talent professionals have if they wish to use testing in their selection and assessment process:

- Use a trained psychologist or qualified consultant to select and apply tests as required (probably the most common approach).
- Be trained in, or have staff attend and qualify for, specific tests or ranges of tests (this can cost many thousands of pounds per suite of tests).
- Employ consultants to design organisation-specific tests and train and authorise the organisation's staff to use them (expensive but effective).
- Buy off-the-shelf tests from publishers and send the completed tests back to the publisher for scoring and report generation (relatively cost-effective but delivers only generic expert system-generated results).

Assessment exercises

Assessment exercises are a simulation of the sort of task the person would be expected to do in the role in future if recruited. Some competencies that are role requirements cannot be reliably evaluated using interview questions or some form of testing. The softer skills sometimes required within roles are better demonstrated by observable behaviour. This is where assessment exercises really excel by providing a vehicle for candidates to show their empathy, communication and collaborating abilities.

They are designed to be reliable, so different people will be able to perform them and the assessor should see similar sorts of results. They should also be designed to allow a differentiation in performance. This means if good candidates perform well, that is evident from what is observed and if poor candidates don't do so well, that can also be ascertained from the exercise results.

Assessment exercises are complex tools and therefore can be expensive to design, trial and test. They can also be time-consuming, needing trained assessors to observe and evaluate the performance of candidates. The consequence of this is that they tend to be restricted to use where there are large groups to be assessed and observed behaviour is deemed to be important. The investment in the design of the test and the training of assessors is then spread across multiple candidates making it more cost-effective.

Alternatively assessment exercises are used in very specific activities where there is no other option to capture evidence of a specific capability. In the vast majority of cases, organisations use predesigned, off-the-shelf, products. There are a number of specialist suppliers in Europe and the USA who can provide a catalogue of scenarios for assessing different competencies at various levels of experience. These are categorised into groups representing specific industries or seniority of roles. There are predesigned exercises available to test young graduate engineers at one end of the spectrum and simulations of complex investment decisions for senior finance roles at the other. The vast majority of these assessment exercises are aimed at the management in organisations. There are fewer off-the-shelf exercises available for more specific technical roles as the economics of design prohibit their development for such a small potential market.

What is essential when using these simulations is that there is a good match between the competencies you wish to assess and the opportunity for those behaviours to be exhibited in the exercise. With very specific competencies it may not be possible to find an existing exercise that reliably creates opportunities for the behaviour to be observed. In this case the creation of bespoke exercises is the only available option or the competencies must be evaluated by some other method such as interview.

Similarly to interviewing, the weakness in the reliability of the results of any assessment exercise is the variability in the assessor's ratings. If the assessor is trained and has experience, the reliability improves. However, where there is a mix of new and experienced assessors there can be a range of scores and ratings given for the same observed behaviour. Experience suggests that even the best designed assessment exercise may not be effective if the assessors are poorly trained or lack the motivation to apply the processes consistently. However, a less effective design can still work satisfactorily as an evaluation tool when the assessor team is well trained and has the will and skill to apply the process consistently.

Individual exercises

There isn't always the opportunity or necessity to use group exercises for assessment. In some cases, either for reasons of candidate confidentiality or because of the lack of candidates for the role, there is an option to use individual assessment exercises.

These exercises can be very effective in providing reliable evidence for certain capabilities. What they can't do as well as a group exercise is demonstrate the soft skills of interacting with others in a work environment. We explore how group exercises work a little later in the chapter.

The most common form of individual assessment exercise is the inbox task. This can be a physical inbox, with letters, documents and other material for a candidate to work through in a predetermined time limit. In this case the task is a simulated work sample, using the skills the candidate may need to display within a role they are applying for. The capabilities assessed will be most likely linked to the competencies of planning and organising, decision making, business acumen and prioritising. These competency labels are not exhaustive, and will differ in some organisations, but give some indication what can be ascertained from an exercise that tests critical thinking and the ability to organise tasks at work.

Some of these individual exercises are now automated. In these instances an email inbox is substituted for the hard-copy material and these can be made even more realistic by the inclusion of interruptions from recorded phone messages. Whatever technology is applied, be it traditional physical documents or the computer-based simulation, the capability of the single individual can be judged against a scoring template containing the competencies required for success in the task. This gives comparability of one candidate against another and against the blueprint, which is the competency profile of the position being assessed. In online and email versions it is possible to automate some of the scoring process to reduce the load on the assessors. In the manual version the task of scoring each of the candidate responses can be quite time-consuming and mentally demanding.

There are other tests of individual performance, some very specific to expert roles, others more generic and applying to wider managerial competence. An example of a more generic individual exercise is the analysis presentation. These are typically mini case studies or managerial recommendation tasks where the individual reviews materials given to them, applies some sort of analytical process and presents their results/recommendations to the assessors.

These can be very effective tools for understanding the individual's decision-making process, their ability to persuade and influence others, and their organisational skills. In these types of presentation exercise, the individual being assessed is the sole contributor and will have the full attention of the assessor when in the presentation element of the task. They are demonstrating their ability to influence and communicate effectively in a relatively formal situation, which can be stressing for some, but they are not in any way competing for attention or airtime. They are in control of their agenda and the way they interact.

Role-play exercises

Roles that require very specific abilities can use exercises that simulate the precise situation found at work. An example of this would be seeing how people deal with customer service issues, crucial for some hospitality management roles or sales positions. It is not uncommon for these to be in the form of a role-play using real actors, or less reliably managers, standing in as the customer. A typical scenario for hospitality could be that the candidate is working in a hotel and a VIP guest has arrived but their room isn't ready yet. How do they cope with this situation and maintain a professional approach?

There is a significant difference between a role-play and other styles of assessment exercise. In role-play scenarios the participants are not given a plethora of information to use in the discussion, but have to rely on their own skill and awareness of how to deal with, for example, an irate customer. It tests the candidate's ability to think on their feet and improvise within reason.

Again, as with other assessment methods, the reliability is dependent on consistent repetitions of the same exercise, which is why the use of professional actors is highly recommended. This is particularly important as there is limited information given to the participants and they can react in a variety of, sometimes unpredictable, ways.

Group exercises

These are very popular activities for assessing certain competencies, particularly teamworking and communication skills. They fall into two main categories: assigned role and non-assigned role exercises.

A typical group exercise would be where four to six people are given a task, often including a common problem or series of decisions to make, and they are observed interacting whilst attempting to arrive at a group conclusion. In these exercises the assessors are evaluating how the individuals work collaboratively and how they communicate when they are not in control of the agenda. In these exercises each individual has to contribute appropriately to demonstrate their capability to the assessors. However, they are in also in competition for the group's attention and they do not have any automatic right to airtime. It is this characteristic of the group exercise that simulates the sort of behaviour, the need to be heard and take part, that you see in many real-life business meetings.

Non-assigned role exercises give every participant the same information about the task, normally in some written briefing notes, and every candidate can contribute to the exercise based on their understanding of the problem or decisions they face. A typical scenario for a non-assigned role exercise is that the members of the group are representing a committee facing some common decision, such as a factory relocation project, and need to prioritise actions to enable the move to go ahead. The common problem they work in is agreeing the relative importance, costs and implications of each element of the tasks about which they all have the same information.

These non-assigned role exercises are the least complex and therefore the easiest to train assessors to use effectively. Their drawback in use is that when a group of participants includes a very dominant or highly confident individual, it is possible that they make all the decisions, take up most of the airtime and leave little space for others to contribute. A more introvert and shy individual working in the same group may not generate much evidence, as their contribution rate would suffer in the face of such a confident and verbose individual.

There is no effective way to intervene and manage this type of group dynamic. What is being observed is probably a true reflection of how the dominant individual behaves and how the more introverted or less confident individual would react in real life. However, there are designs that reduce the frequency of this scenario playing out.

An assigned role group exercise has a core of common information that each participant receives, but, in addition, each role is assigned information relevant to the task but not shared. In these cases the individuals need to decide how to share and what to share in order to maximise their performance but also work effectively on the common exercise objective.

A typical scenario for an assigned role group exercise is that the participants are attending a meeting on behalf of a department of an organisation. Each individual is tasked with a particular set of department objectives they must gain support for. As each participant is representing a different department, the possibility of conflicting objectives becomes apparent and in addition most exercises will have a common overriding problem for the group to address.

This design is more complex and therefore the training of the assessors needs a little more care and attention. The roles should all interact and impact on the final solution, without each one being so discrete that they can be treated completely independently of the whole group decisions.

The big advantage of an assigned role exercise is that they create more equality of opportunity, as each participant has some unique insight or information; the group needs them to interact and take part. Success in this style of group exercise requires even a dominant participant to solicit information and encourage participation from the quieter candidates, as their success is dependent on information they do not have. A second advantage of this exercise design is that the behaviour it elicits from the group is more realistic in comparison to that displayed when there is completely transparent information. If the task of a group exercise is to simulate real life then an exercise which allows individuals to choose how much, or how little, of their information to share is a more realistic mimic of genuine management behaviour.

There is a third category of group exercise, but its use is relatively limited. That is the command or leadership exercise. In this design the exercise is specifically constructed to provide the opportunity for an individual to lead and be able to demonstrate competencies associated with team or group leadership. The exercise format is repeatable but obviously not with the same group. Where a number of candidates are being assessed for their leadership capabilities, a series of unique command tasks would need to be provided. The most common use of this style of exercise in assessment is within the military when selecting young leadership talent for officer training.[6] It is not very common to use a leadership assessment in recruitment selection, but there may be value in such an exercise for gaining feedback related to career development.

360° feedback instruments

A more recently and increasingly popular addition to the assessment toolkit is the use of 360° feedback. This approach requires that a group of people, who know the target individual well, provide feedback on their performance against certain predefined categories of behaviour. It is then processed, collated and presented in a feedback report or summary chart. Typically the contributors of the feedback would comprise the individual themselves, their line manager, their direct reports and then a mix of peers or customers. The concept is to create a 360° picture of the individual's performance which is built up from inputs from all quadrants of their working environment. Where the feedback overlaps and highly correlates there is reasonable level of confidence that this represents a consistent picture of the individual's performance. Where there are clear differences in reported performance, then there is an opportunity to explore why in certain circumstances behaviour and performance differs.

There are two main formats of 360° feedback in regular use with organisations. The first approach is to use online text and rating-scale based tools to gather and collate feedback. These applications automatically send out email requests for feedback on the individual using scales to represent the criteria being measured and to capture the contributor's rating. These are then automatically collated and processed to produce a chart or expert system report showing some overall rating. In some variations there are spaces for the contributor to write free text reasons for their ratings, in others it's a purely numerical or icon based scoring mechanism.

A typical example of one scale and how it is scored is shown in Figure 6.1. It requires the contributor to rate the candidate on a specific dimension, by using behavioural examples linked to their experience of working with the target person. The scale used in this example is very common. In this case it has seven possible responses represented in a Likert scale.[7]

For the person you are providing feedback to please indicate your rating by ticking the box that represents your thoughts in relation to their work behaviour when you answer the specific question for each section shown on the left of each screen.

Performance Management	Disagree Strongly	Disagree	Slightly Disagree	Neither agree Nor disagree	Slightly Agree	Agree	Strongly Agree
S/He sets realistic work goals							
S/He regularly gives feedback							

Figure 6.1 Example computer-based 360° questionnaire input scale

Assessment centres

Assessment centres are events that combine a number of different exercises and activities to assess candidates. Many of the world's best companies, and many government departments, use them as a means of selecting talent at various levels. They have become popular because, as a method of selection, they are seen to be the most reliable and valid predictors of future performance compared to other available assessment methods.[8] They were pioneered for use in business in the 1950s by leading US organisations such as AT&T (American Telephone and Telegraph). At the time psychologists were very active in devising more scientific methods to help business become more productive and better at matching people to roles.[9]

In essence, they combine the best of many of the more scientific approaches outlined above and, in doing so, minimise the gaps some techniques leave. Their design enables supporting and collaborating evidence across all of the competencies or criteria being examined. Selecting the best mix and ensuring all the competencies are balanced in the design of the assessment centre is a complex activity, normally carried out by an occupational psychologist or expert consultant.

An assessment centre's purpose is to allow candidates to present their best evidence of their fit for a role, and for the organisation to make a decision as to whether they pass or not. There is an implied moral and ethical obligation to give feedback to candidates on their performance but the primary task of an assessment centre, and the purpose of the evidence gained, is to make a hiring or promotion decision, not support the development of the individual.

There are a number of defining features of assessment centres, described below.

Multiple candidates

In assessment centres there is a need to compare candidates against a template or blueprint, which is the criteria for talent, and in most cases against each other. If you have multiple candidates working through assessment exercises and activities at the same time it is possible to compare and select the best from those that pass the criteria. It is perfectly acceptable for entry-level talent to be in a place openly competing for roles with their peers. It can be less comfortable for more established candidates who might be applying from a competitor organisation and wish this to remain in total confidence. It is not ideal for them to turn up to an assessment event to find their colleagues are also attending. It is also not considered to be acceptable to have open and transparent competition for executive roles, where individuals demand confidential treatment and in some cases news of a rival executive's interest in a role could impact stock prices or other commercially sensitive business metrics.

Multiple activities

An assessment centre employs a range of activities to test and examine the competencies or criteria that the organisation believes are essential for success in a role. This is typically a mix of interviews, group exercises, tests and individual exercises. The reason for employing the mix is to cover the whole set of competencies in a short period of time, with at least two sources of evidence for each competence. For example, teamworking may be examined in an interview but also tested with observed behaviour by watching the candidate work in a team in a group exercise. There are a number of advantages to using multiple activities. The first is that not all competencies are easily displayed in each activity, therefore using a range increases the opportunity for evidence to be captured. Not every candidate will interview well, so by using additional activities these candidates also get an opportunity to show their skills and capability in a different scenario. The mix of activities increases every candidate's chance to demonstrate a range of their abilities. By using different activities it reduces the risk of errors that poor or less experienced assessors bring to an assessment centre.

Multiple criteria

In an assessment centre, no single competence is dominant in the assessment decision. In most assessment centres the design will be capturing evidence of between six and nine competencies. Therefore, if a candidate is particularly strong in one area, for example communication, it doesn't necessarily have an impact on the overall decision, as there is an additional set of scores for each of the other competencies. Using a range of criteria reduces the halo effect sometimes experienced in activities such as interviews. This is where a competence that has been excellently demonstrated, for example communication, positively influences the ratings the assessor attributes to other behaviours. In addition, the use of a range of competencies builds a portfolio of evidence that helps predict future success rather than basing a decision on a single capability.

Multiple assessors

Assessors are the key component of the whole selection process. Their evaluation is what makes a good employment decision. In the talent management process, the decision to hire is committing the organisation to considerable long-term investment. However, most assessors carry baggage, and have a personal career history, strong preferences and unconscious cultural biases that influence our best efforts at objective decision making.

In order to reduce these unconscious influences on decisions, assessment centres create a joint evaluation process, so no one person is over influential in making the final decision. As each assessor would normally only see a particular candidate in one activity, they must rely on their colleagues to assess the others. The final decision always takes into account a range of perspectives and evidence from all the assessors. Whilst not completely eliminating the effects of a senior, confidant and possibly dominant assessor's personality in the integration session, it does reduce its negative impact significantly.

Development centres

Many of the same tools and techniques employed for assessment centres can be applied to existing talents in order to better understand their future development needs. In that case the organisation is running a development centre. These events are run in a very similar way to those for selection decisions, but the depth and nature of the feedback is focused on the talent already employed. The primary purpose of a development centre is to generate useful feedback on performance and potential for existing employees. That means they generally take longer to run in order that depth of evidence can be observed, and the feedback process is the primary output. There are many models of development centre but most include some face-to-face feedback with participants post centre, in a comprehensive debrief leading to some format of development planning. In other designs the feedback is provided in real time, during the centre, to allow the performance of participants to develop as they continue and participate.

Talent management professionals often use development centres as part of a gateway process from one pool to another. So it is not uncommon for graduate hires having completed a development programme, or fast-track scheme, to undertake a development centre to see if their experience and potential is now sufficient for them to join the more senior high-potential pool. If they meet the criteria for the next most senior level of talent, it demonstrates to some extent the efficacy of the initial selection and development programme and, if not, it may lead to some additional development plans to ensure they regain their career trajectory.

The assessment continuum

The process of selection should be robust, evidence based and consistent throughout the pipeline, even if the method may vary to account for the different levels of experience of each segment. A robust assessment process is one that is reliable and clearly allows decisions to be made based on sound evidence of the individual's capability. The capability being evaluated will be most likely demonstrated by a mix of competencies, which can be assessed, and their experience, which should show in their results at work. The most senior roles in any pipeline are more dependent on experience and performance and the more junior roles on competencies and potential.

Figure 6.2 shows the concept of assessment in a pipeline as a continuum. The left of the diagram shows the entry-level mix of data, which is a different combination to that of senior executives. However, the consistent thread across the entire talent segment is some form of objective assessment. In the central area of the continuum is the sweet spot, a balance of pure assessment data and on-the-job performance data. At the most senior end of the continuum, results and on-the-job performance data is more prevalent and, for this segment, relevant.

Figure 6.2 shows four talent segments, which are represented as Graduates, EU DPP (European development potential pool), Executive Successors and Executives. This was

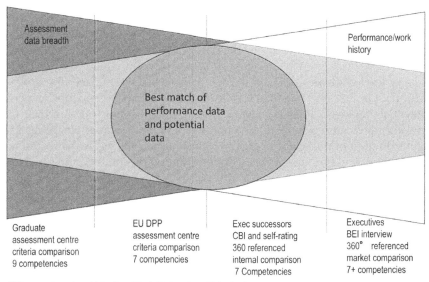

Graduate
assessment centre
criteria comparison
9 competencies

EU DPP
assessment centre
criteria comparison
7 competencies

Exec successors
CBI and self-rating
360 referenced
internal comparison
7 Competencies

Executives
BEI interview
360° referenced
market comparison
7+ competencies

(CBI = competency based interview; BEI = behavioural event interview)

Figure 6.2 An example assessment continuum

the model employed in Sony Europe Gmbh for many years to represent their leadership pipeline from entry level through to the incumbent executive roles. Each of the four segments used objective assessment as a means of selection into, or out of, the talent pool. The need for a consistent process across the segments was accepted at all levels of the organisation. What was necessary was a different methodology at each level, as the approach to assessing the performance and potential of a senior executive needed to be considered fair and appropriate for their status, which entailed using different techniques.

Seven of the competencies remained consistent throughout the segments and were assessed at entry level through to the executives. However, there were two additional competencies assessed at the graduate intake level, to try to gain more information on potential, where there was little work experience to evaluate.

In this example the pipeline was focused on selecting and developing leadership talent. This was defined within Sony using their common competence framework, which for leadership consisted of the following:

Influence & Negotiation

Building People Capability

Communication

Strategic Thinking

Analytical Skills

Leadership

Personal Responsibility

Each of these competencies was designed to be discrete, so that it did not overlap with the definition of another competence. Each was designed to measure some aspect of what Sony considered important for leadership within their European business units. This model was valid and in use during the European business for the period from 2000 to 2010.

For entry-level graduates the level of each competence was judged in terms of suitability for the role now and potential for the future. For the older and more experienced high-potential employees these competences were to be demonstrated in their current roles and also show more potential for appointment to more senior management within 18 months. In both of the senior pools the competencies were evaluated based on current performance and business results with the addition of some cognitive testing.

Assessment choices – a guide to the most appropriate mix

In order to give some guidance on what might be the appropriate mix of assessment tools and techniques we will use the Sony Europe leadership pipeline example. This is not because it should be considered as a benchmark for ETM, but that as an integrated talent management approach it demonstrates the need for different assessment tools for different segments. Finding the balance of evidence in each segment requires some flexibility in the tools and techniques chosen.

Figure 6.2 shows the four segments or talent pools that Sony deemed critical to its business success. An analysis carried out by the HR team had shown weakness in the leadership pipeline mostly as a result of a significant change in the business's competitive environment. The business environment had moved on but the way we managed and led the business had not. Therefore the talent most important to Sony in this stage of its evolution was general management and commercial leaders, but we needed people with a different way of thinking about business to that which we currently had.

Young professionals – graduate-level talent

The issue with hiring young professionals into a business is that they have limited experience, therefore not much past work you can evaluate in terms of performance. However, they can still be measured in terms of potential if you create the right assessment process and you are confident about your definition.

In Sony during the year 2000 there were three different graduate recruitment schemes for entry-level talent across Europe, each with conflicting entry requirements and disparate aims. The starting point for the revised talent strategy was to consolidate these into one, align the competencies with the overall leadership model and invest in the development of a new assessment model. This consolidation enabled a single definition of potential and performance for Sony's younger talent. In addition to the nine competencies, of which seven were core to the leadership model, the requirement to succeed was at least six months' work experience in a second country, business fluency in English and it was desirable to have two other European languages. This requirement was based on a need for internationally focused future general managers. Their academic requirements were set relatively high, but were varied in terms of subject content as the roles would be placed in different functions such as Sales & Marketing, Supply Chain, HR and Finance.

The selection approach used for entry-level graduate talent in Sony Europe was a two-day assessment centre. It was conducted with the aid of consultants and internal assessors made up of HR managers representing the different business units in Europe.

Rationale for the entry-level assessment centre

At the young professional level of entry there is often a huge pool of potential candidates. In this case the organisation openly invited applications from any nationality. It was aggressively marketed as an international programme. Given the lack of restrictions on nationality and relatively wide field of subjects accepted, it was necessary to build in other ways for candidates to self-select out of applying, in order to get only the employees of choice.

To this end, the organisation made a decision to require fluency in three European languages with English mandatory. The result of this specification meant that many good, but not perfectly matched, candidates did not continue their application. In practice this meant proportionally less British and American candidates completed their applications as their education system creates fewer graduates likely to be fluent in the two additional European languages. This was much less of an entry barrier for many Dutch, Swedish and German graduates.

A second filter was the requirement for six months' work experience gained outside the home country of the applicant. The rationale for this was they would travel extensively as part of their development and career, so someone who had already chosen to gain work or study experience in another country would be predisposed to such mobility requirements and have already demonstrated their curiosity for working in another culture.

The first two filters were to some extent automated as completion of the online application process with its built-in rating system rejected those that didn't fulfil the base criteria.

The third and final selection filter was the assessment centre where the nine competencies were tested over the one-and-a-half days centre. The design was a classic mix of tests, interviews and exercises, both as an individual and as part of a group.

	In-Tray	CBI	Group Biere Bleue	MGIB	Analysis Presentation	OPQ
Managing Change and Innovation		✓✓	✓			✓
Personal Responsibility and Achievement Orientation		✓✓	✓✓			✓
Analytical Skills / Decision Making	✓✓			✓✓	✓✓	✓
Building Relationships (incl. Customer Focus)			✓✓		✓	✓
Commercial Awareness (incl. Cost & Profit Mgt)		✓✓			✓✓	✓
Influence, Negotiation and Impact (incl. Communication)		✓	✓✓		✓✓	✓
Planning and Organising	✓✓	✓✓				✓

Figure 6.3 Example entry-level assessment centre mix

Figure 6.3 shows the matrix, the table of activities at the assessment centre matched against their respective competencies. Sony Europe's graduate programme has since been changed and improved, but this version still serves as an example of an appropriate mix of tests, exercises and interviews.

'Bier Bleue' was the name of a non-assigned role group exercise; the MGIB is a commercially provided set of cognitive tests; OPQ was the same commercial provider's personality questionnaire and the in-tray and presentation were individual exercises bought from a specialist provider.

The MGIB tests specific cognitive ability and the OPQ personality preferences related to the profile for the graduate talent pool. The group exercise provided some strong evidence of the candidate's interpersonal skills, and the individual exercise their organisational and analytical ability. The right mix of exercises and tests gives a reliable cover of all the competencies required to demonstrate potential.

The team of assessors were trained in the use of the assessment centre exercises by an external consultant who also provided technical assistance to the centre manager. The consultants used were employed by the test publishers so could offer supplementary input on specifics of any of the assessment tools, should the assessors so wish.

As a result of attending the centre, the candidates were either rejected, with the offer of some telephone feedback on their performance, or those who passed were given a contract with Sony Europe.

It was considered perfectly acceptable for a graduate applicant to attend a one-and-a-half days assessment centre with other potential candidates. At best they received a job offer, at worst they received detailed feedback on their ability, which would assist them in any other recruitment process and an all expenses paid trip to a European capital city.

Mid-level talents – management high potential

Many organisations have some form of talent pool for what is widely known as high potentials. This is the often the mid-level of talent, more experienced than the graduate recruits and generally already showing good levels of performance within their current roles. For this pool to work it's necessary for the organisation to have a clear definition of what makes someone 'high potential' in relation to this segment, and also create a way of objectively assessing it.

The Sony DPP was originally the only nominated talent pool in the organisation. Prior to the creation of the talent strategy this was 'the only show in town' for anyone who considered themselves high potential. As a result it was historically used as a means of highlighting people who had performed well and who were thought to fit the business and could be future senior managers. However, it was also used to reward people who were not high potential, just high performers. This typically happened when there were pay freezes or other restrictions on increasing reward. That meant that the 350 people listed as high potential in the early years were certainly not all of a similar capability or of comparable motivation.

With this segment, the first step was to work with the organisation and agree a new definition of 'high-potential manager' for the mid-level pool. Eventually the consensus arrived at:

Already performing at rating A or B for two years of last 3.

Business Fluent English, minimum TOEFL[10] score of 90.

Passed the criteria at the DPP Development Centre

Possess an International Mind-set

The performance management system gave us the first criterion, as all these candidates were already employed. The second criterion was introduced to standardise the evaluation of English fluency; previously, this was judged by line managers, some of whom were not themselves fluent in the language. The DPP development centre was introduced as a means of giving feedback to the candidates and at the same time set a new threshold for the sort of potential the organisation expected in this pool. Finally, the international mind-set criteria was agreed as a way to underline the organisation's expectation that this pool would move, relocate, work on extended assignments overseas or travel over 50 per cent of their time, as a normal part of their work.

The clarification and communication of this new transparent criteria meant approximately 45 per cent of the pool declined to remain in the programme. Another 10 per cent failed to meet the language criteria. The remaining potential candidates were given a timeline for attending an internal DPP development centre to give them assistance with their development plans and also be a process to decide if they retained their status as part of the pool.

Rationale for the mid-level talent development centre

Existing employees are more sensitive to any suggestion of assessment or questioning of their talent. However, there are more opportunities to measure their performance from their existing roles, assuming that there is already some form of appraisal system in place. The issue for the organisation is to ascertain if their mid-level management talent has sufficient potential for future promotion or to move to a more challenging role. This evaluation is for the organisation to make, but the results now become shared property, with the data being useful for development planning for any individual, regardless of whether they reach the entry threshold for the pool.

The advantage of using a development centre is that it has all the validity and reliability of the assessment centre process, but with the added acceptability of being about the individual's development. Should a candidate not meet the threshold for being accepted into the pool, there would still be detailed feedback to the individual why they have not passed, and more importantly what might be done to close the gap.

A development centre still requires someone to evaluate the evidence that is generated. In this example, senior line managers (not of the direct reports but always from another business unit) were supported by HR business partners carrying out the role of assessors. Also in this approach, one where feedback and evaluation is shared between assessors, the line managers have complete visibility of the emerging talent pool. The use of the HR managers added some consistency across different centres. The decision to use line managers was a conscious choice to give them more responsibility for choosing and evaluating talent, so that they felt this was their process and not some black box that HR was controlling. Sony wanted assessment of talent to be thought of as a privilege, something that is respected as a skill and a task that not every manager would be allowed to do. We did not want it to be seen as a chore to carry out on behalf of HR.

This DPP development centre was delivered over two days. The additional time was necessary as the detailed reports written for every participant required more time to write after integrating the evidence collected by the assessors. The reports were given to the participants and then shared with their line managers in a face-to-face debrief. In addition a comprehensive discussion and planning session was conducted with each participant typically lasting two to three hours. These debriefs were focused on future learning opportunities and usually included some discussion on next steps in terms of promotion or gaining parallel level experience. The purpose of the planning was to fill gaps in their capabilities and enable them to meet their potential.

The result of redefining and communicating expectations, evaluating individuals and feeding back their performance in the development centre reduced the pool from over 350 to around 80. However, all of this group were considered highly motivated and high-potential managers. This new smaller pool was able to provide management capability for the whole European business, as all were mobile, proven high performance and considered as high potential.

Senior-level talent – executive successors

In most organisations there are normally plans in place for successors to the most senior team, the company executives. However, there are not so many businesses where the same group, the executive successors, are assessed using an objective process. It is still very common for their current and past performance to be used as the sole basis for their inclusion into any succession plan or senior pool. In this example from Sony, the decision was made to evaluate as objectively as possible the group of people considered most likely to succeed the incumbent executive teams.

It was considered inappropriate to do any form of group assessment at this level. In addition to the cultural sensitivity of senior management candidates being asked to work together in some form of evaluation, it was also agreed that at this level talent was more about their proven leadership and less about the skills of teamwork. What was an important factor to take into account for their future was how their capabilities were applied with their direct reports and their peers. Sony wanted senior executives who could lead people and work well alongside their colleagues.

This talent pool membership was assessed as individuals, but using the same objective framework of competencies and performance requirements used in the lower level groups. Again the necessary level of performance was a mandatory level A or B for the last three years, but in addition there was a review of their historical bonus awards, which was supporting evidence of their success. Table 6.3 shows the mix used for this talent pool in the example discussed.

Their capability was assessed using a process of 360° feedback. A group of contributors selected from the individual's peers, their line manager, direct report and customers was interviewed in person using a very structured process. The participant was also interviewed in depth using a technique called behavioural event interviewing. The final report was compiled based on this comprehensive collection of perspectives.

Table 6.3 Senior-level assessment mix

Assessment technique	Capability assessed	Comments
Competence-based Interview of participant	Seven competencies focused on, interview duration two hours.	The interviews were conducted by the same person, the senior assessor, for the total management population of approx. 80. This reduced the chance of any interviewer variability.
360° input interviews	Minimum of six contributors, mandatory boss, two peers and two direct reports. Boss interview 60 minutes. Peers and reports 40 minutes.	The boss was interviewed face to face by the senior assessor. All other contributors were interviewed by the second assessor, either in person or, where impractical, video/ teleconference.
Cognitive tests	Tests of numerical reasoning and verbal reasoning in mother tongue were completed.	The test was selected to represent senior-level ability. Norm tables for each language were used.
Personality questionnaire	OPQ32[11] was completed and an expert system report generated.	Used because of its reliability and range of European language versions.
Performance history review	Review of appraisal data for last three years.	This formed part of the final report for the candidate and was discussed with the boss.

The addition of two cognitive tests and a personality profile completed the total assessment data for each participant.

An extract from one anonymous report, this time from another organisation using this approach, is shown in Figure 6.4. The content is drawn from all the interviews, so includes perspectives from the candidate as well as their contributors. In this version the candidate was already a senior manager running a large engineering site. The example shows the competence being evaluated at the top, Team Leadership, and the summary evaluation and feedback in the comments below.

Rationale for the senior-level talent assessment

The choice to use the 360° interview for individual assessment was taken because it provided a reasonable depth of data on existing employees adding information that was absent from their appraisal reports. It was considered a more personal and respectful approach to people who may already have held reasonably senior positions, whilst at the same time ensuring they knew they were being still being evaluated. Once the decision to conduct the interviews was agreed it was then considered a good opportunity to include cognitive testing and get a more complete profile.

The use of tests such as verbal and numerical reasoning at this level filled some gaps in the senior profiles. In the past they may have been recruited on the basis of an interview alone. The use of tests also gave some useful information to each individual

Team leadership

Has a clear vision of what is to be achieved and effectively articulates the strategy to others. Sets challenging targets, inspires and motivates people to work towards the goals. Is visible, present and respected in the workshop. Knows, and is known by most people. Has excellent people skills, engages and supports the team with a collaborative and participative leadership style. Delegates effectively, empowering and trusting others to execute. Monitors performance, recognising, praising and rewarding individuals based on merit. Recognises and takes action on underperformance, making people accountable for results.

Andy is seen by the majority of the contributors as a strong team leader. He himself places great emphasis on getting the right team in place, both in the role of Site General Manager and with his additional role as Project Director of XXXXX. Many of the contributors comment on Andy's excellent listening skills, adding that he doesn't just listen to you, he often builds your understanding of a subject or concept as he restates and checks with you what you have said. Andy's preferred management style is to delegate and to do so with full accountability. He is not someone who likes to oversee the task that he has given to one of his team. At least that is the case when he has his team made up of the right people. His reports are happy with this approach, feeling they are trusted to act within their sphere of operation and that they only really need to consult or report upwards when there is something that will have a wider impact on the site, either internally with another division or externally with local politics. Whilst most are set specific targets, each of his team have the understanding that these are theirs to manage. If they are on track to achieve them there is little discussion other than normal reporting. His team are expected to share any surprises before they happen. No one reported that their targets were too demanding or too ambitious – maybe there is room for more stretch in some?

Andy's ability to build a strong team is commented on by his boss and his peers. His team run the site on a day-to-day basis in his absence. He spends up to three days a week either travelling or at the sister site, yet his team feel he still has a full overview of what is happening and can comment on many of the issues that the site raises. They see his role as Project Director on xxxx as complimentary to his SGM role and potentially help secure the future of the site.

However not all contributors see the team working as well as it could. Decisions tend to be made on a one to one discussion with Andy and a functional head. Until recently there has been no regular review meeting where there can be a round table discussion and more shared decision-making. As individuals the team functions well, but there are limited forums for team discussion on whole site issues. The relatively new change in instigating the site reviews meetings may change this.

Figure 6.4 Example section from a 360° assessment report

about their strengths and weaknesses. Participants also gained some insight from the information shared from their personality profile. Candidate's final reports were compilations of the whole picture showing their strengths, their development needs and any concerns contributors raised, without compromising the source of the input.

The benchmark, or comparison group, in this Sony example, was other participants across the organisation, business unit or divisions. It was not seen as necessary to compare individuals to the external talent market. What became a useful by product of a common assessment framework was the ability of the executive team to compare talents right across the business using the same language and same rating system.

Executive-level talent – assessment of the top team

When the talent under scrutiny is the current executive group there may be arguments put forward that there is no reason to assess potential, as they are already in the most senior roles, and current performance should be visible and obvious. However, there are strong counter arguments that can be made, particularly if the organisation wishes to have a genuine strategic talent management approach.

Senior incumbents are most often in place due to their success in the past. They have achieved their position based on a reputation as people who deliver results. It also means that they are powerful and therefore, at times, difficult to challenge. However, they are also the senior role models and determine the culture of the organisation. If the organisation wants to be seen as a truly open and a transparent place of work then adopting one set of rules for some and different ones for the most senior executives is incongruent with this ideal. An additional selling point, when proposing to assess the top team, is that the top talent needs to understand the process by which their potential successors are selected and prepared.

Finally, the demands of organisations change over time, sometimes at a very rapid pace. If the current incumbents need to change their capabilities they may need some support in doing so. All of these arguments provide a sound rationale for some form of assessment of the most senior team.

A much stronger reason exists when a new CEO or president is appointed. In this situation a review of the strengths, weaknesses, motivations and limitations of their team is invaluable, particularly if it can be seen to be independent. When there is a merger or acquisition taking place, the due diligence of the senior team is a common scenario where executive assessment is conducted.

In the example of Sony, and other enlightened organisations, the need to have the senior team independently evaluated was about demonstrating transparency and the need to develop a culture of performance.

The specific Sony approach has already been well documented,[12] but the method is gaining acceptance as being appropriate for this level of senior management. One of the world's largest shipping and logistics organisations is following a similar path: 120 of their most senior management are currently undergoing a 360° review conducted by one of the top executive search firms. Similar to the Sony example, they are using their own competence framework and their preferred selection of psychometric tools. In this case they have chosen some tests focusing on thinking agility and another personality profiling tool. What is similar is that by using an independent organisation to carry out the evaluation, and one whose brand carries gravitas, they have reduced some of the anxiety and resistance to the idea of senior-level assessment.

The results of these comprehensive assessments feed directly into this organisation's deployment plans, ensuring that they have their most strategic roles being carried out by their best talent. Given the nature of their business the wrong match can damage their profitability very quickly. Assessment at this level was both a new challenge operationally to conduct, as well as a change to the culture of the historically, conservative business.

At this stage in their career, their motivation to relocate and take on new challenges is still important and is their drive to maintain their own performance. This therefore requires assessment and rating. The personality profile helps bring some new information to this domain, but the evaluation relies heavily on the skills and experience of the assessors. This particular example is a very specific industry with few competitors, so the market for strategic talent is quite small, and therefore very demanding. The top team have decided that they can use senior-level assessment to uncover under-utilised capability and where it is deemed necessary make changes to better match the talent they have to their most challenging roles.

Rationale for executive-level assessment

In the two examples outlined above there was a common desire to have complete information on their talents, from entry to senior incumbents. Entry and mid-level talent had traditionally been assessed in both organisations, but never in the most senior groups. This change is not always seen as necessary or welcomed by the senior group. However, an audit of capability can be very revealing.

In a different example the audit of senior talent produced results that when plotted onto a potential/performance matrix, showed significant, organisational-level blind spots.

The example is illustrated in Figure 6.5. It has been made anonymous for reasons of commercial confidentiality but it shows the distribution of the top team of an international technology group. When labelled by function it demonstrates a weakness in current roles and more worrying when looking at bench strength. In this instance it changed the organisation's short-term talent search tactics in order to plug a significant hole in their organisation.

In this case, when this slide was presented to the CEO with the supporting reports it became evident that suspicions about the sales talents were confirmed and now there was strong independent evidence to suggest a change in recruitment priority. Each of the roles shown above was at the European executive level.

The clear benefit of using a reputable, executive, search firm is that they already have a very good understanding of the market for talent at this level. Within Sony, it was used as a means of testing the quality of the incumbent and also what it would take to find a replacement if there was no bench strength to succeed. With talent of this level, comparison internally has some limits due to the size of the population you could use as a comparison. The external agents always have a greater pool as a comparator.

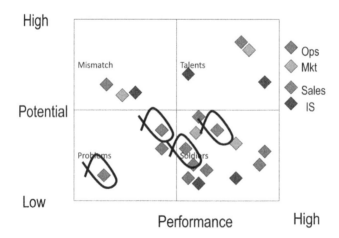

Figure 6.5 Example talent distribution – global technology organisation

The consultants from the search firm were asked to answer three questions for each role and the incumbent. The three questions used to guide the assessment were:

> If the role was vacant and the incumbent was assessed would they be on your short list?
>
> If not, why not?
>
> If so, would they be the recommended candidate?

As part of the candidate's confidential feedback sessions these three questions and the consultant's observations were discussed. It made individuals think about their contribution and also about their value to the organisation. In some cases it led individuals to reassess their next career step.

Factors to consider in selection and assessment choices

Deciding on what form of assessment to use is an important issue in the success of ETM. If the wrong approach is chosen, not only can it waste time and effort, it may negatively influence the senior team leading to less support for the process.

It is unlikely that practitioners are starting from a completely blank sheet of paper and there is nothing existing within the organisation. However, an ETM approach requires assessment that is both reliable and valid for the criteria you are seeking to measure, but also efficient. If what exists is not effective then something else needs to be selected to support the aim of objective assessment. Some of the key factors that need to considered are described below.

What is the criteria being measured?

Some criteria can be effectively measured in interview but others cannot. What evidence needs to be gathered will determine the mix of methodology.

How acceptable is the proposed method in this organisation?

Not all methods are equally suited to different cultures. In some organisations the notion of testing candidates' cognitive ability is not considered appropriate; even more so when the group being assessed are senior incumbents. What other means are there available to achieve a similar evaluation? What is the status of the group which needs to be assessed and what method would be acceptable and yet still effective?

Can we manage the process with the people we have?

If your assessors are not qualified in testing then you will have a need for external support should this technique be chosen. If a competence-based interview or similar is used, do you have assessors with the confidence and skills to carry this out consistently? Do you have the support/admin staff to manage the mix of activities in the assessment process? What would external expertise bring and what problems would it create?

How long will you need to complete the assessment?

This is a factor for the talent team, the assessors who take part in the evaluation and the candidates, regardless of whether they are internal or external. A thorough assessment can take two days to conduct and even more time to fully evaluate. What is the realistic time requirement for the process and is it appropriate considering the importance of the decision? Are there any review dates that the data is specifically needed for?

How reliable is your assessment process?

Can the activities you have selected provide clear evidence of the criteria you wish to evaluate? Are the tests or exercises easy to replicate over time and do you have faith in their ability to produce good evidence every time with different assessors? What additional performance data do you have access to?

Is it cost-effective?

The only way to objectively answer this question is to measure the alternatives and make a judgement based on the cost of failure and the cost of success. When using assessment the 'no decision' is also a positive decision. Not selecting a candidate based on solid evidence of lack of capability is a positive selection decision, just not a hiring or promoting one. So any evaluation of cost-effectiveness should factor in not only the ratio of assessments to hires, but also the cost saving of not hiring the wrong people and having to repeat the process at a later date.

Key review questions

Are there any objective assessment processes currently in use?

How competent and confident are the HR team at assessment techniques?

What different approaches are needed for each segment of the talent population?

Where will there be resistance and what will reduce the anxiety of that group?

Notes

1 Where the international business language is English it is common for non-mother tongue applicants for roles to have to prove their proficiency with a verified test score. TOEFL is widely recognised as one such reliable and comparable test (http://www.ets.org/toefl).
2 David McClelland was very influential in the development of competencies as a central tool in selection. McClelland, David (1973) Testing for Competence Rather Than for Intelligence, *American Psychologist*, Jan, http://www.therapiebreve.be/documents/mcclelland-1973.pdf.
3 Arvey, R. and Campion, J. (1982) The Employment Interview: A Summary and Review of Current Research, *Personnel Psychology*, 35, 281–322; Moscoso, S. (2000) Selection Interviews: A Review of Validity Evidence, Adverse Impact and Applicant Reactions, *International Journal of Selection and Assessment*, 8, 237–47; Macan, T (2009) The Employment Interview: A Review of Current Studies and Directions for Future Research, *Human Resource Management Review*, 19, 203–18.

4 Structured interviews are seen to deliver better results, particularly for newly trained or inexperienced interviews by reducing the reliance on the individual interviewer to create and ask questions that will solicit useful evidence of the competence. The structure is also seen to help the interviewee give a more rounded account of their experience as it structures their responses to the areas of the role the organisation finds most useful in predicting job success. See McDaniel, Michael A., Whetzel, Deborah L., Schmidt, Frank L. and Maurer, Steven D. (1994) The Validity of Employment Interviews: A Comprehensive Review and Meta-analysis, *Journal of Applied Psychology*, 79.4, 599–616.

5 Psychometric tests for selection and assessment can be grouped into two categories, cognitive ability tests, sometimes called aptitude tests, and personality questionnaires. Aptitude tests are measures of specific elements of intelligence whereas personality questionnaires measure specific personality traits. These two psychological constructs show meaningful correlations with employee job performance. Scientifically valid psychometric tests that can accurately measure these constructs provide a good predictor of job performance to organisations.

6 The use of command tasks as part of the Sandhurst Officer selection boards is well documented. See Army Recruiting Group (2008) Are You Ready to Become an Army Officer? Produced for the Ministry of Defence, https://www.army.mod.uk/documents/general/Officer_level_3_V_LowRes.pdf.

7 For more information and a clear explanation of the Likert scale, see http://www.simplypsychology.org/likert-scale.html.

8 Gaugler, B.B., Rosenthal, D.B., Thornton, G.C. and Bentson, C. (1987) Meta-Analysis of Assessment Center Validity, *Journal of Applied Psychology*, 72, 493–511.

9 A short and interesting history of the assessment centre approach, both in the non -business application of military selection and with AT&T in the 1950s, is available from: http://www.icpctraining.com/assess/assessdocs/index.html. In particular, see Moses, Joseph L. (n.d.) History of the Assessment Center Method (AssessmentHistory.doc) available to download from this page.

10 Test of English as a Foreign Language or TOEFL is a standardized test of English language proficiency for non-native English language speakers wishing to enroll in US universities. The test is accepted by many English-speaking academic and professional institutions. TOEFL is one of the two major English-language tests in the world, the other being the IELTS. (Source: Wikipedia, https://en.wikipedia.org/wiki/Test_of_English_as_a_Foreign_Language.)

11 The OPQ tools is now part of the assessment suite of CEB. An example of what the questionnaire scales look like is available from: http://www.shldirect.com/en/assessment-advice/example-questions/personality-questionnaire.

12 Originally published in 2004 by Critical Eye, the Sony Executive assessment process is available from: http://www.change-capability.com/downloads/TalentWalktheTalk.pdf.

Chapter 7

What is the best way to encourage the development of real potential?

Introduction

The purpose of any talent management process is to provide the business with the people capability to deliver its strategic aims. In a few cases this can be achieved just by recruiting the right skilled talent and letting them apply their abilities in the right place. More often than not, it's about moulding and developing raw talent to fit the way the organisation works and also the changing demands of the business. If the talent concerned is part of the young professional pool it will, by necessity, need some sort of planned development path to increase their confidence and ability, and to ensure they remain with the organisation.

This chapter focuses specifically on the approaches to the development of capability – the right mix of confidence and ability that will allow a talented individual to thrive and enable the organisation to get a return on its not insignificant investment.

Clearly there are very different demands at the different levels of seniority and career stage. What an ETM approach does is ensure that the development interventions map across to the individual's career development, whilst at the same time ensuring that the right skills are gained to perform in their current role. In addition the development plans should be preparing them for future, more challenging, roles. Development must try to meet two agendas: the individual's desire for career progression, and the organisation's need for high performance from its human assets.

Observations on common characteristics of talent

As clearly outlined earlier, the ETM approach is based on the position that not all employees contribute equally to value creation in the company. Some people match the organisation's definition of talent whereas some others don't. At least that should be the case if the talent management strategy is genuinely differentiated and is focused on driving organisational success. What this means in practice is that people identified as talent cases will tend to be in the top right of the talent matrix, regarded as both high potential, and high performance.

This profile of the individual tends to share some personality traits or generic characteristics. These can be split into the three areas alluded to in the discussion on defining potential in Chapter 3:

- High achievement orientation – they want to do well, and will push themselves to excel.

- High intellectual curiosity – they are smart, want to learn things and develop themselves.
- Socially highly skilled – they tend to be good at working with, and influencing, others.

These traits are not necessarily present to the same degree in all talents. Younger professionals, for example, often have to gain more experience of working collaboratively, as their academic success may have been more a result of individual hard work and determination than teamwork. However, in the assessment process it is still possible to see the preference for working collaboratively, even if there is limited experience of it within their career. The other two traits seem to be stable across the career life cycle of a talent. The drive to work hard and get things done is an innate, or at least an intrinsic, motivation for their work. They do not normally put in effort solely contingent on the offered reward. Similarly, their intellectual curiosity sets them apart from more average performers. It is this that ensures they stay relevant as their career develops and the demands of the market, technology and the environment changes.

The reason for opening the chapter with these observations on frequently observed traits, is that being aware of them allows the talent professional to tailor some of their development interventions appropriately – taking into account what might be most effective.

If the talent segments, represented by the different pools in the organisation, are generically driven and highly motivated, any intervention aimed at developing individuals or groups will work better when the challenge level is suitably high and when success is dependent on them working to the upper limit of their personal ability.

Similarly, if the generic shared trait from young professional to senior executive is a high level of intellectual curiosity, then successful interventions, either for individuals or groups, need to be ones that challenge their thinking. Too little intellectual challenge will allow them to cruise or sit back and relax, rather than engage and learn from the debate of new ideas.

Finally, the demonstrated level of social skills tends to be quite high across the spectrum. The strong recommendation I offer organisations is to create opportunities for them to learn in a network and to develop new connections. Success in large complex organisations, both public and private, isn't just dependent on technical ability and hard work. The nature of complex businesses also requires the talents to have a well-developed personal network. This will of course develop organically over time, but learning is both an individual experience and a social phenomenon. Organisations can harness the two and create great learning experiences that also build the talent network within the business.

The rest of the chapter will explore a range of approaches to developing capability in individuals and in the organisation's talent pools. The different segments represented by the pools sometimes require quite different approaches, but the three common traits are worth bearing in mind regardless of level of seniority.

Defining the development path

For some specific skills, training may be required when first joining an organisation in order for someone to be able to perform in their new role. Alternatively, the same may be required when there has been an internal appointment and the new role requires learning new skills. This is very much tactical training and development, and whilst it is necessary and helpful, it is not strategically important with regard to the ETM. This skill support will happen regardless of the status of the new hire or new appointee.

What is more important for the talent professional to consider is the short and long-term development of strategic capability. For a business to succeed in its chosen strategic plan, it requires the right people to implement it. This means people with the capabilities that the organisation has deemed strategically important.

In Chapter 2's example, Fast Fashions agreed on a limited number of strategic capabilities, some of which were a development of existing strength and some were brand new, and related to current weaknesses. In Fast Fashions' case, 'e-tailing' became a strategic capability deemed necessary for its future success and one that it realised it currently lacked. Its development plans focused on building a new academy programme to rapidly build the management population's understanding of what Fast Fashions meant by 'e-tailing' and also a view of what the competition provided. In parallel, its recruiters were seeking to attract new talent from competitor organisations who already had experts in this capability.

If there is a demand for a capability directly linked to the organisation's strategic aims, then this becomes the priority development need. Of course there will be additional generic needs requiring development support: the usual suspects of managing projects, time management, leading teams and presentation skills. All of these are in some way useful at developing generic capability. However, this is just creating the same abilities as your competitors and other large organisations. In contrast, focusing on the strategic capabilities, as defined by the executives and agreed that when present drive the success of the organisation, is a means to really contribute value. The development path provided across the segments should have a range of interventions that develop these critical, few, strategic capabilities, as a priority over other management development and executive education. Strategy, as Michael Porter reminded us, is all about focus. Focusing on the few strategic capabilities will increase their rate of development and also drive positive results. Spreading development too widely will slow down the achievement of business results.

The short-term development for individuals should be identified as part of the normal organisational appraisal process. This typically annual process should focus on future performance and the skills and new experiences that may aid the person in the current role. The process would normally be the same for all employees. However, those employees also considered members of specific talent pools, should also be the subjects of a wider, talent development review, where longer-term development opportunities can be explored.

Talent reviews

Many organisations have historically held succession-planning meetings. The purpose of these groups was to populate a hierarchical plan with likely successors to selected senior roles. It would not be uncommon for each of these roles within a business to have up to three potential successors identified by name. In addition, they would be ranked in order of role readiness. This approach is time-consuming and assumes that roles in the future will be very similar to how they are structured now. What seems to be the most effective format for replacing this relatively mechanical process is the emergence of talent reviews or talent forums.

The purpose of a talent forum is to specifically review a sample of the total population of people in the pool. They should also assess the overall bench strength and the development opportunities and needs of the whole group. These reviews may also discuss specific named candidates in regard to known future internal appointment. This should form part of the development discussion and not just be triggered by an immediate vacancy.

Typically, the talent review group is made up of HR and senior line managers from across the organisation. The purpose of these reviews is to discuss small groups of talents, in rotation, regardless of their current role, but with a view to considering their long-term development in line with the strategic aims of the organisation. The underlying assumption in this approach is that the pool will provide multiple candidates for many of the roles in the current hierarchy, not just specifically named individuals for each position.

The combination of the normal development needs diagnosis arising from the standard appraisal process, and the longer-term focus and wider agenda of the talent forums ensures that the whole organisation's capability is considered.

Designing effective development interventions

There has been a growing consensus amongst management thinkers that the most effective form of development, particularly for high potentials, is gaining new experiences. What appears to be particularly important is that the experience is of something the individual finds challenging. There is substantial research evidence[1] that shows certain specific types of experience provide more potential for development and capability growth than others. McCall, a leading writer in the area of leadership development, suggests the following five experiences as being pivotal for many of his research contributors:

- Starting from scratch
- Turnaround
- Change in scope
- Special projects
- Move to staff

Whilst these five areas are not meant to be exhaustive, they are examples of the type of challenging work experiences that seem to have the most impact on capability development. In addition, they found many opportunities that were specific to an individual's early career. In many cases, the type of early work content they had and their own initial supervisory experience was quite influential on their development. The first time an individual is responsible for the work and performance of others, is often viewed as a rite of passage in their career.

Focusing on the most common five elements, McCall suggested from his investigation that each experience created a particular form of learning:

Special projects created learning about handling cooperation and collaboration not always with authority.

Move to staff roles seemed to highlight the difference between hands-on operational management and the more reflective, persuasive style needed in central staff roles.

Starting from scratch created lessons in the importance of prioritisation, and also about building self-confidence when they needed to take quick decisions.

The lessons experienced in trying to turn around a business showed people how to make tough decisions and also be persuasive about their plans.

Finally, the most common lessons learned from a change in scope were to delegate and develop others when the role required more than was possible by themselves.

McCall's findings, supported by later research from management development writer Alan Mumford,[2] showed that not only was real work experience the most effective way of creating learning opportunities, they also found that, of these, many were linked to a significant person. That significant person highlighted in their research was almost always a boss, not very often a peer, colleague or subordinate. This finding should influence the selection of any development roles. A challenging new work experience where the boss is open to a talent working with them and is able to foster the right learning environment, is the ultimate goal for the talent professional.

The consensus seems to be that experience is the most effective development tool, but that doesn't preclude the use of other more traditional methods. There is certainly a place for management education and other approaches that are not work based. However, the focus should always be on what will be most effective in developing the capabilities that allow the individual to create most value for the organisation. That is the best way a talent professional can support the organisation and help it meet its strategic objectives. The real skill for the talent professional is balancing this organisation-level need with the development ambitions of the various individual talents.

Approaches to developing capability

There is a myriad of different ways to create opportunities for development. Each has its positive aspects and its drawbacks. The following section reviews a number of approaches and aims to guide the talent professional on the benefits of each with particular focus in relation to creating an ETM strategy.

Management education

It is likely that at some stage of a talent's career they would really benefit from attending a programme of business education. Many talent pools contain the people who the organisation wishes to lead part of the business at some point in the future. To do this effectively they may need additional educational input to supplement their current experience and their existing education. Historically, many large organisations defined their talents by default of their inclusion on one of the prestigious management programmes. Invitation to the 'Warwick Business School Development for Young Managers' programme meant you were a high potential within Nestlé UK. For many years at Sony Europe it was inclusion in the IMD, two-week, management programme that defined you as a high-potential talent. It became commonplace for organisations to look to business schools to develop programmes for their most valued talent. The use of prestigious partners offered some visible high-status reward for being selected. However, some of these programmes became the output of being high potential, rather than a vehicle for its development.

The benefits of using such a provider, normally a business school, to deliver management education programmes is the perceived quality of their material and the status that attending confers on a participant. It can also mean that the participants can be part of a large alumni group, a network that has its own value. Using a renowned provider can give the organisation access to some of the world's most respected thinkers in any chosen field, so a carefully selected school can also offer some potential commercial benefits.

There are advantages to using these high cost providers, but also drawbacks. Many schools want to offer their core content, sometimes with very little effort put into tailoring it to the specific needs of the organisation and the unique challenges it faces. Even some respected schools often wish to follow their faculties' research agenda ahead of the commercial priorities of their clients. Over the majority of last two decades, programme designs offered by some of the major business schools were no more sophisticated than stripping out some content of their MBA (Master Of Business Administration) and offering it into a two-week format. There was a tendency to treat all managers as prospective MBA students and not a high-fee group with specific needs related to their organisation. However, conducting a robust briefing and insisting on having an iterative design meeting should minimise this tendency and create a bespoke proposal that is more effective.

The school's reputation and kudos is built on the strength of the faculty, and some leading professors are widely considered as business superstars. When the school can list world-class professors and authors on its faculty, it becomes an aspirational institution and a place that attracts talent. However, its superstar talents have limited teaching time and many other more lucrative opportunities to earn fees. If your organisation chooses a school because of the reputation of the lead faculty, you should also ensure that any contract ties those staff members to the programme. Failure to specify who delivers the content may mean a second-tier teacher and a less than inspired set of participants.

The final area for attention is the content of the programme. In many schools the case study is the preferred method of teaching, with lectures coming a close second. This tried and tested format works as an academic approach where the participants, who are paying very high fees to attend, are motivated and are primarily there to study. With managers, who already work and have other life experiences, there isn't always the same disciplined leaning. It is in this scenario where a good school or skilled education provider will add value by creating learning experiences that are more realistic and meet the needs of a more experienced group. Action learning is gaining popularity as a method for experienced participants and seems to be gaining ground over case studies with some of the better schools.

There is a belief from some providers that their reputation is reason enough to work with them. There is certainly some kudos for the business and the individual participant from partnering with schools with international reputations, such as London Business School, INSEAD or IMD. However, there is also a tendency to be tied exclusively into their faculty when doing so. The freedom to follow and engage the best faculty and thinkers regardless of their tenure is sometimes a greater advantage than the benefit of having very close ties with one particular school. In addition it is more cost-effective to buy expertise only as and when there is an identified need.

The rise of the masterclass

In the final years of my employment at Sony Europe the organisation decided to review its executive education needs with its long-term programme provider. The company had enjoyed a long-term relationship with one of Europe's most prestigious business schools. Over the previous 15 years they had designed and delivered a two-module, 10 day duration, executive education programme with regularly updated material, but a similar design and format throughout.

The agreed talent strategy required some focused education and development to support the rapidly evolving software business. Sony historically had been focused on hardware and a corporate decision to design and integrate more of its own software applications required its managers to understand the added value, and the different business challenges, that this created.

The development need was identified for managers who were in the talent pool as high potentials and therefore would be leading some of our operational units and functions at country or European level in the near future. Sony wanted this talent group to be aware of the challenges this change in the company strategy meant, for them and their competitors.

Nothing in any of the provider's material dealt with this theme. The extensive search with the current provider for faculty who were interested in this area resulted in a poor match to the business's requirement.

Following this failed search, it was widened to all top-tier European business schools. The specific brief was for a short, high-impact masterclass, exploring the challenges and implications of a strategic switch from just hardware to one of integrated software and hardware.

One school showed more interest and greater flexibility than many of the others consulted. It was engaged to create a one-off masterclass for a group of high potentials. It was its first relationship with Sony and its enthusiasm for creating something of value was very clear.

As a result of this successful initiative, the two-module standard programmes were abandoned in favour of the creation of a series of specific topic-focused masterclasses led by a range of emerging faculty stars from some of the best business schools in Europe. The masterclass format allowed a better match of a very company-specific development need, to the new and rising stars of the European faculty, which contrary to the views of the previous provider, were not all based in Switzerland.

Masterclass formats are now very popular offers from many of the leading business schools in Europe who are having to respond to the more demanding, and increasingly competitive, executive education market.

Action learning

This approach to learning was pioneered by Reg Revans,[3] an educationalist based in the UK who explored better ways to bring learning direct to the workplace and relate to real-life situations. His approach has now become a favoured methodology for organisations that want to develop their managerial talent, but at the same time want that process to be grounded in real work. Action learning sets are small groups of peers who meet to discuss and review, then consult with each other, on challenges that they face as individuals. It has its grounding in experiential learning theory,[4] seen by many theorists and practitioners as the most effective explanation of the way that adults learn. Each learning set is made up of four to seven participants normally with similar levels of work experience and status.

In practice, this approach provides organisations with huge flexibility and yet ensures that responsibility for learning remains with the participants. A typical programme would take place over a number of months with small groups, of either assigned or self-selecting participants, meeting frequently to reflect on their challenges and successes over the period since their last meeting. With some introductory skills training, to enable them to understand the process of action learning, the group can practically run itself. The use of mentors or external coaches is common where the group is seen to benefit from an independent perspective.

Action learning, or its various derivatives, has become a central development methodology for a number of large organisations. Companies as diverse as Microsoft, Samsung, Dow, GE, Nestlé, Sony, Deutsche Bank, Boeing, Sodexo, Novartis, Nokia and many others use action learning to solve complex problems, develop leaders, build teams and expand corporate capability. The real advantage these companies gain is that the development experience is closely linked to real-life problems and is not a theoretical investigation with sometimes limited relevance.

Development assignments

Experience is without doubt a great teacher, but sometimes the price is high. In order to be constantly developing, there needs to be a variety of opportunities to learn, not the same experience repeated throughout the individual talent's career. As highlighted earlier there are a few significant experiences that seem to act as catalysts for learning, and routinely show up in research on management, talent and leadership development. The five most positive are: *starting from scratch*; *turnaround*; *change in scope*; *special projects*; and *move to staff*.

These may, or may not, appear as opportunities for an individual during their normal career path. If that is the case significant learning is possible. However, that is not likely to happen for everyone present in the talent pools, without some positive intervention from the organisation. Talent professionals and senior management will need to proactively identify and instigate some of these key opportunities.

The concept of development assignments have been around for many years, typically used by global organisations as ways of filling geographically far flung management roles and at the same time testing their high potentials. What is becoming common is for the organisation to identify a number of specific roles that regularly offer development opportunities and that can be reserved or ring fenced just for emerging talent. These development roles can provide the chance for talent to experience one or more of the five significant learning situations.

Roles that are challenging and offer new experiences that shape future management expertise and confidence are usually present in most large organisations. What has been proven to be effective is when a number of these roles are used to rotate high potential talent. This gives the business unit a regular supply of great people, and the individuals a chance to learn and develop.

This concept of development roles or assignments can only be agreed at the highest level in the organisation. Talent is a company asset and not the prerogative of a single business unit or manager. It is therefore critical that the best opportunities to develop the talent are available and that may, for some individuals, be a move to a reserved development role.

These roles should be significant enough to offer a challenge, but not so business critical that they cannot survive any early mistakes or learning errors. This is a fine line to draw, but one that must be considered if risk is to be mitigated. If development roles don't offer enough of a challenge then they will be seen by talents as a soft option and become less attractive than real business unit responsibility and, on the contrary, if they are so demanding that they restrict the talent's ability to learn, they will not work.

These development roles could be flagged on the organisation's recruitment system so if they become vacant at any point they must be pushed to the talent review for consideration and subsequent appointment. In some organisations there is a virtual internal talent agency ensuring that the vacancies in-house are scanned for potential talent as a priority before they are opened up to other internal candidates, or ultimately to the external market if there is not an appropriate fit. This ensures, if at all possible, that every development role is taken up by a member of the talent pool, and that talent pool members are automatically considered as a priority for filling them.

Mumford[5] makes a very valid point that not all development roles and assignments offer the same scope for development. However, he also adds that many would be much better with just a little preparation. He comments that many new roles are considered great learning opportunities in general, accompanied by the hugely inspiring comment, 'you're bound to learn a lot from this next role', without any specific plan to maximise what can be learned. He calls this the big O – a vague amorphous learning opportunity – whereas he suggests that a development assignment should be a mix of the big O and a lot of identified smaller Os. Figure 7.1 shows this concept with some additional overlaid examples of the smaller Os. Defining the development goals in any assignment will encourage a focus on them, both from the individual and from their supporting line manager.

In some organisations there has been a trend towards designing the graduate development programme as a 'Cooks Tour'.[6] Successful candidates went from department to department, or division to division, in order to gain a broad understanding of the organisation. The underpinning belief was that in future general management roles understanding of the nature of each part of the overall puzzle would be an important contribution to their success.

It seems reasonable, but as with other common sense approaches there can still be problems. If the modules are too short for significant learning to take place, or for them to make some other positive contribution, they become nothing more than basic work experience. High potentials thrive on results, and the rotation model, if not carefully designed, will lead to them being given less significant roles and simpler activities. Managers will sometimes reserve them the less challenging activities, as for them the graduate is just one more example in the sequence of transient staff that they have to put up with. This neither maximises their learning

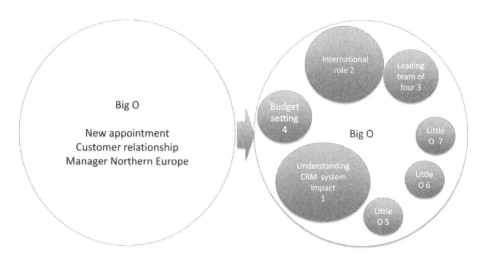

Figure 7.1 Example of development opportunity creation

Based on an idea by Alan Mumford in *How Managers Develop Managers*.

nor gives them the depth of understanding of the department or division. If business units or divisions are to be seen as 'schools', places where critical skills can be learned from experience, then sufficient time, and a role with direct involvement, should be given in that rotation. In that way the capability identified as synonymous with that 'school' can be learned in some depth. For example, experience in dealing with consumers and understanding their perspective may require someone to take a role facing customer complaints. If that is a token role, with limited responsibility to take action or is simply a taster, the individual may not value the learning or see customer satisfaction as having a significant relationship to business success. A carefully chosen rotation with some ability to find solutions could provide a really valuable development experience and underline the importance of customer satisfaction to the organisation.

There is a key role for the line manager when a talent takes up a new role, in assisting them to identify not only the major learning opportunity it might present, but also the many specific smaller challenges that the individual can learn from. Identifying the smaller Os in Mumford's model is something that the line manager can really contribute to, as they know the rotation's scope and where the best experiences could come from.

Without doubt the line manager is one of the most significant people to influence the development of any individual talent. They can make a challenging role possible through their support and positive feedback, or they can make it impossible by ignoring the need for development and short cutting any learning. However, they are not the only people who can play a significant role in the development of talent in an organisation. Mentors and coaches have a place, but they also enjoy a different type of relationship.

Graduate talent rotations

One of my clients, a large transport infrastructure provider, recruits around 30 graduates each year for its entry-level global talent pool. The development programme they join has three rotations each of around six months, normally to a different part of the company and often in a different country. Whilst the placements are not explicitly designed to reflect the primary experiential learning opportunities outlined above, each of their rotations follows a similar path.

The first rotation takes place when they first join the organisation and starts with their sponsoring division or business unit. It is always placed into a factory or operational site and in a role that requires a lot of hands-on work. Many, but not all of the company's graduates are engineers, so placing them into manufacturing areas or with production teams tests their ability to work with different levels of employees and also introduces them to the practical end of the business. If they are non-engineering graduates, recruited for roles such as HR, then their first placement will be as a junior HR officer in a manufacturing site. The rationale is to put them somewhere operational and close to the people who make the products. In this way they start to appreciate what the company is about and it also start to build their credibility. The reality of working on a manufacturing site grounds the work for the graduate and ensures that they realise that their status as talent is not automatically conferred but needs to be earned.

The second rotation is normally in a functional role on another site. These placements are into a role that is more analytical rather than operational. Within these rotations the graduate is tasked with creating savings, increases to productivity or some improvement in quality. Many of the graduate talents are highly analytical and following their first rotation have gained some operational experiences. This second rotation is designed to allow them to apply their theoretical knowledge, gained from college, and build on their first placement's operational experience to propose some improvement to the business they are placed in. This special improvement project is done in addition to their main role and the performance objectives as dictated by their line manager.

Finally, the third rotation is usually being the executive assistant to a senior figure in the business. In some organisations this is labelled 'the bag man'. Their role is to provide admin, analysis and logistical support to their new executive boss. In practice, it means attending and preparing materials for board meetings, client meetings, regional conferences and any other activity that the senior executive might require assistance with. The rationale here is to ensure that they have visibility of what a senior leader does in the business and also that they demonstrate that they are willing to do the hours, the travel and the hard work required of top management. A not insignificant side benefit is that by accompanying their boss on their schedule they meet and gain visibility with the network of senior executives in the organisation. Whilst these are not pure staff roles, they do enable the graduates to see, and work at, the organisation's centre. They have achieved a move from operations to staff within their first two years' experience of the organisation.

At the end of their rotations and before their two-year anniversary, the graduates are ready to work in their first main role. They will have built a network, gained some credibility and also offered some return on investment by proposing some improvements to their business. If they complete the full two years they are rarely short of offers within their sponsoring division of potential roles.

Coaching and mentoring

There are two important helping relationships that can be encouraged as means for supporting talent development. These roles can be called upon at any stage in the individual's career to help them achieve their potential, both as a recipient and as a practitioner. Some of the best coaches and mentors are those individuals who have benefited from this type of support themselves in their own career and therefore appreciate the value it can add. Both of these helping relationships are normally independent of the management reporting line, and as such offer an additional unbiased source of experience, counsel and support. However, many of the techniques of coaching are just fundamentals of good management, so can be used by any line manager with their reports in their daily interaction.

Whilst coaching and mentoring share some skills and techniques, they come from quite different perspectives.

The coaching relationship

The first issue with any helping relationship is the motivation of both parties. The coach must want to be part of a helping relationship, just as the person being coached must be open to learning from the process. It is therefore critical that there is a process of mutual self-selection. As the relationship is one where trust is absolutely essential, any obligatory or enforced coaching is starting out with a low probability of success. The right coach matched with the right individual learner can have a hugely positive effect on the individual's confidence and capability, and not insignificantly on the development of the coach's ability.

The following features distinguish coaching from other helping roles:

- It tends to be a short duration process or intervention.
- It tends to focus on specific needs rather than general development.
- It focuses on performance issues agreed by the individual and the coach, or manager.
- As an approach, it can be used by a line manager to concentrate on one aspect of capability.

When an individual is operating as a coach they are offering help to someone who is openly seeking it. In most cases the focus is on developing their performance in a skill-based area or in the realm of decision making at work. The coaching role is one that offers guidance, feedback and insight. What the individual being coached chooses to do with that information is really their decision, and forms part of the learning gained from the interaction. Whilst good coaches encourage a discipline of action planning, as this often helps embed the learning, the implementation of any change of behaviour is up to the individual talent. It's their choice, taken from a range of options explored with the assistance of the coach.

There are many schools of coaching, and almost as many qualifications available from the myriad of awarding bodies. There are schools of thought that advocate non-directive listening-based approaches, based on the belief that the role of the coach is not to suggest but to just act as a sounding board for the individual. There are others that believe that more directive and instructional approaches are the most effective way of helping others learn. The truth of the matter is that no one approach fits everyone's need. A reflective approach can work in some circumstances and an instructional style in another with the same person. It's the experience and knowledge that the coach has that will help them select something effective in order to maximise the learning of their individual. In some cases that means using their superior experience to spell out the various options available and the consequences and benefits of each choice. At other times it will be teasing out these very same options from the discussion and thinking of the person being coached. All that really matters is that the person benefits from the process and is learning effectively. If they understand more about their own performance, and what they can do to enhance it as a result of the insight they gain from the coaching conversation, it has been successful.

The skilled coach often follows a process to help them understand the individual's needs before being able to offer some insight to their issues. Again there are a number of competing models and frameworks. What is more important than which framework is used is that the coach is always focused on the individual's success and learning, rather than slavishly following a prescribed model. A great question for any coach to ask themselves when working with someone is: Will the person learn more from a more telling style or from drawing out the issue from them? In this way the coach keeps the learner at the heart of their conversation.[7]

Coaching is also a very powerful development opportunity for the coach. The process encourages a deep self-reflection on the part of the coach, searching for useful insights and novel ways to represent situations to enable the person they are working with to understand different perspectives. It's also a process that demands highly tuned communication skills, particularly active listening and the ability to be flexible in their own critical thinking. All of these skills are in demand for the more senior roles in many organisations and can be developed through practice in a coaching relationship, as the coaching manager.

Coaching Voldemort

A number of years ago when working as a consultant I was asked by an old colleague to speak to his boss and Group CEO about a potential coaching need they had in one of their UK-based businesses. I agreed to meet his boss at their European HQ in Germany and discuss their request. The business was a large Internet services organisation operating across Europe and the USA.

Their issue was that they had acquired a good business, from a young dynamic entrepreneur, and as part of the sale inherited its management board. One individual, the self-titled CFO (Chief Financial Officer), was proving to be difficult to manage from a distance and this had become more of an issue as the group had appointed a new Managing Director; a role he thought he should be the automatic appointment for. In this illustration to protect confidentiality, let us refer to the CFO as Steve.

The coaching need was about the behaviour the individual exhibited with his colleagues and his direct reports. He was described to me, by the Group CEO, as dogmatic, dictatorial and lacking in respect for the new organisation. There were numerous examples of people who had complained to the headquarters about his behaviour including one who cited him as the reason she left. The CEO wanted to solve or at least remedy the problem before the new Managing Director came on-board in a few weeks' time. However, currently there was no UK line manager to deal with his behaviour and in the interim the business was effectively being run by this individual. In the past, and with the previous management, Steve was considered a real talent and someone to encourage.

My first response was to ask how much Steve knew about his behaviour and how serious the issue was to the organisation. I wanted to check what he already understood. The answer was not so surprising, that no one in senior management thought it was their role to deal with the situation from Germany and they felt it was the CEO's job to fix him or fire him. The CEO rightly recognised he was unable to fire someone for something they had never witnessed, addressed previously or even directly raised with the individual. In addition the CEO did not have the time nor, he admitted, the skills to tackle what might be a very difficult set of conversations.

I agreed to have a discussion with Steve and talk about whether he wanted any help, and if so would he want it from me. This was the first stage in a process to build a relationship and check the motivation of the individual. Three things became apparent from the initial difficult first conversation:

Steve had never been told of the organisation's concerns about his behaviour.

He did what he did with the very best of intent for the company.

He was feeling threatened and anxious about his position but wanted to stay.

After a very frank and open exchange of views Steve agreed that talking and working with someone independent of the organisation might be worth exploring. Although he didn't like what he heard me describe, he said he respected me for being honest and direct. We agreed how we might work for the next three months, and to review the process at that point, to see if there was any value in continuing.

The following weeks of meetings and exercises explored how Steve might work in future, what the positive and negative aspects of any change were for him and what he valued at work. The discussions were always very task focused, as Steve was very reluctant to share any information that was not, as he saw it, related to his work objectives. He was an intensely private individual who found discussing anything he saw as gossip, small talk or potentially personal as out of bounds.

(continued)

(continued)

The process was slow and challenging, but ultimately helped Steve see work in a different way, no longer aiming for a role (that of the subsidiary Managing Director) that he could not do, nor would enjoy. He was a very proud individual who held the belief that at work you needed to be seen to be strong and not let any personal relationships build with colleagues or direct reports in case you needed to discipline them. This view softened over time, but not without its difficulties and personal challenges for Steve. He was a strong introvert and set demanding targets that his team didn't always meet. The respect for him as a manager did improve, but there was still little in the way of any relationship with his team or colleagues.

The results were mixed: Steve kept his job for a year, but ultimately moved onto a new company and similar role. This was his choice but not one that he took lightly. He wanted to do a good job for his new Managing Director and stay in his role, but found the open management style of his new boss challenging. In his next role he returned to work for his old entrepreneur boss, who was now on his third start-up and wanted familiar faces around him.

Steve seemed to demonstrate a more relaxed approach to work as a result of a single insight that came from one of our coaching conversations. He believed, to be successful, he needed to have the top job in the company and that achieving this status was somehow his right. However, when we explored his strengths, his motivations and his dislikes, it was clear that the top job would not be something he would enjoy or do well. This seemed to be a relief to him and in future he could concentrate on being a great CFO. Steve is thriving in his new role working with a boss who values his efforts and who manages his behaviour.

The mentoring relationship

The second helping relationship that can be provided is that of mentor. The term has many different meanings but a reasonable working definition would be:

> A protected relationship where an influential person provides help, guidance and advice to someone over a significant period of their career outside the line management relationship.

The person offering the guidance and advice is called the mentor, and the recipient of the insight the protégé. This relationship is much less concerned about immediate skill and capability development, but is focused on the longer-term career and the significant decisions facing the protégé.

In contrast to other helping roles, mentors provide:

- longer-term assistance, through a significant period of a person's career;
- insight and guidance on more general development needs, such as next career move;

- a sounding board for difficult choices where the mentor may have experience of the politics of the organisation or the impact of the cultural norms;
- access to a network within, or external to, the organisation.

Mentoring does share some aspects of coaching, in that much of it is reflective and based around a conversational process. What is usually different is that the mentor is often more senior in status and therefore most often in age. A mentor's role is also to guide and advise not just outline the range of choice the individual has. In this sense they are more influential and the trust and respect that they hold needs to be kept at a very high level.

To be an effective mentor, the person must really understand the deep workings of the organisation. Many of the issues that face a younger talent are about the nature of decision making within the organisation and this is directly affected by its culture and its politics. These are difficult things to formally teach but something that respected mentors can guide their protégés through. It is difficult to research or study the politics within a large organisation, but a wise mentor can steer someone through the minefield that they have experience of.

Matching mentors and protégés is not easy, as there needs to be a strong motivation on both sides for it to work. Also some of the conversations will be about difficult work-based, and in some cases personal, decisions. It is primarily for this reason that mentors should be outside any line reporting relationship, so that they can be independent and as unbiased as possible about the protégé's issues.

The descriptions above will, for some, conjure up images of 'management Yodas' sitting in big chairs dispensing executive wisdom to eager initiates. This is far from the truth: much of the time the conversations happen in coffee areas in informal catch-ups and quiet words of advice. Formal review appointments can be scheduled, and a six-monthly programmed meeting is strongly recommended, but the nature of mentoring requires more flexibility than that. They are someone to call on when you have a difficult decision or just want someone to listen and offer a viewpoint. This makes it more personal, and in many ways more informal than coaching.

For the most senior roles in an organisation, the choice of mentor is more difficult, as there are no more high-level executives to offer guidance. It may be that the board members have significant people outside the organisation, but still known within their personal network, that they can seek guidance and advice from. If this is the case, they are using their network to mentor them informally. However, an alternative and more professional means of delivering mentoring at this level, is the use of external coaches. Mentoring senior team members in confidence is the realm of the expert executive coach.

Again, there are positive and negative aspects to using external coaches to mentor the top team, but there really are few internal alternatives. External coaches can operate in the mentoring model if they are well matched and have the level of experience that the protégé would find valuable. Senior teams are by nature full of confident and competitive people, who find it difficult to ask for help or show weakness. Confiding in a trusted external adviser provides them with excellent development support just when they are facing their most demanding career roles.

Most executive coaching supports two different capabilities: the softer skill of managing people and their own performance, and business-specific coaches who bring experience of the industry or functional expertise.

Many executive coaches that specialise in people-related development issues are often expert in HR management or qualified business psychologists. For the business-specific coach it may be necessary for the sake of their credibility to have held a significant senior role in their career as well as holding some relevant academic qualification such as an MBA. It may not be entirely necessary for every organisation, but a solid career history, high-level functional background, or the presence of an academic accreditation, is a sign of some expertise and professional ability.

External coaches acting as mentors and being their independent trusted adviser is very useful for the many senior executives, just as long as the personal chemistry works. It's not impossible for executive coaches to be appointed, but far more success comes from those personally chosen by the executive being coached, as the relationship is deeply confidential and sometimes very personal.

In some national and organisational cultures the notion of coaching is seen as remedial or only for people who have issues with non-performance. In others the use of an executive coach is a sign of the individual's value to the organisation and as such is seen as a status symbol. If the issue arises about the utility of coaches for people who are already considered as high potential, then you should reflect on this quote from Atul Gawande, an author, surgeon and staff writer for the New Yorker magazine:[8]

> There was a moment in sports when employing a coach was unimaginable – and then came a time when not doing so was unimaginable. We care about results in sports, and if we care half as much about results in schools and in hospitals we may reach the same conclusion.

His article shows that there are few fields where effective coaching and mentoring could not positively impact on the talent's development, regardless of whether they are doctors or musicians. Think of any world champion athlete in any sport and then think if they still use the services of a coach. Why would they stop if the coach helped them improve performance?

In a similar way to coaching, the process of taking a protégé and being their mentor is also an opportunity for development; particularly of more senior managers who are willing to take the time and effort to share their experience and wisdom. The experience of taking some responsibility for developing your organisation's future leaders can be very rewarding. This can be a great way for someone whose career is well established to add even more value.

Coaching and mentoring – the cascade mechanism

There is a perfect cascade of impact and influence if the organisation is able to use its whole talent pipeline to help develop its capability. Figure 7.2 shows how this has already worked in one large European business. Each of the four identified talent pools were offered the opportunity for coaching, from people who they selected from a database of willing and trained coaches. This was managed in some ways like a dating agency, setting up a range of initial meetings for prospective coaches and their talents needing coaching at three levels, and letting the pair decide whether they thought it would work. The rationale was that you were coached from a member of the talent pool more senior than yours. This generated the expectation that if you were a talent

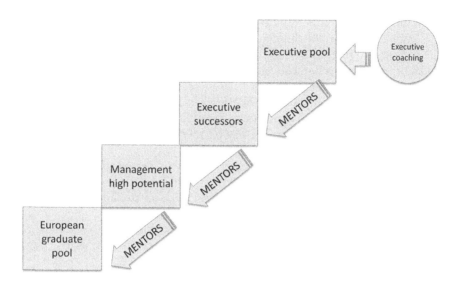

Figure 7.2 Cascading coaching in practice

you were open to coaching as method of learning, both in terms of receiving it and in providing it. It also increased the visibility of the younger talent to each more senior pool in the organisation.

In this example, the executives in the most senior pool were encouraged to engage with external, executive coaches to mentor their development and also develop them as coaches for the next pool in the pipeline. The successors were matched with high-potential managers, not in their own function or division, to provide them with the opportunity to coach and mentor emerging management talent. Finally, the high-potential managers were engaged as coaches for the talents in the graduate pool. The benefit of this approach is that there is a visibility of talent from the top to the bottom of the pipeline. It was not unusual for talents to be spotted through a coaching relationship, then discussed in the coach's business network and offered an appointment later in their career. This approach built strong networks and increased the overall visibility of talent in the organisation.

What is even more beneficial from an ETM point of view is that this cascade process sets the expectation for what being a talent meant in this organisation. Coaching was considered a part of being a good manager and that meant being open to receiving it as well as developing the skills of providing it.

Teaching others – Business school/university liaison

There is an oft quoted saying from Aristotle, 'Those who know, do. Those that understand, teach.' Development opportunities for talents can come from many different sources. One that is sometimes underestimated and overlooked is encouraging your emerging talent to share their understanding with others. As a learning experience, teaching really is second to none. It requires a level of preparation and understanding that transcends just carrying out the role at work. As such it requires the person to really think through their communication approach, their prepared material and then try to pre-empt any potentially difficult questions. It also contributes to developing the confidence in sharing their ideas and their impact and presence in front of a group.

The benefit from undertaking a visiting speaker role for the talent involved doesn't stop with the skills development, but includes increased prestige within their personal network as well as in the academic world. This has an additional benefit for the positive image of the organisation with future potential employees who may be in the audience. It also ensures the faculty of these partner schools understand what sort of talent your organisation wishes to recruit in future.

Most business schools encourage partnerships with organisations and regularly invite guest speakers to add some real-world examples to their teaching. Increasingly the technical schools are encouraging guests from industry to demonstrate how their research makes it into applications for the business world.

The range of benefits from this sort of intervention is potentially enormous and the effort required in establishing them as part of the talent development portfolio relatively small.

Developing capability – core competences

The approaches outlined and explored in this chapter are not meant to be exhaustive. There are many other ways to create development opportunities for talented individuals. There is a limited role for online and blended learning, but in most cases this is more suited to skills and knowledge acquisition rather than developing more general capability. In addition there are numerous inventories, questionnaires and surveys that, when used carefully, can add information and useful insights to individuals as part of their development. My experience suggests these are most effective when used in conjunction with some coaching or mentoring support so that their findings can be placed into some career context.

The different approaches discussed so far do share a core feature – they develop individuals in a more holistic way and focus on general capability. ETM has a both a short-term objective of filling the essential strategic roles with high-quality talent, and a longer-term perspective that is to build capability throughout the pipeline. By focusing on general capability, the pipeline will have both depth and width. The people who are selected into the pools will have the depth of ability to take on a new challenge, and the breadth of understanding of the organisation to ensure they play an effective part in it.

Specific skills and knowledge to carry out the core of the role is still the realm and responsibility of the line manager, and will require some organised training interventions. However, the building of capability and confidence is the role of the talent professional and this is something that requires a strategic approach and not a tactical response such as a training programme.

Key review questions

What are the core capabilities that need to be developed?

What would be the most effective experiences to develop them?

Where in the organisation do these experiences exist?

How many managers have the skills to coach or mentor the talent in the organisation?

Notes

1 Chapter 3 of McCall, Morgan W. (1998) *High Flyers – Developing the Next Generation of Leaders*, Harvard Business School Press, Boston, MA is a summary of the research and examples of the seven experiences with the most potential for leadership development. See also McCall, M. W. (2010) Recasting Leadership Development, *Industrial and Organizational Psychology*, 3, 3–19. doi:10.1111/j.1754–9434.2009.01189.x; Marquardt, Michael J. (2000) Action Learning and Leadership, *The Learning Organization*, 7.5, 233–41.

2 Alan Mumford has written about learning styles and how managers learn and develop. With Peter Honey they devised a diagnostic questionnaire about adult learning, called the Learning Styles Inventory. Mumford's career and research focuses on management development. Mumford, A. (1993) *How Managers Can Develop Managers*, Gower, Hampshire, UK.

3 Professor Reginald Revans is the originator of action learning. Revans's formative influences included his experience training as a physicist at the University of Cambridge. In his encounters with this talented group of scientists – several went on to win Nobel-prizes – he noted the importance of each scientist describing their own ignorance, sharing experiences and communally reflecting to learn. He used these experiences to further develop the method in the 1940s while working for the Coal Board in UK. Here, he encouraged managers to meet together in small groups, to share their experiences and ask each other questions about what they saw and heard. The approach increased productivity by over 30 per cent. Later, in hospitals, he concluded that the conventional instructional methods were largely ineffective. (Source: Wikipedia, https://en.wikipedia.org/wiki/Reg_Revans.) Revans, Reginald W. (2011) *ABC of Action Learning*, Gower, Hampshire UK.

4 Still one of the best books covering how people learn from experience and the theoretical underpinning is; *Organizational Psychology, an experiential approach to organizational behavior*. (1984) David A Kolb, Irwin M Rubin and James M McIntyre, Prentice Hall, Englewood Cliffs

5 Mumford, A. (1993) *How Managers Can Develop Managers*, Gower, Hampshire, UK, 35.

6 The Grand Tour was the traditional trip of Europe undertaken by mainly upper-class European young men of means. The custom flourished from about 1660 until the advent of large-scale rail transport in the 1840s, and was associated with a standard itinerary. It served as an educational rite of passage. Though primarily associated with the British nobility and wealthy landed gentry, similar trips were made by wealthy young men of Protestant Northern European nations in Continental Europe, and from the second half of the eighteenth century, by some South and North Americans, among others. The tradition was extended to include more of the middle class after rail and steamship travel made the journey less of a burden, and Thomas Cook made the 'Cook's Tour' a byword. (Source: Wikipedia, https://en.wikipedia.org/wiki/Grand_Tour.)

7 The best way to understand the process of coaching for developing talent is to seek out and explore a number of different coaching frameworks. These two books offer different models but are both written by respected practitioners. There are of course many other schools of thought but these offer a solid starting point: Gallwey, Timothy (2003) *The Inner Game of Work*, Thompson, New York; Whitmore, John (2002) *Coaching for Performance, Growing People, Performance and Purpose*, Nicholas Brealey, London

8 Gawande, Atul (2011) Personal Best, Top Singers and Athletes Have Coaches, Should You? *New Yorker Magazine, Annals of Medicine*, 3 Oct.

Chapter 8

Which roles need the very best performing talent?

Introduction

The whole purpose of any talent management strategy is to ensure that the organisation has the right people in the right place at the right time. Therefore doing everything efficiently in terms of recruitment and development and then deploying the talent to the wrong place would be a potential disaster. At best, it would result in limited positive impact on the organisation; at worst, a negative effect would be noticed.

Organisations have multiple options in order to fill their vacancies and make appointments to roles. The most common reason for any appointment is to respond to an immediate need. A person leaves the organisation, either as part of the normal turnover of staff or because they have received and accepted another offer. This role is then backfilled with whoever is known to be available to the hiring manager, or with someone who shows an interest in the internal advertisement. Failure at this internal stage generates action for an external recruitment campaign.

Whilst there is nothing fundamentally wrong with the line manager hiring who they want or the best of who's available, from a talent strategy perspective it has a few flaws. The first is the ever-present temptation just to fill a vacant role as soon as possible with whoever is available. No manager likes to run their department with less than their allocated resource. This conflicts with the wider strategic view that any new opportunity is a chance to upgrade the talent pool of the whole organisation. The second significant flaw is that the hiring manager may not have visibility of the talent and potential that already exists in the organisation in another function, division or geographic location. Without this visibility, they cannot make a decision that would be aligned with the wider talent strategy.

Finally, there is the issue of the quality of the line managers themselves. The well-known adage 'A' players hire 'A' players and 'C' players hire 'C' players is based on research evidence. Confident, capable line managers hire people who will challenge them, who are experts and high performers, as they value these traits themselves. 'C' players, who survive in the organisation and do what they need to meet job requirements, rarely if ever hire someone who will out-perform them, challenge their thinking and be potentially difficult to manage.

If the organisation treats every single hire as a component of the larger strategic plan, then its decision making can be more effectively structured. If the role is a strategically critical role, an 'A' position or one that the organisation deems pivotal, the hiring decision should be managed differently from that of a simple hire to fill a vacant seat.

To ensure that the best people are placed in the most crucial roles, the organisation needs to bring together the two concepts discussed in Chapter 4, the map of the critical roles and the assessment profiles of the people in the talent pools.

The organisation can then use the available assessment and performance data to ensure that the right talent is deployed to their most critical roles. If this match is carried out effectively there should be a measurable impact on overall performance of the role. Matching the best available people to the most demanding and strategically critical roles is the key to ETM.

Placing the right talent in the right role is the right starting point for creating high performance. However, an additional factor requires consideration and that is the way the talent is managed, with particular reference to the approach used to motivate and incentivise high performance in that specific role.

The rest of this chapter will explore the practical considerations that affect the deployment process. Some are formal restrictions placed upon the organisation by external agencies, others are to do with the talent's personal circumstances, and yet others are to do with culture and politics. In addition, the issue of performance management will be discussed, with reference to some important factors that need to be considered to ensure that the organisation achieves an ETM approach.

Who owns talent?

One of the crucial questions to address when thinking about deployment is that of ownership. When the organisation is relatively small the question rarely arises. The idea of a department not offering the best people to do important roles in the organisation would not be an option. With limited resources and complete transparency the best people will be known and the most important roles will be obvious. It would be commercial suicide for a small organisation not to use its best human assets in the most demanding roles. However, in larger organisations this level of common sense seems to disappear and inter-department or cross-divisional rivalry becomes a confounding factor.

It is common in large, complex organisation structures to have business units, divisions, and regional and national country operations competing with each other as a normal part of business life. Europe can be measured on its results and then compared with the Asian region. The Nordic cluster of countries is measured for performance against results from Eastern Europe and the food division is compared for profit and productivity with the beverages business. The drive for success has created metrics and league tables that mean senior managers compete in their own organisations at least as much as they try to beat their competitors in the market.

In these circumstances, and this seems to be the case in reasonably large minority of organisations I have worked with, it is difficult to ask managers to be altruistic about their star players. It would be difficult to blame a manager in the German subsidiary who doesn't wish his best talent to be taken to support the troubled Austrian business and leave him to find, develop and retain another in their place. However, this is exactly what happens and means that many talent management efforts fail to deliver on overall organisational success. Not because they lack talent overall, but they are not deployed for the best interests of the organisation as whole.

The shareholder is much less interested in who has talent in reserve, particularly if the results are not as expected. A company could not write in its annual report, 'we could have done better but all our best people were in the wrong place and we couldn't get agreement to move them'.

However, for some organisations this statement would not be too far from the truth.

Two things handicap talent management success more than anything else. The first is the secrecy that some organisations place on being considered a talent. This reluctance to treat people as adults and tell them the expectations the company has of them results in the wrong people leaving for pastures new. The second is treating talent as a local issue rather than an organisational asset. This means that the talent that is often the most able to succeed within a role is not identified by their managers, who fear losing them to another part of the business.

In Figure 8.1, from which the business name has been removed to respect its confidentiality, the ownership of the talent at each level of the organisation is made explicit. There can be no doubt to the managers, who are issued this as part of their talent handbook, where the decision for deployment of talent sits. It makes any discussions about deployment of talent much more about impact of the person in the role and much less about internal politics.

Talent should always be regarded as a company asset. It is not a country or business unit prerogative to retain their talent regardless of the overall business need. Talent is considered by many academics and thinkers to be the most significant competitive advantage an organisation can have, it follows therefore that it cannot be ring-fenced for a specific parochial need, unless that specific local need is agreed to be the most effective deployment for the whole organisation.

Let's explore the second of the problems: that of secrecy, or to be kind, intentionally opaque talent pools. Consider a young professional with ambition; it is not unexpected that they would like to progress as fast and as far as possible in their career. To be promoted they must meet some capability criteria that the organisation deems essential to be credible, and then perform well enough to be noticed. Where talent

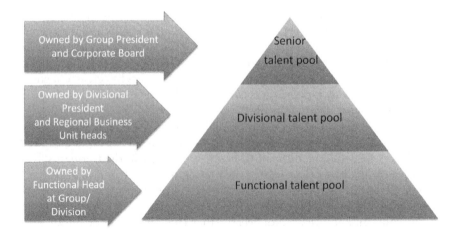

Figure 8.1 Example of explicit talent pool ownership – global engineering group

pools or programmes exist, it should not be unexpected that a young professional would want to be part of it. Without knowledge of the entry criteria and without a transparent assessment process, it becomes difficult for anyone to consciously develop the capability to be eligible.

With limited transparency of criteria, unreliable or subjective assessment and poor measurement of performance, becoming a talent becomes dependent on luck and patronage. Transparency requires telling a talent that they meet the criteria and are therefore considered eligible to be in the pool.

Elite athletes in any sport have clear rules to play to. They are measured using standard processes. Their world rankings in their sports are decided in a transparent manner and they know what they need to do to qualify for a higher level of competition. Of course, luck still plays some part in results, but the basic criteria for performance at any level is laid out and, with coaching, hard work and good performances when it matters, they can make progress.

Without a transparent talent system, the organisation is trying to win the game with players who don't know if they are in the squad and who don't get feedback when they play to tell them if they are meeting the standards to be first team, be on the bench or dropped. It doesn't make sense in sport and it really doesn't make sense in business.

The most common counter-argument to complete transparency is that selecting some small group for special treatment and attention is elitist. They argue that defining some people as more important to the organisation is divisive and unfair. If you re-read this last sentence and find yourself agreeing then you have missed the whole point of ETM.

The truth is, some roles are more important than others and some people are more effective than others and therefore contribute more value to the organisation. It does not mean all other jobs are worthless and the people who do them are not valuable, but relatively they do not require the same attention in terms of talent management, and to give them the same attention would be a mismanagement of the organisation's resources. It may seem harsh but it's true.

However, with a transparent pool criteria and a reliable and robust entry assessment process, anyone who believes that they are talented can apply themselves and try to match the eligibility profile . . . that is fair, transparent and healthy. It treats all employees as adults rather than having senior managers act like some benevolent parent hiding their sensitive children from the truth of the world.

The secret of the Black Magic box[1]

In my early career, when working in a factory as a training officer, I was invited to attend a development programme run by my company's education partner, Warwick Business School. As the only non-graduate on the programme and the only factory employee without a staff position, I was surprised, but delighted, to attend. I assumed it was some sort of pilot event to include non-graduate population staff and some sort of social experiment. The programme was over two weeks, each separated by a group analysis and

(continued)

(continued)

improvement project. The whole experience was challenging, as I was still studying for my distance learning degree and had limited exposure to higher education. However, the work was interesting and so was sharing ideas with other bright young employees. In addition our group had the opportunity to present to the current company chairman and a board member from the Nestlé Global Management Committee.

I didn't attach any particular importance to this programme in terms of my career but enjoyed the process. A few years later in my final role for the organisation, which was the result of a double grade promotion, I was recruiting graduates for the company as the Graduate Recruitment and Development Manager. In this role my boss, the head of the organisation's training and development function, set me a target of having 50 per cent of the graduates I recruited appear in the High Potential rankings of the organisation within two years of finishing their two-year development programme. I enquired what the various criteria were for entry into the pool so that I could align the recruitment process and particularly the development plans to meet these requirements. I was told that these were confidential and at my grade they couldn't disclose them. It seemed to me at the time that there was a black box which talent went into, with unknown career consequences and unknown criteria. I was bemused but tried to recruit the best talent I could, albeit blind to the requirements.

One year later, having accepted a lucrative offer from another company and after taking the difficult decision to leave a company where I had enjoyed a 20-year career, I was asked to attend an exit interview. In the discussion and conversation that ensued, I was told it was a great shame I was leaving as I was in their High Potential pool and had been since attending the Warwick programme some five years earlier. It seemed this was the reason that they could not share the entry criteria or pool listing, as I would have seen my name on the file. It seemed my name had been in the black box all along.

I left the company with mixed feelings. I was grateful to have enjoyed a long career that had given me countless development opportunities but was utterly bewildered by their decision regarding transparency. Their policy of never telling a talent that they were considered so was strange and ultimately counterproductive. If people never knew the company's opinion of them then they had no clear incentive to stay when counter-offers were made. Talents always attract counter-offers and my case was not the only instance from my Warwick Business School alumni.

Black boxes should be for packing chocolates in, not for hiding secrets about the organisation's talent.

The question of where and when

If the organisation has already tackled the thorny problem of transparency, the discussions on where and when to deploy talent can be carried out in a more open and consistent manner. It allows better decision making when people and places and options can be openly discussed with a group of interested senior managers.

There are many ways to answer the question of where to place talent. If there is an organisation-wide process for tracking talent, as many HR software suites do, new vacant opportunities can trigger a search in the online pools of potential. However, with an important resource and critical roles to fill, a more concerted effort would be more effective. Selecting the wrong person, or moving a talent at the wrong time, could be counterproductive and potentially create a negative impact on the business.

In Sony Europe, the process was tackled by an internal agency. This worked for positions and talents up to and including the Development Potential Pool. Just as an external recruitment agency would scour its database for matches to openings and pitch these to corporate hiring managers, the internal team where briefed to operate in a similar way. The central function for talent, the People and Organisational Development team, had two team members whose role was to be the conduit for talent placement across the European business. They would be the expert recruitment consultants for line managers who had open positions above a certain grade. The process, managed by the central team, was designed to ensure that internal talent had the initial visibility of any new roles as they became vacant. The line manager had an obligation to interview candidates that were matched from the talent pool, but there was no compulsion to hire. Using this internal agency approach, the team increased the visibility of talent to a wider range of line managers who might normally recruit locally known candidates or externally, without knowing the range of capability that already existed in the organisation.

This system worked very well for the graduate population and the young high-potential pool, as the agency model efficiently brought together the pre-assessed talent and the hiring managers. The central team built a great reputation for being accurate with their matching, and the talents themselves proved to be good hires. It quickly became the default method for getting young mid-level management posts filled. It was simple, low cost and highly effective.

For more senior and experienced talent, where appointments were more strategically important, a different approach was created: that of the talent forum. This was a regular meeting of the business units' most senior managers, a senior consultant from the People and Organisational Development team and a senior manager from a parallel, but independent, business unit. The structured process reviewed a sample of the senior talent in the business unit or division. The purpose was to create a discussion about succession and development plans for their talent. In the course of a year, every talent was reviewed at least once through a rotating schedule. This was in addition to their own individual performance review with their current line manager.

The mix of senior business unit manager, talent professional and third-party senior manager was designed to enable an open and robust discussion. The third-party manager's role was to be devil's advocate and ensure that all possible options were discussed. The role of the talent professional was to ensure that assessment and performance data was prepared and interpreted correctly and to share the organisational overview of talent, so decisions could be made in context. Each meeting would last a full day and take place every six weeks with different participants.

There were three main decisions to take in these forums. The first was the filling of known senior roles and building a proposal for the business unit's board to approve. The second was for potential development moves, where the objective was to build the capability for the individual talent for future application in a more senior role. The third was around succession. For each individual discussed, the question was asked: 'How many of the senior roles in the organisation could they fit into?' The aim was to understand the strength and depth of the talent pool bench players.

These forums proved to be quite time consuming, but highly valuable. It became a status symbol to be one of the senior managers who represented their business unit on the forums. By default they became the gatekeepers for talent for their part of the organisation.

Similar review groups operate in other organisations, some with different processes and most with different names. What unites them is the desire to make deployment the result of considered discussion and shared opinion of what will make a difference to the organisation's success.

Tale of two cities, two industries, two methods

One of my client organisations based in London operates in the dynamic digital marketing sector. It prides itself on providing its own clients with an end-to-end digital marketing service, everything from big data analysis of the economic impact of advertising through to the delivery of award winning, creative, media advertising. It operates in a highly competitive market but is respected within it as one of the world's biggest and best digital media organisations.

Talent is highly mobile amongst the 8 million people that make up the promiscuous London employment market where the organisation is based. Retaining good talent whilst growing its presence globally is critical to the organisation's continuing success. Its creative and technical talents can easily move to another agency without having to relocate or spend too much effort on job search. As a result, the attrition rate for its staff had been over 30 per cent as people listened to the calls from head-hunters and moved to pastures new. In some cases this was as easy as crossing the street to a competitor.

As a strategic response, the Head of Leadership and Learning instigated the use of 'Talent Circles' to ensure that critical talent is discussed openly, and their performance reviewed and acted upon to ensure the organisation retains the people it needs to fill strategically critical roles.

Their Talent Circles meet with the 'High Potential' individual present, alongside the line manager, a talent professional and the senior HR business partner. The initial focus for the Talent Circle is the development path for the individual, but this doesn't exclude discussion on their next career move, actions to prepare for it, how to develop their capability and targets for improvement.

The rationale for the Talent Circles is to create visibility and raise the talent's profile, whilst generating opportunities for the creation of development plans and positions. The results to date suggest that this review process has reduced the number of talents answering calls from head-hunters and has already had a positive impact on the organisation's attrition rate. Whilst in the past there existed an informal career development path, the talents were not always aware of it or felt consulted on it. Results so far show a reduction in the rate of leavers, particularly in the key talent segments and an increase in proactive development actions.

Elsewhere in Europe, in the cosmopolitan city of Berlin, another client has instigated its own review and deployment process called 'Talent Days'. These full day meetings of business unit managers and HR professionals review and discuss the population of high-potential talent in their part of the organisation. The purpose is two-fold: to populate their unit's succession plans, giving them some confidence in maintaining future capability, and also to deploy people into currently vacant critical roles. In this organisation they have already taken steps towards full transparency, with talents being told they are in the succession pools for roles above them or, in some cases, roles that are parallel in the structure to them. This use of parallel moves is more prevalent in flat management organisations where succession is not always about an appointment upwards.

The total population of high potentials in each division, around 80 people from a business unit of 1600, are reviewed in this way at least once during a year. In these meetings the talent professionals provide the latest assessment data and performance management ratings so that each talent can be viewed objectively. In the past it was uncommon to use assessment data so explicitly and discussions about deployment and appointments were more focused on senior managers' opinions.

The creation and agreement of a clear set of definitions for all aspect of the talent management process has been a significant step forward. The concept of a 'critical position' is now articulated for the whole business, something that was a matter of opinion and disagreement before the Talent Day process was instigated. In this organisation a critical role has at least two of the following three characteristics:

Has specific competencies or expertise that cannot be developed in less than three years within a role.

Is at the top of the functional hierarchy (head of a business unit or regional function).

Has a negative financial impact on the organisation if the position is vacant.

In addition, this process reviews the performance and potential of each candidate against recently clarified definitions for both. Now the managers attending the meetings share and use the same language and have become much more objective in their discussions than previously observed. Decisions are now based on objective evidence about the talent and, after agreement, which are the most important organisational priorities.

One of the criteria for being a high potential in this organisation is that you are included in one of the succession plans. Whilst not everyone in the succession plans are high potential, all of the high potentials are in a succession plan.

These meetings are about specific individuals and the purpose is to match them to critical roles identified from the business plans, and to offer development routes for those not

(continued)

(continued)

yet ready to move. The participant managers are always at least one level above the talent being reviewed, and the individual talents themselves are not present.

The Talent Days are a bottom-up process, so results from one day's review feeds into the next level above. In this way the talent across a global organisation employing over 30,000 people, can be managed in a systematic and reliable way. Eventually, towards the end of the process, the Executive Board members have complete visibility of their potential successors, knowing that it is the result of a comprehensive review of the talent across the whole organisation.

Whatever format of talent forum is used, the final objective in all cases is for the organisation to have the best talent in the most critical positions. In the terminology of *Topgrading*[2] and also that of the authors of *The Differentiated Workforce*,[3] it's about '"A" players in "A" positions'.

Following the example shown in Berlin, defining what is critical or strategically important is the start, with the matching of potential being carried out by robust discussion and debate. Chapters 3 and 4 explored some of the processes and ideas behind defining talent and how to determine the critical roles. What is needed is a forum where these two high-level actions are followed up by management decisions on deployment. It is the correct deployment that earns the return on the investment.

Performance in role

Let's assume that the right person is now in the right position. As the result of an in-depth discussion at a circle, forum or talent day the talent has been appointed to a critical position as defined by the organisation and considered strategically important in relation to business success. The next concern of the talent professional is to ensure that these individuals are able to perform to potential and make the impact that is expected of them.

This is not a central responsibility for the talent professional but a coordinating and monitoring role, supporting the talent by ensuring that the line manager has, and can use, some form of performance management system.

Without doubt, other than the individual themselves, the most influential person in relation to someone's performance in their role is the line manager. With a conscientious and supporting line manager a talent's true potential can be reached and they can perform in role as expected or even exceed expectations. However, a great talent with a disinterested or sceptical line manager can make it difficult to achieve anything of real value to the organisation.

Whilst the talent professional cannot dictate how managers work with their reports, they can monitor some basic indicators of support – such as how often and how comprehensively the appraisal or performance reviews are completed. It's a matter of judging both quantity – the frequency – and quality – the content of any development plans, feedback process or follow-up support.

Role of the line manager

Alan Mumford,[4] a well-respected management development expert, identified two streams of support for performance that the line manager should have direct involvement with. The first is the formal expectations of the organisation for any manager of people. These include:

- the performance appraisal meeting;
- analysis of development needs;
- sponsorship of training programmes/activities;
- goal and target setting.

The second stream of support is concerned with the informal opportunities that could be presented in any role and that the line manager could use to enhance performance. These include:

- establishing specific learning goals;
- giving regular feedback;
- direct coaching;
- setting an example as a role model;
- providing higher levels of responsibility.

Clearly the more formal expectations are easier to monitor and control, and so these tend to be measured in most organisations. An HR department can monitor the completion of the appraisal process and audit the managers who are responsible, particularly if the appraisal system is linked to a software application. In many cases the HR system also records the goals set by and for individuals. It's also relatively easy with a learning management system to acquire reports of who is nominated for programmes and who has attended them. All of this gives the HR team some confidence that their performance management approach is working. However, that confidence may be misplaced if the recorded actions are not creating high performance for the talent concerned.

If the line manager is complying with the process instead of embracing it to deliver better results, the system is not working. How many times are appraisal forms submitted late or on the deadline set by HR? Is this a sign of someone complying rather than taking the role as a line manager seriously?

The second set of support activities Mumford identifies are much more discretionary on the part of the line manager and therefore much harder to monitor and evaluate. It is the managers who embrace these who will encourage the talents that work for them to reach their potential and, with it, higher performance.

Line managers who understand that their role is not to control, but to create the conditions for high performance, are still in the minority in some organisations. An ETM approach requires that the line manager's role should be considered as one important factor in placement and that wherever possible strategic roles are managed by people who care about the development of potential. Talented people will realise more of their potential if their managers are considered supportive.

Performance management choices

The basic purpose of all performance management systems is to reward the desirable behaviours that the organisation wishes to see in its employees. It is the things that people get rewarded for that tend to get repeated or that they strived to achieve. Behaviours that get no reward, or have negative consequences, tend to be pursued less and therefore these die out over time. This paradigm comes from the behaviourist school of psychology resulting from Watson, Thorndike and Skinner's research carried out during the middle of the last century.[5]

In an organisational setting the required performance should be directly linked to success, and therefore the strategic aims of the business. These performance goals can be often broken down to represent measurable Key Performance Indicators (KPIs) such as an increase in revenues, reduction in costs, reduction in cycle time, raised levels of quality or improved customer satisfaction.

As the late management guru Peter Drucker[6] is attributed to have said: 'What gets measured gets done.' Performance management requires both goals and measures, and these measures should also include the range of behaviours your organisation wishes to see acted out.

To ensure that the organisation does get the results it wishes, what is needed is a mechanism that matches individual capability with challenging, but achievable, goals. In addition, there should be a process for giving performance feedback, one that offers clear indications about progress or distraction from the expected target.

Just as the behaviourists were suggesting the strong link between reward and performance, other schools of psychology were providing additional insights that have influenced how we design performance management systems. Locke and Latham[7] researched how goals, and the process of goal setting, impacts on individual motivation and success. The essence of their theory suggests that goals need to be agreed upon not just dictated; that these goals should be challenging to the individual if they are to provide any additional motivational effect, and they should have some form of feedback mechanism, so that progression and attainment can be monitored.

Their research and ideas have significantly influenced current thinking regarding goal setting practice as an integral part of the performance management system.

There are a range of different performance management systems, all with their advocates and detractors. Some are based on traits, with the underpinning assumption that the presence of the right traits will drive the right performance. Others are almost entirely focused on behaviour with the corresponding assumption that this is all you need to measure and manage to drive success. Yet other schools of thought prefer to focus on the skills and knowledge required to complete the role and therefore assume that these are the keys to performance. Finally, there is the results-based performance management school that assumes the means are not as important as the ends and therefore focus entirely on driving the outputs more than the inputs.

In this section we will look at one hybrid approach that seems to meet the various psychological conditions required for a performance management system to work. This choice does not suggest that this is a perfect model or that the approaches and assumptions made by others systems cannot work in the right organisational context. However, it seems that the structure and assumptions behind this hybrid model are robust enough to work in most organisations and is therefore a generic model that can be used by practitioners as a template to modify and deviate from. All really effective performance management systems are customised to reflect the organisation they are operating in, but at least starting with the hybrid template will offer a framework to build on.

Effective performance management

Given the strong evidence presented in support of goal setting theory it makes clear sense to base a performance management system on its underlying principles. This means that performance goals should be agreed with the person who needs to attain them. The second condition should also apply; that they are challenging in terms of the use of skills and abilities. Finally, they should have a means of gaining meaningful feedback about progress or the lack of. Most systems based directly on goals are referred to as Management By Objectives (often abbreviated to MBO). This approach has proven popular, particularly over the last two decades, with a wide range of organisations. MBO tends to be used for entire employee populations not just those in the talent pools.

The basic model of MBO is to take the strategic goals of the business and break these down in a cascade approach, so each person's goals, when achieved, contribute to their manager's, or to the department's goals. By the aggregation of all individual targets, which should be aligned to the business goals, the assumption is that the organisation will be successful overall.

In theory, this model makes perfect sense and all participants should be able to see their contribution having some impact on one or more of the organisational goals. In practice, this whole approach relies on the skills of the manager setting and agreeing goals so that they do in fact contribute and are not merely functional tasks that the role demands. A skilled manager can take their overall targets and, through discussion and dialogue, agree with each individual the appropriate contribution for each of their team. This would be the process for all staff including any high-potential talents they have working for them at the time. When carried out skilfully this approach can be really motivating for the individual and also provide much needed clarity to the whole team or department about how they contribute to business success.

The problem in practice is that many managers, particularly those appointed to their first people management role, do not possess the necessary skill to carry out MBO effectively. Where an organisation launches a new appraisal system, performance management approach or development review process based on MBO, there is frequently an accompanying skills and communication training. This is not always the case when people are appointed in the months and years following the launch, when the process is embedded into daily activity and is not the latest HR initiative. It is not uncommon for managers to be conducting appraisal meetings and performance reviews with nothing better as a guide than their own past experience of being reviewed.

It is therefore critical if the performance of your talent pools is to be maintained, and preferably enhanced, that the managers who are their direct bosses are skilled in the process of goal setting, and understand some of the psychological principles behind it.

However, for high potentials, those who still have more to give in terms of their capability, and more development to undergo, even well-crafted targets are not enough.

Performance, and particularly high performance, is about consistently doing what you are expected to do or more. Many of these targets are concerned with sales, costs, customer satisfaction or productivity, and are easily measurable. It is more difficult to measure the progression of a talent's potential. What is required is some other aspect of their overall capability besides the scores associated with hard business metrics. This is where competencies come back into their own and enable reviews to be conducted that target performance in a way which encompasses how people work, as well as what they achieve as a result.

This dual approach to performance is the core to the hybrid model. It is based on MBO plus a focus on the development of key capabilities that are described by core competencies. A good performance review will set and agree targets that are quantifiable in both hard business measures and also in terms of competence development. An example of one such hybrid appraisal form is shown in Figure 8.2. What is illustrated is the format for recording an appraisal meeting and where any notes resulting from the conversation should be captured. In many organisations this is now online or a function of a wider HR database, but regardless of the medium, the format for a hybrid approach should place importance on quantitative targets for the business as well as qualitative development goals connected with competencies

There is no magic formula for the documentation that accompanies any such discussion. The simpler the better, so that both parties, the talent and the line manager, don't focus too much on the paperwork, and concentrate their conversation on performance. In many organisations the drive for efficiency has digitised everything, resulting in appointment for performance reviews being triggered and tracked by the HR system. Fields are provided on the system to capture data, and in some systems there is even an attempt to automate the appropriate choice of development path from pull-down lists. The aim of all this data capture is for the centre, HR and other senior managers, to have at their fingertips a real-time picture of their human capital: its goals, its development plans and its performance. What are more effective than any complex data capture system are high-quality conversations about performance that allow a talent to make changes where necessary and receive honest feedback about their work. If this can also be captured online, following the conversation, then that is a bonus, but the focus should not be on the documentation.

As Einstein was falsely reputed to have once said: 'Not everything that can be counted counts and not everything that counts can be counted.' It seems this oft quoted insight was actually made by the sociologist William Bruce Cameron. The exact same sentiment is true with regard to performance management. It is much more important that it takes place and the managers are skilled in the process rather than they spend all their time and energy filling in data fields for senior managers, so that they can feel comfortable that they are managing the business.

The frequency of appraisal or performance reviews is a question frequently raised when thinking about talent. For the members of the talent pools who are prequalified as high potential and high performance, any mechanism that helps them continue in that way of working should be pursued. If the 'requirement' of the organisation is to do annual appraisal then that is excellent as an audit, but not really satisfactory as a way of enabling high performance or development of potential. A good line manager would naturally see the benefit of a more frequent approach and reviewing the results every quarter would not be excessive. The time invested would almost certainly justify the effort in terms of increased performance.

For the segment of younger talent, often represented by members of the graduate scheme, the need for more frequent reviews is quite clear. For most of their career to date, which will be dominated by academic study and internships, they have been given regular grades for performance, by their faculty and their internship bosses.

Performance Review and Development Plan

Name: John Doe   Date of review: 1 April 2015

Reviewing Manager: Steve Smith

For the next 6 month review period the agreed performance targets are:

	Description of Objective	Measurement / Expectation
1	Reduction of inventory for business by introduction of a just in time order system, working with supplier base.	Reduction of 30% of Stock Keeping Units by end of year.
2	Audit full supplier database and reduce suppliers to no more than 3 per SKU and maintain security of supply.	To be completed in 12 weeks. £5K expected savings in administration work.
3	Tender new contracts for supply of workforce safety equipment, to meet corporate policy. Remain within approved costs.	New suppliers in place, 16 weeks. On cost or below approval limit.

For the next 6 month review period the agreed capability development activities are:

Competence Area	Activity or Experience	Expectation
Business Acumen: The ability to link long-range visions and concepts to daily work. Business Acumen moves from understanding specific business areas and acting on them to understanding business fundamentals and strategies to a sophisticated awareness of the impact of the environment on strategies and how external factors affect choices.	Work with corporate strategy team, via 3 week secondment, on preparation of next business unit strategy presentation for coming 3 years. Focus on gaining experience of integration of business unit strategic plans to group plans. Line manager to arrange secondment terms with Corporate by end of week 15.	On completion to be able to work with senior manager on strategic planning activity following secondment, and take responsibility for liaison with group.
Communication: Transmitting and receiving information clearly and communicating actively to others by considering their points of view in order to respond appropriately. It includes receiving information, understanding, and responding openly and effectively in interactions with others. Competence in communicating across diverse contexts is critically important, particularly taking cultural differences into consideration.	Present department results at regional conference. Within 2 months. Work on preparation for post presentation questions, to build confidence at answering live questions after meetings. Line manager to give feedback on rehearsal one week prior to the conference.	Increase in responsibility at senior management meetings deputising for line manager. Need to seek out feedback following conference and act on any areas for improvement.
Team Leadership; The intention to take a role as leader of a team or other group. It implies a desire to lead others and an ability to inspire, enthuse, and motivate others. Team Leadership is generally, but certainly not always, shown from a position of formal authority. The 'team' here should be understood broadly as any group in which the person takes on a leadership role, including the enterprise as a whole.	Lead stock keeping team in warehouse audit. Manage team, schedule of work and initial audit training for 5 people. Line manager to review audit plan before commencement.	Week 20–22 audit completed. Ad hoc team drawn from existing staff. Seek feedback from team members on leadership approach, post audit.

Figure 8.2 Example hybrid appraisal form

It has become an expectation that they get feedback on performance. There is no reason to stop the process just because they have joined the organisation for a career.

Many organisations' graduate schemes use a review at the end of each development rotation and as part of the objective setting process for the next one. This means over a typical two-year graduate development scheme, a young talent will have eight reviews, two annual and six in relation to rotations. Whilst this takes some management time, experience suggests it does positively impact on the speed of learning of the graduate and enhance their potential impact on the business.

Two essential appraisal skills

Experiential learning theory suggests that the most effective form of performance management is when the process of setting goals and giving feedback on them are closely linked. In practice this means agreeing goals and then setting dates for feeding back on progress, not leaving it until next year's annual performance review. What follows from this is that the skills of goal setting and giving accurate feedback are essential for the manager carrying out the performance management review.

Goal setting as a concept is incorporated into almost all training curriculums for appraisal. In many training programmes the idea of SMART goal setting is seen as the standard for creating well-formed goals for subordinates. SMART being the acronym for:

- Specific – is the goal specifically described and not an amorphous aim.
- Measurable – can the goal be measured in some form, either continuously or summarily.
- Agreed – agreed by the subordinate and the manager.
- Realistic – is this possible in the time and with the role's resources.
- Timescale – is there a deadline or target for completion that makes sense.

Whilst the inclusion of SMART goals will improve the effectiveness of performance management generally, what would really improve the specific performance of any talent being managed is that the manager understands the principles behind goal setting theory so that they can then adapt these to the individuals situation.

Goal setting works best as a motivator, which is the primary reason for using performance management, where the goals are agreed with the individual not just delegated to them. The process of agreement is not a means for negotiation, or a way to reduce the challenge or level of performance. In practice, the dialogue about what is an appropriate goal is something that sets the level high enough to challenge the talent, but still within the range that the individual sees as a stretch, but possible. This principle, of setting goals on the upper boundary of what the individual thinks is possible, comes from the work of Locke and Latham in the 1990s and more recent studies of high-performance states, sometimes called Flow,[8] from the American psychologist Csikszentmihalyi, a professor based at the University of Chicago. Setting goals too low, or not challenging enough, can result in lower than average performance as boredom and complacency sets in. Setting goals above what is considered possible, if stretching, can also result in lower performance, as performance anxiety impacts the individuals and they revert to extrinsic excuses for non-achievement. A well-crafted and individualised goal creates intrinsic motivation,[9] a drive from within the talent, rather than something incentivised by others. Agreement to the goal is the individual psychologically contracting to the challenge and in doing so internalising the goal as being theirs.

The reason agreed goals that are on the boundary of capability are so effective is that they provide personal challenge but don't over-reach the individual. For people already prequalified as high potential, the opportunity to push themselves and demonstrate to others what they are capable of is generally welcomed, but the line manager needs to find the boundary and not push the talent over the edge. Finding this boundary is a negotiated process that results from an open coaching style dialogue.

So the first essential skill is to understand goal setting beyond the basics and be able to individualise a goal to get the best possible performance. The individualisation part requires that the manager is open to listening and able to reflect to the talent their options and choices so that they can select the activities and challenges that will bring their potential out.

The second required skill is that of coaching through feedback. This reflection and provision of feedback is, in essence, the start of a coaching relationship. Wherever I have designed performance management processes for organisations, either as a staff member or as a consultant advising clients, I have encouraged them to embed coaching skills within the appraisal training for managers.

This chapter cannot cover the details of coaching in any depth, but the focus of the line manager in the performance management process is to listen and provide feedback on how the individual is working. From this a number of potential choices arise that can form suitable development experiences. Again the dual skills of listening and giving feedback can help guide the individual talent to rise to the challenges and take the opportunities available to them. It's the conversation about performance that matters not the format for recording it.

Conclusions – deployment and performance

As we have already discussed the purpose of any ETM process is to provide exactly the right talent to enable business success. The deployment of the right people, those that have demonstrated their high capability through assessment and performance, is what makes an organisation competitive in its market.

When the organisation understands its talent is a significant business asset and one that is difficult to replicate quickly, deployment decisions can be made based on the returns a placement will generate. The most effective way of making crucial deployment decisions is with a group of senior managers and at least one senior talent professional. In that way both the business units and the whole talent strategy are represented. Managers who don't understand how strategic talent contributes to success may need some sort of sanction if they block the movement of potential around the organisation, whilst holding some misplaced view that they should retain their best people just for their own department.

If the 'A' player who is placed in an 'A' position is given the right, ongoing support, and that means appropriate goals and coaching to aid their development, there is no reason why they cannot realise their potential and make a significant contribution to the organisation.

To support the talent's line manager, there should be an effective way of managing their performance. This chapter has used a hybrid performance management example, one that combines hard results with more qualitative measures of their behaviour in the role. The hybrid model can be adapted to suit many organisations' needs but would still need to combine the two threads: personal capability development with some measure of contribution to the business goals.

Finally, remember that the process is much more important than the documentation. A great coaching conversation can unlock potential and increase performance, a fantastic all-encompassing paper form will never achieve the same result.

Key review questions

How are deployment decisions made now, and by whom?

Where are the organisation's best talents currently being deployed?

What measurable impact is the organisation's performance management system having now?

What changes would significantly improve that level of impact ?

Notes

1 In the 1980s, a hugely successful TV campaign for boxed chocolates used the line: 'Who knows the secret of the black magic box?' You can read about the success of the affordable luxury product campaign at: http://www.dailymail.co.uk/news/article-2397937/Now-thats-magic-The-adverts-helped-Black-Magic-chocolates-SAVE-Rowntrees-brought-luxury-masses—just-14p-box.html.
2 Smart, B.D. (2005) *Topgrading: How leading companies win by hiring, coaching and keeping the best people*, Penguin, New York.
3 Becker, B.E, Huselid, M.A. and Beatty, R.W, (2009) *The Differentiated Workforce: Transforming talent into strategic impact*, Harvard Business Press, Boston, MA.
4 Mumford, A. (1993) *How Managers Develop Managers*, Gower, Hampshire.
5 The research of Watson, Thorndike and Skinner was centred around how behaviour was somehow contingent on reward or punishment. As a behaviour was rewarded, by food for their animal subjects, or punished, by electric shocks, they could shape the responses of their subjects with some precision. Their experiments with animals led to theories about reward and performance that have stood the test of time but also made their way into mainstream management. For a general overview see https://en.wikipedia.org/wiki/Behaviorism.
6 Peter Drucker was one of the most quoted and cited management thinkers of the last 100 years. He was a practical thinker who inspired many novel approaches to management and business improvement. His work is now kept alive at http://www.druckerinstitute.com/peter-druckers-life-and-legacy/.
7 Locke, Edwin A., Latham, Gary P. (2002) Building a practically useful theory of goal setting and task motivation: A 35-year odyssey, *American Psychologist*, 57.9, 705–717.
8 Csikszentmihalyi, M. (2007) *Finding Flow: The psychology of engagement with everyday life*, Harper Collins, New York.
9 A really well written exploration of motivation at work, and particularly the role of intrinsic motivation as a driver of high performance in all realms of life, is *Drive* by Daniel Pink. Whilst not being an academic study, more of a management book, it takes past research and more up-to-date studies to explore the idea of why some people thrive when others fail at challenges. Pink, Daniel H. (2009) *Drive: The surprising truth about what motivates us*, Riverhead Books, New York.

Chapter 9

How can I ensure I reward correctly and retain the organisation's talent?

Introduction

An ETM approach must cover all the full range of talent activities. Reward has often being regarded as the domain of the compensation and benefits specialists within the HR team, and has as such been a thorn in the side of talent managers who wish it to be part of their strategic approach. For many years compensation was considered to be the role to aspire to within HR, as it seemed to be essential for career progression, and was considered a critical role in the function. Holding the reins to salary and benefits and sitting on the compensation committee for senior appointments, the role carried a lot of kudos. However, for the purposes of ETM there is a need for a more holistic approach that links reward, in its broadest sense, to the retention of strategically important assets, namely the members of the various talent pools within the organisation.

This chapter examines the role of reward in the process of retaining these assets. It starts by exploring the concept of salary bands and what level of reward should be paid to each type of performer. This builds on the recommendations about high performers in strategically important roles identified in Chapter 4. The limited resource, that is the salary budget, must be spent in a way that maximises the return. We also look at how salary links to other rewards elements, such as performance bonuses and equity. Finally, in terms of reward, the chapter looks at other motivators or incentives that are non-monetary. The aim is to explore the options an organisation has at its disposal when considering the issue of rewarding talent with the explicit aim of retention.

Reward is very contingent on what each individual values. You cannot easily motivate someone with an increase in salary if they have already reached their personal economic wage, one that matches their perceived need. The level of reward is also dependent on the risk that losing the specific talent brings to the organisation. Some individuals are just more costly to replace but would have a significant negative impact on profits if they left tomorrow. In order to be better prepared for any eventuality the organisation should undertake some form of talent risk assessment or commercial risk audit. A simple format for carrying out a risk assessment is illustrated later, which should allow readers to create a more customised version suitable for their own situation.

Motivational aspects of reward

There are many respected motivation theories that try to explain performance at work. Some of these theories have become keystones of management training, even though their relevance to work is at times questionable. Whilst not wanting to conduct a full academic review of them, it is useful to examine some of the relevant issues that are highlighted.

Abraham Maslow's hierarchy of needs is probably the most widely taught motivation theory,[1] seemingly part of every management college curriculum across the globe. It is enticingly simple, based on the idea that as basic physiological needs are met, humans aspire to higher level needs such as making an impact on their group or society until ultimately they are fulfilled by achieving their personal potential. However, there are problems with this model, particularly in relation to motivation at work. The main critique is that there is no evidence that the hierarchy model works in practice within employment, as most of the research that Maslow conducted was with students in academic situations. If that was not enough of a sample error, to make it an even less representative, they were mainly his psychology students. The premise in the theory that a particular level needs to be satisfied before moving up the hierarchy is also countered by many people's personal experiences and numerous anecdotal accounts. If you are interested in the idea of self-actualisation and achievement of personal mastery then do read more of his original work. However, as a guide to work-related motivation, Maslow isn't so helpful other than suggesting that it's not all about money – other things motivate those that already have what money can buy and thereby satisfy their physiological needs.

A more promising explanation came from the work of Frederick Herzburg and his concept of hygiene factors and motivators.[2] His work highlighted, more specifically, the factors that people in work reported as dis-satisfiers and those aspects that they found motivating or increased satisfaction. He labelled some of the common factors necessary for satisfaction as hygiene factors, their absence being dissatisfying, but their presence not offering any further motivation. One such hygiene factor was salary; not enough for the role was considered dissatisfying but adding more than a personal threshold was seen as no longer influencing any higher level of satisfaction. Higher levels of satisfaction came from other elements of work, such as additional responsibility or freedom to act. In some cases there was a direct link, so more responsibility created more satisfaction and motivation to do well.

As a theory, Herzburg's has more utility to assist building a reward strategy related to talent retention. There are also critiques, but the core messages are sound, that everyone has basic requirements that need to be addressed – 'hygiene factors' and that the things that motivate or satisfy people are not always costly. This insight suggests reward systems should concentrate on more than just salary bands and bonuses, as these have a limited motivation value other than marking the status and value of a specific role.

In regard to the specific needs of talent professionals, there is a much more interesting model of motivation from Harvard psychologist Professor David McClelland.[3] His research and associated theory focuses on specific drives that people report and demonstrate in their working lives. The three drives identified in his need theory are:

- Need for Achievement
- Need for Power
- Need for Affiliation

What McClelland's research indicated was that some people were clearly motivated to achieve because they had an innate, intrinsic requirement to achieve challenges. They pushed themselves to complete goals as part of their personality makeup. It wasn't so much a conscious choice but to some extent just how they were wired. They gained their personal fulfilment from meeting a challenge as a result of their own effort. This means feedback on performance is critical to them and that goals should be set that can be attributed to hard work, not dependent on some external circumstance. He labelled this drive, 'Need for Achievement'. McClelland particularly focused on drives at work but clearly this innate drive influenced their sport and social activities as much as their career.

He also recognised that others in his study were more motivated by the feeling of belonging that being part of a group, team or society can bring. People in this segment were keen to collaborate and want to comply with the group norms and cultural requirements. In short, their personality has a requirement to be liked by others and they want, and need, to fit in. McClelland called this drive, 'Need for Affiliation'. Again these people reflected this need in their non-work relationships and activities.

The third drive his research indicated was that connected with being in power or control. People who aligned with this drive showed signs of high status consciousness, held a personal desire to be in control, displayed a need to be right and enjoyed high levels of discipline. What was an important factor in their motivation was being seen to be in a position of status and control – being important. He labelled this drive as, 'Need for Power'. Again these drives manifested themselves outside the work situation.

All three drives seem to be consistent across genders, culture and ethnic backgrounds. There are two that are more likely to feature in people who demonstrate high performance and potential: whilst not exclusive, many people who feature in high-potential programmes express a high drive for achievement, whereas others are very driven by the opportunity to lead or be in a position of power. Each of these two drives can be, to some extent, harnessed in a reward strategy.

Those people with a need for achievement will be more interested and motivated by the challenges that work can provide. This need for constant stretch goals can be incorporated to the deployment decisions already discussed in Chapter 8. Finding assignments that meet the organisation's need for a talented high performer whilst also matching the motivational need of the individual is one way of encouraging longer retention. If your drive for a challenge was constantly being met within your organisation, why move?

A similar consideration must be made to those individuals that display a need for power. The opportunities that could be offered to them should encompass a role that is perceived as high status and has significant freedom to act. If it manages other people then their need for being in charge is also satisfied, again reducing the likelihood of retention problems. In both cases salary is less important as a motivator, unless the pay grade reflects on their perceived status.

Herzburg's research suggests that a good reward policy reduces as many of the dissatisfaction elements as possible, including pay, and increases the number of positive motivators, such as responsibility and freedom to act. McClelland agrees this is effective for those people who have a drive for achievement or a drive for power. Responding appropriately requires some flexibility in the reward policy and some understanding of the needs of each individual talent.

Pay as a means of retention

All three motivation theories outlined above would agree that increasing pay in itself doesn't motivate higher performance. However, in some roles the pay is visible and therefore a public indicator of worth and value to the organisation. This is particularly important in sales roles where high performers are often fêted and given public recognition amongst colleagues. Getting pay wrong will definitely, negatively affect motivation and therefore, potentially, performance. It's also why in some sales organisations rewards such as exotic holidays are proposed for the highest performer, as the status of being the winner is disproportionately motivating compared to the relatively low cost to the company.

Many large bureaucratic organisations have complex and restrictive pay systems. They are managed to ensure consistency and are an attempt at fairness. However, an ETM approach advocates a few simple principles to ensure that regardless of the structure of the salary bands within the organisation there remains recognition that some people contribute more value and have more strategic impact than others.

In Chapter 4, the concept of 'A' positions, those with strategic impact, and 'A' players, those individuals who are both high potential and high performance, was explored. In Chapter 8 it was argued that there is a clear need to deploy 'A' players into 'A' positions'. What is required from any organisation's pay and reward policy is that it has the flexibility to ensure that the salary offered reflects the critical nature of the roles and the significant additional value that these players bring to the organisation.

In practice this means creating quite broad salary bands for the 'A' players in 'A' roles, which allows the pay to reflect their true contribution. The funding of these broad bands can be supported, to some extent, by the appropriate banding of pay and reward for the 'B' players in support roles, and any savings from relatively low salary payments in the non-strategic roles. Total salary costs, if aggregated over time, could be similar to a more traditional approach. However, increases in reward for the 'A' players would be contingent on increases in performance in their strategic roles. If the role was genuinely strategic, this would translate into a cost saving, an increase in revenue or a customer satisfaction increase. All three could be translated into a monetary value – which would justify any increase paid in reward.

Figure 9.1 shows this principle in chart form. The diagram shows total reward for 'A' roles, 'B' roles and 'C' roles. The 'A' roles with 'A' players in place have a wide salary band starting well above the median in the market, with a very high upper limit. The principle underpinning this approach is that if these people are strategically important and contribute exponentially to the success of the business, having any cap is counterproductive if the pay is contingent on performance. Figure 9.1 reflects total reward, which is made up of base salary and any bonus element. Finding the right combination of these two elements can also impact on performance and motivation, both positively if the mix is considered fair, and negatively if the mix is considered unfair.

The 'A' roles should, as a guide, be banded with the upper 25 per cent of the market rate, as these talents will have profiles and capabilities that are in heavy demand. If they perform well in the role the band should be broad enough to reflect that. In those roles where any bonus element is related to measureable impact on revenue or costs, capping it would be counter-productive and illogical. You would have to agree, capping a bonus that is tied to high performance and has a clear line of sight to strategic goals is ludicrous. However, setting bonus achievement beyond what is possible is also ludicrous, as it just acts as a sign of an organisation that is demanding and unrealistic. People generally do not try to achieve goals that are they think are genuinely unattainable. The right level to set a bonus trigger is where the individual believes its achievement would be tough, but possible, and that the reward offered in return has 'valence';[4] it's desirable to them and they would value it.

In the UK, with the aftermath of the banking collapse and the economic recession that followed there is a marked reluctance to pay really large bonuses. The media, and a great many in the general public, have criticised the use of very large bonuses to retain people in the banking sector. Given the way the banks have performed in recent years the awards are widely regarded as unjust. This is entirely natural where the performance of the organisation is not directly linked to the individual's contribution. In the banking sector very large bonus pots had become an expectation and cultural norm, not a means of driving success. Where high performance makes a significant contribution, i.e. in circumstances where the specific role has clearly made a measurable impact on profit, cost savings, customer satisfaction or share value, then an award should not be questioned. A company can really only understand this if the concept of strategic roles and performance management is well defined and the link between the two can be measured reliably.

Elsewhere in the structure of the organisation, the pay should reflect what it takes to get competent people able to carry out the role and not more. Therefore the 'B' roles should reflect the market rate, so the band starts on the median for that specific role, the range being there to reflect performance in the role over time. Bonus payments can be justified if the individual roles contribute indirectly to the success of the organisation's strategic aims.

The 'C' roles are non-strategic so should be paid no more than market rate, if they are already filled. As these roles are not strategic, and could in many cases be outsourced, there is no imperative to even pay market rate should they become vacant. There is also no case for additional incentives in these roles. If a 'C role' is carried out to world-class levels of excellence then there would be no more positive economic

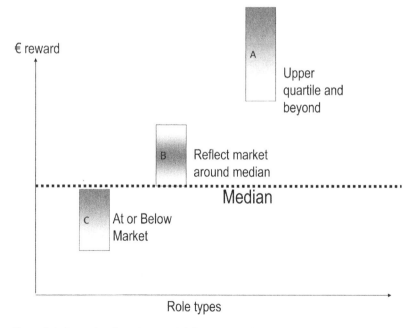

Figure 9.1 Example of total reward differentiation by role

impact on the organisation's goals than if it was done to a merely satisfactory standard. There is no performance management justification for paying any bonus in these roles. There might be an argument for a company-wide, profit-related, bonus element paid to all staff regardless of impact, but this is not really performance management, more a means of general motivation and wider employee engagement. It may have some positive effect on staff retention, but in the 'C' roles, retention is not a critical issue.

The salary band chart in Figure 9.1 can often generate powerful, and sometimes heated, debates in HR and management meetings. The clear implication from Figure 9.1, and the underlying principles, is that some roles are much more valuable than others and should be prioritised in terms of financial resources. This is a logical conclusion if the idea of 'A' roles and 'A' players is embraced, but sometimes it only becomes completely transparent to managers what this means in practice when the issue of reward is openly discussed. Regardless of the banding structure that the organisation has in place, an open and transparent discussion with the senior management team will always provide some value to the talent professional. In the worst case scenario, it will at least have informed the senior team of the difficulty of rewarding real talent without reference and influence on salary. In the best case scenario, it may encourage them to support a more transparent and results-based system of reward which would reduce the risks of attrition.

Reward assumptions

When using an ETM approach there are some implicit assumptions made about pay and reward. They directly affect the way the HR and talent professionals think about compensation.

The first is that fairness and equality is not the same thing. For those managers who believe that the reward principles outlined above are somehow unfair, they should consider the inequality potentially felt by talents who know they produce high value but are paid average salary. It is these talents that will leave the organisation, not because the pay isn't enough, but because the pay reflects the value that the organisation attributes to their contribution. Status is conferred and measured by economic worth and that is reflected in the salary or reward package of talents. Pay alone may not be enough to motivate them to perform higher, but a lack of it will distract them and lead to dissatisfaction and eventually to them seeking opportunities elsewhere.[5]

In a differentiated approach, one where talents are rewarded for their overall contribution to the company's success, the assumption should be that there is no limit to the overall package. However, reward should reflect their measurable value to the organisation. This means if a talent really is the best available in that particular capability, then the rate will be commensurate with that fact. This very clear linkage of value to reward reflects in the motivation of the individual and their attitude to the employer. The individual who is motivated by challenge or power and is paid something commensurate with their value is not likely to leave for something similar elsewhere.

In a more traditional reward approach, the market rate in the industry would set the benchmark for compensation. However, this does not take account of the fact that the best performers in the role create significantly more economic value for the organisation than an average performer. To attract and retain the very best performers, there needs to be an employee value proposition that is much better than average – salary is only one part of that offer.

Many job-grading techniques used by organisations, and supported by specialist HR consultants, do not reflect the realities of strategic talent. Many of the scores that determine how important a role is considered to be are based on organisational structure – not economic impact. Only a very individual approach can really determine how much value a specific role in the organisation can add when filled by a high performer. An aggregation of that role description from the consultant's database of competing firms is not always so useful, as this will lead to a figure based on the market average, not something that represents someone who is market-leading talent. If you base your reward package on the average for the role in the market, this will become apparent to applicants when they read the recruitment advertising. Consequently, it will attract people who consider that fair for their contribution – an average performer.

Retention – other factors

Pay, as discussed, needs to be right to remove dissatisfaction, but will not always motivate people to produce their full potential and their best performance. Organisations are always looking for something else to give them the edge in attracting and retaining the best people. The highest rated employers in competitive markets really take this to another level.

Google is consistently rated as one of the world's most desirable employers and one of the best places to work. A recent article outlined their talent retention strategies at a number of their worldwide sites:[6]

Work any hours, as few or as many as you like if the work is done

Rewarded with a beach side office week for hitting three months targets

Free gourmet meals in the canteen

Free haircuts at work

Pets at work (only in the early days of the company)

Cash payments when you have a child and extra time off to bond with it

Death in service benefits of 50 per cent salary for your dependents for 10 years

Other companies without the vast resources of the Internet giant may have reservations about some of the perks on offer for the Googlers. However, a more creative approach to recognising an individual's needs and what they would perceive as a benefit, can be considered.

An example of this creative flexibility comes from Nestlé. When they operated a cutting edge research facility, located in the north of England, and needed some of the best scientific talent available they tailored the working hours to suit individuals. One young scientist wanted to do the role over 3.5 days of 12 hours shifts rather than a full week, to accommodate his relationship and family situation. This young specialist could operate with colleagues in different time zones on two other continents in his long working day, and a second researcher also interested in this pattern for different reasons could follow on for the second part of the week. This was considered an advantage in the global world of research. Nestlé gained an accelerated development track for some of its work, carried out twice as fast as normal, and the individual got the time to spend with his young family whilst being able to do world-class work. This was a cost-neutral decision, but highly valued by the young talent involved.

Other organisations such as Microsoft, and Johnson and Johnson have instigated concierge services to offer bespoke services to its staff, such as collecting dry cleaning, booking car services and arranging restaurants. If these are offered as performance incentives, they may have limited impact, but as part of building a culture of support and ease of work they can remove some of the daily frustrations that may entice people to search elsewhere.

Still one of the most important issues for retention of valued staff is the availability of a development programme and the issue of individual career progression. A recent CIPD survey of talent management suggested that career development is still considered the most effective retention activity by companies and yet is one of the most cited reasons for leaving in exit interviews.[7] When it comes to scarce talent, the organisations that can offer a plan for individual development and show a robust process for career reviews fare better in the retention stakes.

A focused approach to development means managers talking to their staff and finding meaningful solutions, not necessarily some form of organisational scale intervention. This is why so much emphasis was placed on managers' coaching in Chapter 7. What is clear from research and anecdotal experience is that talents in general really want to fulfil their potential and they place a high expectation on organisations to assist them.

Risk assessment

As outlined earlier, there are a number of ways to reduce any potential retention problems by addressing the basic elements of total rewards and by adding benefits to the employee value proposition. In most organisations these processes are addressed across the whole organisation as part of the pay and compensation review. There will be some elements that need to be addressed differently for the specific segments or talent pools, whether that is in the area of reward or additional opportunities for development. However, a more proactive approach may be to concentrate just on the strategic talents and try to highlight any retention risks before they become a problem.

Given that ETM suggests deploying the organisation's best talent to the most critical roles then losing a key player from one of these strategic positions must have some negative impact on the business. Estimating the probability of this occurring, the risk, will allow a more proactive and pre-emptive approach to retention.

Risk is an estimate of the likelihood of a circumstance occurring. In talent terms this would be an assessment of whether a particular person might leave the organisation, and if they did what would be the impact? The greater the risk and impact, the more important it would be to reduce the likelihood of this happening by taking some mitigating action.

A process can be used that is not dissimilar to the due diligence that may be undertaken by the HR team on the target management as part of a takeover bid. There are a number of key questions that need to be answered:

- Which are the important roles to assess?
- What is the specific value of the role to the organisation?

- How is the current incumbent performing in the role?
- What is the risk of them leaving, short term and medium term?
- What is the impact on the organisation if they did?
- What can be done to reduce or mitigate the risk?

Answers to these questions can create an outline plan of action to minimise the risk to the organisation, and the size of the impact, should the talent choose to leave. Table 9.1 shows an example of a risk assessment grid. These grids summarise the results of a review process undertaken by a senior management team for the respective business unit.

Nothing in the risk assessment process will necessarily be new information, at least not if the line manager of each talent is already aware, but the process of bringing this disparate range of information together in one place, with a senior team taking action, reduces the potential for any unexpected negative business impact. The first time the organisation hears a talent was unhappy in their role should not be as they conduct an exit interview.

Reward and retention conclusions

Talented employees are the ones that will always have a choice of where they can work. For some of these talents that opportunity is constantly being offered by headhunters and calls from ex-colleagues. An organisation can do many things to ensure that it retains as much of its key talent as possible, but to do so requires a differentiated response, as outlined in ETM.

I have heard senior executives in businesses say that a high turnover is healthy and nothing to be concerned about. At the same time, when questioned, these executives have no idea which sort of person is leaving, their economic value to the organisation or the scarcity and expense of finding a replacement. Attrition of high-potential employees is never a good thing. But to arrest it, you need to understand what high performance and potential is, and who has it.

If your organisation has a high turnover of 'B' and 'C' roles then there is a problem, but not one that will significantly impact overall success. It can be resolved by recruiting from the market additional competent staff to do these supporting roles. Alternatively, for some of the 'C' roles, the services of a specialist supplier can replace the need for an employee. However, if your business is losing people from strategically important 'A' positions which you have filled with high-performance 'A' players, your organisation is in serious trouble. Without the clear definitions of roles and talent, a strategic talent map and a succession pool with already assessed bench strength, the organisation will not be able to respond quickly to losing a key person.

Responding to a rising trend of losing people in strategic positions requires that you measure the retention rates of key talent as a minimum performance indicator. A useful KPI would be the number of 'A' positions that are currently filled by 'A' performers. How many are vacant or filled with 'B' performers would also be a helpful supporting measure. Finally, an additional hard measure is: What is the typical cost of recruiting an A performer into an A role? There is little advantage in measuring the retention costs in other recruitment segments, such as 'B' and 'C' players, as these roles should not directly affect success.

These simple, and readily available, metrics allow the organisation to start to measure the impact of an ETM approach where it matters most in the strategically important

Table 9.1 Example talent risk analysis grid

Role	Incumbent	Risk	Notes	Action	Bench
Head of EU Supply Chain (Barcelona Site)	T.J. Van Helden	Short term Medium risk High impact	Wishes to be nearer family back in Belgium, and currently travelling significantly in role (50 per cent).	Discuss and look for opportunities to move home to Belgium, cross-functional role with 12 months.	No existing replacement in pool based in Barcelona, need to find and train successor.
Marketing Head, Data Storage Product Group EU (Hague)	S. Stone	Short term Low risk Medium impact	New to role, recent appointment, within 6 months, performing well to date.	No action required. Monitor performance.	No current named successor but plan to replace in two years so review talent pools.
Head of Consumer Sales (Germany)	G. Schmidt	Medium term Low risk High impact	Gert Schmidt will retire within the next two years, but is really respected by clients in the German market. He will not leave before agreed dates.	Appoint Dieter Dagler to support Gert in transition to role. Bonus Gert regarding mentoring Dieter.	Dieter Dagler will step into designate role within 12 months. Dieter will need a successor for his role.
Customer Account Director France (Lyon)	D. Lapin	Short term High risk High impact	Currently unhappy with role, has discussed with his boss regarding promotion to VP and a bigger remit to take in EU customers.	Need to discuss his next career move whilst not impacting on the French region performance. He has a key relationship with some large contracts. Consider short-term target with bonus element.	J. Demarche is named as a successor; also has strong relationships in region.

roles. The measure of effectiveness of any reward system is: How much does it drive business success? Measuring the key roles and their impact is a more effective way of doing this than reporting on everything that the HR system can report.

Key review questions

Does your pay and reward policy align to your stated business objectives?

Can you reward extreme high performance with uncapped bonus?

How is retention currently measured in your organisation?

Does the organisation address retention risk with its key talents?

Notes

1 Maslow's work in the 1950s created an interest in the idea of a 'needs theory of motivation'. This easy-to-understand model created a lot of interest from managers looking for something to explain why some people were motivated by different things but wanting a simple explanation. For a great overview of the model but little critique, see http://www.businessballs.com/ maslow.htm. An interesting article which does offer some critique is Denning, Steve (2012) What Maslow Missed, Forbes/Leadership, 29 Mar, http://www.forbes.com/sites/stevedenning/2012/03/29/what-maslow-missed/.

2 For a review of Herzburg's theory and some useful critique of applying it in business, see Mind Tools Editorial Team (n.d.) Herzberg's Motivators and Hygiene Factors: Learn how to Motivate Your Team, MindTools, http://www.mindtools.com/pages/article/herzberg-motivators-hygiene-factors.htm.

3 Need theory, also known as Three Needs Theory, proposed by psychologist David McClelland, is a motivational model that attempts to explain how the needs for achievement, power and affiliation affect the actions of people from a managerial context. This model was developed in the 1960s soon after Maslow's hierarchy of needs in the 1940s. McClelland stated that we all have these three types of motivation regardless of age, sex, race or culture. The type of motivation by which each individual is driven derives from their life experiences and the opinions of their culture. (Source: Wikipedia, https://en.wikipedia.org/wiki/David_McClelland.) A more in-depth understanding of McClelland's work can be gained from reading his work, particularly McClelland D. (1988) *Human Motivation*, Cambridge University Press, Cambridge, UK.

4 Expectancy theory also influences how goals and rewards are perceived. For a brief explanation, see https://en.wikipedia.org/wiki/Expectancy_theory.

5 The concept of the economic efficient wage applies to talent. For a simple overview of the concept, see http://www.economicshelp.org/blog/glossary/efficiency-wage-theory/.

6 For a recent article outlining why Google is so successful in its talent management process, and particularly in retaining people when they join, see Casserly, Meghan (2012) Here's What Happens To Google Employees When They Die, Forbes/ForbesWoman, 8 Aug, http://www.forbes.com/sites/meghancasserly/2012/08/08/heres-what-happens-to-google-employees-when-they-die/; also Matsangou, Elizabeth (2015) Secrets of Google's talent retention success, *EuropeanCEO*, 15 Jun, http://www.europeanceo.com/business-and-management/secrets-of-googles-talent-retention-success/.

7 CIPD in Partnership with Hays (2015) *Resourcing and Talent Planning 2015*, CIPD, London, http://www.cipd.co.uk/binaries/resourcing-talent-planning_2015.pdf.

Chapter 10

What are the next major challenges for talent professionals?

Introduction

This is the final chapter of the book and the place to pull together the threads of ETM. It's also the part of the book where some of the current debates and emerging issues concerning talent management are addressed. Whilst it's not the time to bring in new ideas or concepts it is the place to link the ETM approach to some of the challenges that talent professionals face from the competitive marketplace, and at times from their own managers.

As discussed in the first chapter, the time for talent management to make a significant contribution to business success is now. The era of technology as a competitive advantage is short lived, as reverse engineering and copycat versions of the new gadgets or platforms are quickly on the market, with some of the second to market clones outselling the organisation that developed the original concept. The difference between the organisations that manage to survive and thrive and those that go under is their ability to attract, manage and retain the best talent available.

Microsoft is one such case: as its dominance of the operating systems and office productivity applications was ebbing away, its people were enthused to reinvent themselves by new CEO, Satya Nadella.[1] He asked them to think of themselves as the 'new kids on the block' and challengers, rather than corporate behemoths. In this early stage the signs are good, with new services coming to market that were not core to Microsoft's existing Windows-dominated strategy, and devices that had a real chance of competing with the market leader Apple. The new future for Microsoft needed to be 'Cloud Services and Devices'.

Nadella knows it is his people, the same ones he had already seen grow the software business, that can reinvent the future. Nadella knows that talent matters and that no amount of market share or history of dominance will protect the company. Good people deployed in the right way can make that difference. They are now making good progress in the tablet market, in smart phones and in the services that support the increasing mobile-dominated market.

Talented people make organisations resilient, as they bring the intellectual and creative capability to drive change and respond to changing market demands. With the right people in the right place at the right time, an organisation has the highest chance of success in its chosen field.

ETM – the process revisited

In the previous nine chapters the various elements that make up an ETM approach have been outlined. In some of the sections there have been choices discussed, with the pros and cons of each highlighted. The talent professional needs to make careful decisions on which of the options are best suited to their own situation and their organisational need. There's no perfect recipe for an effective talent strategy but with a carefully selected mix of constituent parts and some guidance on what it takes to use them well, any competent talent professional can improve their role's impact on the business. In order to re-emphasise the integrated nature of this approach let's briefly review the key steps in ETM.

Understand business strategy

Any organisation's strategy should be built on its core capabilities. Any talent professional who doesn't understand their own organisation's strategy and how its core capabilities drive it will struggle to be effective. This really is critical to being effective and credible with senior executives. Spending time building a real depth of understanding is never wasted, as the more you recognise the driver of business success, the more your talent processes can be tailored to deliver them. For a master class in strategy I cannot recommend Richard Rumelt's *Good Strategy Bad Strategy: the difference and why it matters* enough.[2]

Understand the market

Understanding the organisation's goals and strategic aims is just the starting point. The talent professional then needs to place this strategy in the context of the market and its competitors. Knowing what your key competitors are doing will widen and deepen your understanding of the market for talent. If no one else in your industry is exploiting the capabilities you need then finding and retaining talent will be relatively easy. If you and the competition are all chasing the same scarce resource, that requires a different, more creative, response.

An understanding of the competition and the market allows a creative talent professional to identify new pastures, rather than follow the herd and resort to the poor tactic of making a higher offer. In addition, an understanding of the company's strategic capabilities will enable you to find transferable skills in talent pools from other industries. For example, supply chain expertise is a core capability for the rising home delivery services, an industry whose growth is driven by Internet shopping. Great logistics people are in high demand, particularly those with a sound grasp of technology. Sourcing your next head of outbound logistics from Amazon, Hermes or DHL might be very expensive. However, the UK military is downsizing substantially and has world-class logistics expertise that is very technologically savvy. Find new places for recruitment where there are candidates with the transferable skills but much less competition.

Defining your talent

'If you don't know where you are going then any road will get you there', wrote Lewis Carroll in *Alice's Adventures in Wonderland*. Without a clear and transparent talent definition, you are unable to choose a road that will lead to success.

Vague descriptions of talent are destined to failure or at best result in mediocrity. It is only when organisations really understand what capabilities drive their success and can articulate these into a definition of the specific talent they need that a strategy to attract, recruit, develop, deploy and retain them can be developed.

As discussed earlier, there are those within organisations who believe that talent definitions are elitist and are designed to separate out specific people for special treatment. They are entirely right, but instead of this being seen as somehow unfair, it should be considered the exact opposite, the only fair way of rewarding contribution. Only by identifying the talent that does make a difference can the organisation invest in them disproportionately and reap the rewards of doing so. It would be business mismanagement to do otherwise.

The talent definition for each organisation should be specific to its goals and strategic aims. This is not the place to adopt best practice or do what your competition is doing. Adopting Google's definition of talent will not make your organisation into Google.

Planning strategically

The purpose of any talent management approach is to have the right people in the right place at the right time. This means creating a plan that captures all of these elements. Step 1 in the plan is creating the map that defines which roles are the most strategically critical: the 'A' positions within the organisation. Following this mapping, there should be an audit of what talent already exists in the organisation, effectively uncovering who your 'A' players are. These two factors allow a gap analysis to be made. The talent professional now has the base facts to start their planning process. The perfect outcome is all the 'A' roles are filled by 'A' players and there is a reserve in the various talent pools to cover attrition, growth and special projects. If the gap analysis shows some void, a recruitment process will need to be undertaken to help fill it. The organisation also needs to be attractive to the type of person you need to execute your plan.

Finally, the strategic talent plan is only as good as the information it is based upon. So the strategy will need to be reviewed in light of any change in the organisation's direction. It also means that the data about who is high potential needs to be reliable and based on objective evidence.

Attracting the employees of choice

All organisations need a set of profiles that attract the segments of the talent pools that are critical to its success. The employee value proposition needs to be clear and compelling to compete with the rivals for your staff. Earlier we reflected on the marketing principles that might guide a talent professional to really target their opportunities. In the current busy market a multi-channel approach is advocated ensuring the message is consistent, always present and attractive. The new mantra should be: think marketing, think social media and think mobile.

Remember that what is cool and exciting in terms of a career move for a young 20 something talent may not be the message that will be considered attractive to a senior executive with need for a new challenge.

In terms of finding a new role, personal recommendation still comes high up the ranks of successful approaches. A good talent strategy will harness the current pool of talent to attract more like them, either from using their profiles in digital media channels or more effectively from their network. Good talent managers need to embrace marketing and PR methods and use their network to build a strong employer brand.

Don't rely on the wider corporate brand attracting the right talent; the two things are different concepts.

Selection based on objective evidence

If the employer brand is strong and the value proposition is attractive, you will have plenty of candidates applying for a career. The problem now is finding that elusive employee of choice. All organisations have selection processes, it's just some are much more effective than others.

For some organisations, those without a clear definition of talent, the hiring manager sees someone who matches their own unspoken criteria, and they use their unstructured interview (still the most common tool) to confirm their unconscious decision to hire. In the military they call this 'Decision Based Evidence Making'. It is not useful, but only too common an approach, where the manager justifies with post hoc evidence something that is already decided.

Evidence Based Decision Making is more robust, repeatable and effective. It ensures that the candidates are selected based on clear criteria linked to the talent definition, and therefore to the business strategy. It also means that the process is fair and transparent. What it does require is a skilled assessor pool, however the organisation achieves it.

Earlier we outlined many of the different tools that can be used but also suggested the best decisions are made with evidence gained from a variety of sources. As such some form of assessment centre or individual assessment suite is recommended.

Developing the right capability

When the individual is in their new role they need to be able to perform. Talent pools do invest heavily in individuals in terms of their development and the increase in opportunities that the talents receive. The expectation is that they perform in role and realise their potential. This should be encouraged and managed to some extent, with the setting of goals and clear expectations.

In Chapter 7 we explored a range of tools and techniques that could be applied for different development situations. However, the approach that research and experience suggests is the most effective, particularly for talented people, is that of challenging work assignments. Real work responsibility with challenging goals seems to bring out the capabilities of talents and push them towards their potential. Whilst programmed learning opportunities can be effective, they are more orientated towards skills to do the job (training) or increasing knowledge (education). It seems that the most significant development is derived from challenging the individual to learn from their own experience.

What does seem to be effective, and is strongly advocated as part of any ETM approach, is the use of coaching for individuals. This should be specifically tailored to that individual and therefore is something that requires a skilled coach. It is for this reason that it may not always work if it's just the line manager trying to help. A cadre of trained coaches benefits the organisation three fold: it helps the talent develop their potential; enables them to achieve their performance goals and it brings the skills of coaching to more senior managers. It results in a win for the talent, a win for the manager and a win for the organisation.

Deployment and high performance

Putting a great talent into a role that cannot have much strategic impact is a travesty. It will, over time, encourage the talent to leave the organisation and will have wasted all of the time and resources of the recruitment and development process. However, this scenario can happen all too often if the talent is considered to be a local resource and kept within the business unit that initially recruited it. Talent should always be considered as an organisation's asset and should be deployed wherever the business needs it most.

It is understandable to some extent that managers want to keep their best people within their own business, but if that is the case then the organisation will be limited in what it attracts from the market. Most talents like to be challenged and that often means new opportunities elsewhere in the organisation. There are not many businesses that can offer a range of challenging opportunities just within their own unit; so one alternative is that talents seek them elsewhere, sometimes with competitors. Losing talent is bad news; losing talent to a competitor is a tragedy.

As part of the deployment process, talent forums, talent circles and talent days were discussed. Each of these formats differs slightly, but they all share the same intent: to involve senior managers from across an organisation in the deployment decisions for talents. In this way different interested parties have a voice in the discussion but the overall objectives of the organisation are still the focus of the deployment process.

The ETM approach to performance management should always be a mix of both quantitative targets that relate to the business and qualitative targets related to the individual's development. Regardless of which system is employed for the purpose of performance management, the crux of the matter is the performance conversation, not the means of data capture. A clear guidance to anyone setting up a performance management process for the first time, is to not get too excited by the endless features of an HR software package, but focus on line managers holding regular feedback and performance discussions. Having the ability to track and monitor targets across the organisation in real time is an attractive proposition; the reality is that if people are filling in data fields rather than having face-to-face discussions about performance, the monitoring is meaningless.

Rewarding and retaining talent

Psychologists seem to agree that pay is not a motivator. They also agree that it does dissatisfy people if it's not deemed correct for the role. There are ways other than pay to ensure retention. When people are challenged, given responsibility, visibility and the flexibility to work in a way that suits them, their desire to search elsewhere is reduced. The talent management strategy is not effective if you are losing people from the talent pools. To know if this is the case you require a few basic metrics: monitor the numbers in those pools (total talent), and the rate of them in 'A' positions (deployed talent), and finally count the 'A' roles with vacancies. If you have significant under achievement in these three figures against plan, there is potentially a retention issue.

There is a well know saying in HR: 'people leave people'. It's still true to some extent that people don't dislike organisations or brands, they dislike the situation they are in at work, which is mainly embodied by their relationship with their boss. What is important about the talent groups is that they are more likely to cite the lack of challenge when they are exit interviewed than most. The next challenge for them should have featured in a discussion related to performance with their line manager, who could then flag this up for some action.

An ETM approach would include a risk assessment for all critical roles described as the 'A' positions on the role maps. Whilst this does not eliminate any potential attrition; it brings to the surface, in a discussion at a senior level, the risks associated with each role and information that might enable some mitigating action.

Current issues and future trends

Talent management as a function of HR is now around 20 years old; at least that's how long the term has been in common use within the management lexicon. Within those years there has been an evolution of approach, from the initial superficial response of rebranding the recruiting team through to the development of comprehensive integrated systems. It's now commonplace to see the term used in HR organisation charts and many of these roles are in relatively senior positions. Without doubt, talent management has come of age and established itself as a core discipline in the wider HR function, reflected by the subject being part of the core curriculum of many professional qualifications.[3]

There are, as always in professions, a number of areas where the status quo is being challenged or there are contesting opinions. I will reflect on a few here and offer a practitioner perspective, which, of course, is a personal opinion, but one based on years of experience and the pragmatism of a consultant.

Transparency

There was a time, only a few years back, when being part of a high-potential scheme was akin to being in the Masons. Everyone knew they existed and that it was a special status, but the means of entry and benefits it bestowed were not always clear, especially to anyone not in the secret circle. What was implied by this status was that there was a plan and some sort of a career mapped out for you.

Things have moved on in most organisations. First, the issue of transparency has come as a result of a better understanding of talent management being a strategic lever, therefore requiring it to be higher on the agenda of senior management. Second, talent professionals have become more confident about their processes and can easily defend their decisions when challenged.

For the individual, being informed you are a talent is great news and gives some personal recognition, but does reflect the double-edged nature of being considered high potential, which is the expectation of now delivering high performance.

Transparency will continue to become a core issue in talent management. Those organisations that fail to disclose to individuals their conferred status are missing a useful motivational tool and it shows a lack of confidence in their overall talent strategy. What would give them more confidence is having an effective approach, one that is linked to the business objectives.

Employee branding

Over the last decade this concept, the employee brand, has emerged as a hot topic in HR. It seemed at one time everyone wanted to be the employer of choice. In some respects this has been fuelled by the rise in the rating indexes favoured by some of the media. Not having a presence in the latest best 100 companies was somehow seen to be completely negative. Employee branding seminars and conferences sprouted from nowhere as practitioners were told that their brand mattered and they could control it by following a few easy steps. Now there are the additional pressures of comments on the online rating sites such as Indeed and Glassdoor. Social media seems to be where most conversations are held about your brand.

There is no doubt that brand matters in terms of attracting talent. Goldman Sachs was the 'go to' destination for high-flying graduates who wanted to be 'masters of the universe' and earn a huge salary in the city. Following the collapse of the banking world in 2008–09, their brand value for this group of career seekers plummeted. Being rich was one thing, but being loathed at the same time was not so popular.

This is an area where a pragmatic and focused approach will enable an organisation to attract the right people. The right people are the ones who will meet your specific talent criteria and not everyone who just thinks they have some talent. Think of the television show X factor with its countless hordes of hungry hopefuls,[4] most of who have no talent whatsoever, but would still like to pitch. It makes entertaining TV but is not what an organisation wants in its marketing. It is expensive, wastes a lot of time and raises unnecessary hope with the wrong profile of applicant.

What is more effective is to be completely transparent and selective. Be totally candid about what the organisation expects from a successful hire and then be brutally honest about what that takes from a candidate to succeed. What will happen is that people who cannot meet that challenge self-select out and don't apply. Think more like the SAS entry course in the Brecon Beacons,[5] its success rate is about 1 in 10, but many more choose not to apply because of the transparent high expectations.

Globalisation

There is still a high demand for single, country-based, talent management programmes. In small organisations based within a single country it may be possible to have the right people from within the national boundary. However, in any EU country this will inevitably mean applications from other EU nationals. Just recruiting in London opens up the application to a global talent pool.

Many businesses are operating in a global market for their products and services. It makes clear business sense to ensure that your talent pool matches that demographic to a greater extent. In some cases, just the additional languages and wider cultural understanding that a non-home country employee brings will add a business advantage in that specific market. This reason alone explains why a more international talent pool is becoming a trend. However, there are still some circumstances when a home-grown talent will be better. As a Milanese colleague told me, an average Italian salesman is always going to do better in Italy than a great Spanish or English national. Growth and globalisation means a truly international workforce and in terms of talent this is no different.

As talent has become a clear differentiator in business, and as the demand for certain key skills, such as STEM (Science, Technology, Engineering, and Mathematics), has risen, organisations now have to look further afield for talent. The number of engineers graduating in the UK each year is approximately 46,000. In India the number is closer to 1.5 million and China is a close second with 1.1 million. To complete the comparison, the USA has around 100,000.

Initially this meant many companies were getting more applications for their STEM roles from Indian and Chinese graduates already studying in Europe. However, the numbers applying are not high enough and an emerging trend is to take the process to the source. As a result of statistics such as these, organisations are now focusing their recruitment drives for younger talent in the Asia region, with specific assessment centres and dedicated local talent teams.

If your ETM strategy does not take account of where the talent is plentiful and where it is scarce then it's not very strategic. Where else is there a pool of, as yet, untapped talent? Where can your organisation be a first mover?

Technology and talent

There are many ways that technology has impacted on talent management practices over the last few years. The rise in software suites with talent tracking and applicant management functions is clearly of some benefit. Anything that can improve the administration of the processes involved in managing talent is to be welcomed. However, the existence of talent management software does not mean you are being effective in managing talent. What matters, and makes a difference to success, is alignment of talent to results in the business.

Technology can offer options elsewhere in the talent management process. For example there are a number of good systems that anyone can use for video interviews. Skype and Facetime are almost ubiquitous, but there are a number of more professional applications available. What they save in travel time and costs is significant, but they do lose a little in translation. However, they offer an intermediate step in the recruitment process and, although not as easy to arrange as a telephone interview, are becoming an increasingly acceptable alternative.

Social media has already been discussed as a method of having a conversation with your target group talents. What is becoming commonplace is to also use the same tools to vet or verify the profile of potential applicants. There are a number of commercial services that will carry this out for you; alternatively, members of the in-house recruitment team can conduct it. The 24/7/365 world of social networks such as Facebook, Twitter and Sino Weibo leave a digital footprint that doesn't always flatter or provide positive support for an application. It seems more employers are willing to use these platforms for vetting first-level applications, as a matter of course. [6] Even 'Googling' their name can reveal previously unknown images and references that can influence an application.

Mobile applications are becoming serious elements of any recruitment and therefore talent management. Having a great recruitment portal with micro-sites showing how talents will thrive in your organisation is not really effective if they are not optimised for mobile devices. The latest statistics show that over 80 per cent of people in career search use their smart phone or tablet for initial responses and research into opportunities. [7] Whilst the computer is still favoured for final applications, the tablet and phone are becoming increasingly important.

Digital media

Finally, the technology platforms are important, but to some extent irrelevant if your site is not showing up in a search. Digital marketing techniques and tactics are now becoming increasing important in talent management. Search Engine Optimisation is necessary to help the right people to find you, and Pay Per Click advertising may be worth every penny, if the targeting is right. Gone are the days of printed brochures for young talents or paper media, professional journal advertising. The most effective media for finding talent is now through digital channels and it's important that these tools and techniques are understood and where appropriate adopted.

The Talent War isn't over

The War for Talent is not something that can be definitively won, but you can improve your success in the battles along the way. When the trend for talent management emerged back in the 1990s there really was a sense of HR doing something different and changing the focus of their efforts to finding the talented rainmakers of each business. However, the environment changed and so did the need for talent.

Following the banking crisis of 2008 and the subsequent recession in Europe and the USA, the focus was taken off talent and placed squarely on cost reduction, downsizing and commercial survival. As the economies of the west, at least, are starting to recover, the attention has returned to securing the right talent to support growth. Again the need for talent has become front and centre of many businesses. However, the way they are recruiting is becoming more sophisticated and more directly connected to their strategic objectives.

The talent professional who can deliver a truly effective talent management strategy will never be short of work. It's a talent role that requires talented practitioners. This book has tried to convey an approach that does work and when implemented makes a significant contribution to the success of the organisation. This is not because of some secret method or special software code that will eventually be copied, but because it is based on sound principles and a clear line of sight to the organisation's purpose.

In the terminology of ETM the talent professional's role is strategically important. It is one that sources and develops the most critical resource the organisation has: its unique talent pool. This is one role within the organisation that really should be filled by an 'A' player.

Notes

1 Nadella's memo to staff on taking the role is discussed in Wilhelm, Alex (2014) Satya Nadella's Vision For A New Microsoft, TechCrunch, 10 Jul, http://techcrunch.com/2014/07/10/satya-nadellas-vision-for-a-new-microsoft/.

2 Rumelt, Richard, P. (2012) *Good Strategy, Bad Strategy: The difference and why it matters.* Profile Books Ltd, London.

3 The Chartered Institute of Personnel and Development is the leading body for the HR profession in the UK, and it is also the largest professional institute by membership. It certifies the professional standards for HR in the UK and, by default, much of Europe. An outline of its talent management qualifications is available at http://shop.cipd.co.uk/shop/cipd-training/qualifications/learning-talent/talent-management?limit=all.

4 The TV talent show on UK'S ITV channel had 182,000 applicants for its series 5 auditions.

5 The numbers for SAS (Special Air Service) and its sister service SBS (Special Boat Service) are to some extent self-regulating, but success is not high on the final endurance test. See http://www.eliteukforces.info/special-air-service/sas-selection/.

6 Hill, Kashmir (2012) Facebook Can Tell You If A Person Is Worth Hiring, Forbes/Tech, 5 Mar, http://www.forbes.com/sites/kashmirhill/2012/03/05/facebook-can-tell-you-if-a-person-is-worth-hiring/.

7 You can download a great info graphic with the latest survey results for smart phone job search use from http://about.beyond.com/Content/Resources/files/Media/pdfs/MultiScreenJob Search.pdf.

Index

Made in the USA
Monee, IL
12 December 2022

20935840R00105